Language and Social Psychology

Language in Society

GENERAL EDITOR:
  Peter Trudgill, Reader in Linguistic Science
  University of Reading

ADVISORY EDITORS:
  Ralph Fasold, Professor of Linguistics
  Georgetown University
  William Labov, Professor of Linguistics
  University of Pennsylvania

Language and Social Psychology

Edited by

HOWARD GILES and
ROBERT N. ST CLAIR

University Park Press · Baltimore

Library of Congress Cataloging in Publication Data
Main entry under title:

Language and Social Psychology

  (Language in society ; 1)
  Includes bibliographical references and index.
  1. Sociolinguistics.   2. Social psychology.
I. Giles, Howard.   II. St. Clair, Robert N.
III. Series: Language in society (Baltimore) ; 1.
P40.L29   301.2′1   78–21766
ISBN 0–8391–1356–0

Printed and bound in Great Britain

Contents

Editors' Preface: Language in Society Series

For some, the title of this series will imply principally the relationships that obtain *between* language and society. For others, the emphasis will lie on the role language plays *in* society. But whatever the interpretation, it is clear that there are many reasons for the growing interest in the field of language and society. Language for instance can be the medium through which a society may be influenced, conditioned or manipulated: studies of oratory and rhetoric have a long and respectable history, but more recently attention has also been focused on the language of advertising, the language of diplomatic euphemism, the language of political obfuscation.

Conversely, a language may also reflect in some degree certain aspects of the society in which it is spoken, and therefore may constitute a profitable area of investigation for social scientists. It is not merely that the vocabulary of a language may reflect the interests, needs, experiences and environment of the people who speak it. (It comes, after all, as no great surprise that Eskimo has a more extensive 'snow' vocabulary than English does, or that Jamaicans have a large number of words for yams.) A language may also indicate something about the way in which a society is structured, as conveyed, perhaps, through its kinship terms, or its beliefs, norms and values—illustrated, for example, through linguistic taboo, descriptive labels for social and ethnic groups, or in terms for men and for women. The study of conversation, too, may be informative. An analysis of what speakers say and more particularly, what they do not say, can be indicative of the unstated, shared assumptions of particular social groups.

Linguists, too, have a very considerable interest in language and society. Language as it is used by people in their everyday lives must, ultimately, be what linguists describe and explain, and the study of language in its social context provides an essential counterbalance to studies in the laboratory and to researches that concentrate on the linguist's knowledge of his own language. Indeed, it is more than this, since there are many aspects of language, such as the mechanisms involved in linguistic change, which can only be studied in this way. Empirical studies of language in society have produced some of the most interesting work in linguistics of the past several years.

Some work in this field, then, is of especial interest to social scientist, and some to linguists. But there are also many aspects of the study of language and society which are of equal interest to both. Linguists and social scientists have much to learn from studies that ask questions such as what languages, dialects or styles are employed in different situations; what are the social norms for using language in different communities; what social meanings and connotations do different varieties of language acquire, and how may these be manipulated in social interaction? And there are also many ways in which work of this nature can be applied to the solution of practical problems—in second and foreign language teaching; in mother tongue education; in language planning and standardization.

This series *Language and Society* is concerned with all these areas—language and communication, anthropological linguistics, ethnomethodology, secular linguistics, the sociology of language, the ethnography of speaking, discourse analysis, the social psychology of language—and with their applications. Publications in the series will therefore be of interest to linguists and to social scientists, and are intended to provide sound coverage of particular areas of the field while at the same time incorporating up-to-date and original thinking and findings. Language and society as a field of study is no longer in its infancy, but it is becoming increasingly obvious that there is a very great deal that we do not know. This is both chastening and challenging. It is also exciting. This series will, we hope, face up to the challenge and reflect the excitement.

One consequence of the close relationship which obtains between language and society is the extent to which linguists and social psychologists can derive mutual benefit from studies of each other's work. Linguistic forms of every level, and linguistic behaviour of many types, can act as markers of personal and social characteristics, and may provoke different reactions and responses in social interaction. Social psychologists concerned with language may therefore turn to linguists for assistance in the analysis of linguistic forms. Correspondingly, linguistic attitudes and stereotypes can be a powerful force in influencing linguistic behaviour and, ultimately, linguistic forms themselves. Linguists must therefore look to social psychologists for explanatory analyses and concepts in their examination of the social psychological factors at work in, for example, linguistic change. In fact, however, the amount of mutual benefit that has been derived remains as yet relatively small. Social psychologists have only infrequently resorted to linguistic analyses. And, while psychology has had a considerable influence on the study of foreign language learning and teaching, social psychology has had comparatively little influence on sociolinguistics. It is to this latter omission that this book is primarily directed. Written in the main by social psychologists, it is also directed at linguists and sociologists. It shows that multidisciplinary work of this nature is not only valuable but at this stage in the development of sociolinguistics and the social psychology of language, essential.

PETER TRUDGILL, UNIVERSITY OF READING
WILLIAM LABOV, UNIVERSITY OF PENNSYLVANIA
RALPH FASOLD, GEORGETOWN UNIVERSITY

1

Sociolinguistics and Social Psychology: an Introductory Essay[1]

HOWARD GILES

When we examine the field of language in its social context, socio-linguistics, we find it far from unified in its goals and approaches; many commentators agree upon this (Ferguson, 1970; Hymes, 1972). Nevertheless, a reasonable definition of its scope is provided by Fishman (1970:3). He states that

> it is the study of the characteristics of language varieties, the characteristics of their functions, and the characteristics of their speakers as these three constantly interact, change, and change one another within a speech community.

A number of writers consider the area to be a sub-branch of linguistics (e.g., Trudgill, 1974) and not as a truly multidisciplinary endeavour. However, we do find that disciplines such as sociology, social anthropology, and education have made their marks on the field of sociolinguistics and often are labelled as having independent status as the 'sociology of language' and 'anthropological linguistics'.

One discipline conspicuous perhaps by its absence from the above is that of social psychology. However, if textbooks and readings in sociolinguistics are examined (Fishman, 1968; Gumperz and Humes, 1972), we find that social psychological theory has rarely permeated it. There are workers such as Roger Brown and Wallace Lambert who have made important contributions, but overall social psychology has had little impact to date in this sphere. Thus, one of the prime aims of this book generally, and the present chapter more specifically, is to show that social psychological theory and methodology have important implications for the development of sociolinguistics.

If we return to Fishman's definition of sociolinguistics, we see that the discipline is imbued heavily with notions of description and taxonomy. Such activities are of course a high priority, particularly in an embryonic field, and it would be foolish to decry them, as they are an essential foundation for any reasonable theory of language behaviour. Nevertheless, one begins to feel a little uneasy when few attempts have been made to move us from the what, when and where to the why of socio-linguistic phenomena. Hence, if we are going to understand why individuals acquire, use and react to language and its varieties in the way they do, we require a greater understanding of the dynamics of attitudes, motivations, identities and intentions, that is, social psychological phenomena. It would seem, despite the fact that sociolinguists (Labov, 1963; 1966; 1970) have far from ignored these notions, that social psychological theory (and methods) may be able to guide us towards a greater appreciation of at least two, perhaps fundamental, issues: why are speech variables important in evaluating others, and why do people speak the way they do in different social contexts? This book, then, is divided, as our questions are, into two overlapping sections.[2] The first deals with decoding processes of language behaviour, while the second considers encoding issues in a manner that highlights not only what happens, but why. In short, then, social psychology may be able to increase the explanatory power of sociolinguistics.

Before overviewing the contributions to this volume, let us briefly examine the field of social psychology itself. Social psychology is the study of an individual's behaviour in his or her social context. Nevertheless, if one looks at definitions of the field in introductory textbooks and elsewhere, we see that workers have often been somewhat loathe to commit themselves to a consensual framework. Moreover, some writers have construed social psychology as a conglomeration of separate topics (e.g. attitude change, attraction, conformity and prejudice) exceeding the grasp of experimental psychology and having a reliance on the social sciences (Brown, 1965; Insko and Schopler, 1972). In this sense, social psychology has been as lacking in a unified sense of goals and approaches as has sociolinguistics and is constantly undergoing harsh reappraisals (Strickland, Aboud and Gergen, 1976).[3]

For the present purposes, we, as so many other writers have, will consider the field of social psychology mainly in terms of the social influence process (e.g. Hollander, 1972; Aronson, 1972). For instance, Allport (1968:3) states that social psychology is 'an attempt to understand how the thoughts, feelings and behaviors of individuals are influenced by the actual, imagined, or implied presence of others'. More recently, however, some social psychologists are explicitly extending this approach to a consideration of how society and its structure, that is, as reflected along such dimensions as power and control, affect the individual's social behaviour (Tajfel and Israel, 1972). Another feature of social psychology which workers have agreed on is its characteristic methodology. Traditionally, the most appropriate method for collecting socio-psychological data has been to record and revise scientifically the subjective and objective behaviour of individuals in a controlled manner. Again, however, methodology within social psychology has not been without its critics (Harré and Secord, 1972; Agyris, 1975).

As we shall see throughout this volume, social psychologists have many theories about how individuals search for understanding of the behaviour of others and the situation they are in, and about how this mediates to guide their subsequent behaviour in an interactive sense. One of the important ways in which we can influence others, and be influenced by them, is through language behaviour. In other words, much of individual social behaviour is concerned with the decoding and encoding of verbal and nonverbal language variables. It may be then of some surprise (if not concern) to learn that language processes have not been at the core or even periphery of social psychological interests; admittedly, however, such processes have assumed more salience in European and Canadian quarters. Yet if one examines introductory texts and readings in social psychology, few chapters (if any) are afforded language processes. Naturally enough, exceptions can be found (Brown, 1965; Wrightsman, 1972; Tajfel and Fraser, 1978), and important reviews and books have occasionally emerged on social psychological aspects of language (Ervin-Tripp, 1969; Moscovici, 1967; 1972; Carswell and Rommetweit, 1972; Robinson, 1972; Argyle, 1975), but as such, these processes have not played a prominent role in social psychological theory and certainly no current field of 'sociopsycholinguistics' has convincingly emerged.[4] Hence, it is a secondary aim of this book to make explicit the importance of understanding language processes for any worthwhile theory of social behaviour. It is not inconceivable, then, that social psychology and sociolinguistics could profit from a symbiotic relationship.

Let us now overview the main features of the chapters in two sections of the book, underlining the links between them and the story they tell. Needless to say, much of the inherent richness and theoretical scope of each contribution will be lost in this review in order to meet the demands of a concise integrative approach. We shall subsequently highlight the value of this work for sociolinguistics on the one hand, and for social psychology on the other. Finally, we shall conclude this chapter with a consideration of the apparent deficiencies of these research approaches, the need for a fuller multidisciplinary orientation and some potential goals and priorities for the future.

The first section of the book is concerned with the judgemental aspects of the listeners' decoding processes of language. Work in the past has shown that speech style can influence impression formation (Giles and Powesland, 1975). In this context, 'speech style' refers to linguistic features which determine *how* a message is said rather than *what* is said in terms of verbal content. Most of the results, however, were obtained in the artificial context of the laboratory and involved ratings of anonymous speakers. An important feature of this section of the book is that chapters were included which investigated the social significance of language behaviour in a couple of *applied* contexts, namely, the classroom and the courtroom. It will also be seen that a wide range of language variables such as accent, speech rate, pitch variety, voice loudness, interruptions, etc., can have important influences not only on people's general impressions of others, but also with regard to potential decisions they may make about them.

The opening chapter by Edwards concerns the role of childrens' speech, in this case, reading style, as a cue to their teachers' impressions of them and as a potential determinant of their scholastic success. He shows that Dublin children from so-called disadvantaged areas have speech characteristics perceived as different from those coming from non-disadvantaged environments. Moreover, the perception of the former's speech characteristics (poor vocabulary, fluency and pronunciation) led teachers to make negative inferences about their social backgrounds and unfavourable evaluations of their personalities. The data showed that the attribution of disadvantage from speech cues has the effect of inducing teachers towards a *holistic* stereotyped downgrading of the children concerned.

Most of the chapters remaining in this section involve listeners' ratings of taped speech. Edwards's chapter is an important opener to this work as his careful methodology provides evidence that suggests that people find the judgemental task a realistic one, and even admit in an interview afterwards to forming such impressions of speakers on the basis of their language behaviour in everyday life.

The next chapter, by Giles and Smith, continues the educational perspective, but from the other side of the coin: students' evaluations of a teacher's speech styles. This study empirically highlights features of the judgemental process other than direct attribution of a speaker's background and personality. First, the experimental design acknowledges that listeners make judgements about the appropriateness of message characteristics provided them in that particular context. Second, the study demonstrates that listeners can assess how the speaker views *them* from these message characteristics. From the viewpoint of a new theory of speech diversity, these authors were concerned with determining listeners' reactions to the various ways a lecturer from abroad could make an effort to take account of (or accommodate to) the particular features of his audience. It was found that the speaker (a Canadian) was rated more favourably, up to a certain optimal level, the more linguistic features he adapted to his English audience. In general, student teachers appreciated the speaker slowing down his speech rate more so than his attempts to attenuate his distinctive foreign accent and make his peculiar Canadian phrases more intelligible. In fact, convergent accent shifts had little effect on listeners' evaluations of the speaker in this context.

Although the speech variables manipulated in the first two chapters have been shown to have an influential effect on listeners' impressions, without wishing in any way to diminish their obvious importance, we have no means of telling how salient or frequently they occur in the social contexts studied. However, in Chapter 4, Lind and O'Barr are concerned with legal encounters and used speech variables in their stimulus tapes only after discovering their prominence in a prior linguistic analysis of real courtroom interactions. The authors found that law students reacted less favourably to a witness who spoke to a supposed lawyer on tape with linguistic intensifiers, hyper-correct grammar, hedges and rising intonation (a so-called 'powerless speech style') than those who did not incorporate such linguistic features into the very same testimony. Other studies showed that witnesses' patterns of answering the lawyer's questions (narrative versus fragmentary), and their initiation of, and reaction to, simultaneous speech with him (persevering versus acquiescent), affected in a complex fashion listeners' reactions to the witnesses and their statements. An important feature of Lind and O'Barr's research was that they showed listener's *expectations* of how the interaction should proceed for different types of witnesses with the lawyer had an effect on attribution about the witnesses' behaviour. Moreover, it was suggested that when listening to a dyad and being asked to make evaluations of one of the participants as a target person, we assess their interlocutor's speech style in an attempt to determine how he or she may be reacting to them. Such inferences can then, of course, be used by listeners in formulating their own beliefs and opinions about the target speaker.

Chapter 5 by Scherer proceeds one step further in tapping the social significance of speech variables by investigating their impact in ongoing semi-natural situations. The author videotaped different six-man groups in the United States and Germany who were asked to role-play a jury making a decision about a legal case of manslaughter with which they had just been presented. After the discussion they were asked to make certain assessments of themselves and of the other group members, including their perceived influentiality during discussion. Analysis showed that people agreed more or less amongst themselves about who was the most influential person in their groups, and as such, these people were perceived as being more competent and dominant. Speech analyses of the group interaction showed that the influential speakers were quite different from other members of the groups and also varied cross-culturally. In Germany, the speaker perceived to be most influential was found to speak at great length and to use many more filled pauses and agreement expressions, together with a higher rate of articulation and a wider loudness range. In the United States, the influential speaker was also shown to be verbally productive but used many more repetitions, interruptions and a wider pitch of variation. It was also found that the perceived influencer had a different self-reported personality than other members of his group, and that this also varied cross-culturally.

Given that evidence is presented which suggests that certain social processes are marked by speech differently in diverse cultures, the possibilities of communicational breakdowns emerging at different phases of an interaction when decoding a speaker from another cultural background are quite large. In a recent paper, von Raffler-Engel (1977) has highlighted the role of *kinetic* behaviour in such inter-cultural situations. She focuses upon the fact that others' behaviour, such as smiling, body posture, and body movement (which are important aspects of language behaviour beyond the scope of this book), can have important effects on one's assessment of these people. She argues that there are a variety of kinetic cues which are under more conscious control than others, and that there are also a stream of psychological elements in an interaction more or less within the realm of conscious control. Von Raffler-Engel proposes that although differences at the more conscious levels are likely to lead to gross inter-cultural misunderstandings, these are relatively short-lived and easily-comprehended with careful guidance. However, the less conscious elements of a person's psychological and nonverbal make-up, particularly body rhythm, when discrepant from members of another group are difficult to synchronize, and they lead to problems of attribution and communication discomfort, if not to outright breakdown (cf. Taylor and Simard, 1975; Segalowitz and Gatbonton, 1977).

The chapters in this section demonstrate that a wide variety of signals from a speaker can affect our evaluations of him or her. Indeed, Scherer in Chapter 5 presents data suggesting that in some contexts vocal qualities of the target person assessed are more crucial for impression formation than either content or visual cues available. Listeners use the perceived characteristics of speakers and speech styles in making multidimensional inferences of their likely backgrounds, personalities, psychological states, degree of influence over others, quality of their arguments, etc. This judgemental process is seen to be very complex, with the emergent assessment (or even decision) being not only dependent on the listeners' own social and personality characteristics, but on how the other's speech style conforms to social and situational expectations, how it allows inferences to be made about how the target speaker views the listeners, and how others' speech behaviour in the situation provide cues as to how they perceive the speaker as well. Although all authors are rightly cautious in considering the generality of their findings, it is apparent that these studies are of immediate social relevance and concern. It appears that aspects of a person's language behaviour can not only cause discomfort in a relationship, but can have dramatic (and oftentimes erroneous and undue attention in a courtroom) repercussions for the speaker manifest, for example, in a lack of educational opportunities.

It would seem that processes of this kind are rampant in the whole vista of social contexts a speaker enters, including the occupational and medical ones. For instance, Kalin and Rayko (1977) have shown that a job applicant's ethnic accent may well have an effect on Canadian employers' decision about job suitability. These authors found that commerce (and other) students downgraded job applicants they heard on tape (supposedly an extract of spontaneous monologue in an actual interview) when they spoke with a foreign accent when applying for relatively high status jobs relative to an Anglo-Canadian speaker, whereas the evaluations were in the reverse direction when applying for jobs of low status (cf. Hopper and Williams, 1973; Shuy, 1973). Interestingly, the nature of the foreign accent (e.g. whether it was West African or Portuguese) had little effect on listeners' ratings. In addition, judges' personality profiles were ascertained on a couple of dimensions and it was found that the above evaluative tendencies were accentuated the more ethnocentric and authoritarian the informants were (cf. Giles, 1971a). In Britain, Fielding and Evered (1977) also investigated the effects of social accent on listeners' judgements, but in their work they used regional rather than ethnic accents in the context of a doctor–patient interview. They required medical students to listen to a supposed taped interaction between a patient and physician. It was found that exactly the same symptoms voiced in a regional accent were diagnosed as less psychosomatically and more physically-determined than those voiced in a standard (R.P.) accent (cf. Shuy, 1977). Moreover, although the R.P.-accented patient was upgraded on perceived competence and communicative traits, he was downgraded relative to the regional accented patient as more emotional and less sensible.

Although the chapters overviewed in section one were categorized as decoding contributions, it would be an injustice to them to suggest the authors had not considered the encoding implications of their work. Indeed, in Chapter 5 we see that a speaker's personality is associated with his speech style. Chapter 3 also lays considerable emphasis on the 'negotiative' aspects of a dyadic interaction. Similarly, as we move to Part Two, which is concerned with encoding processes, the authors here also pay due attention to decoding considerations in their discussions. Chapter 6 is a useful introduction to section two given that its theoretical stance provides a link between the receptive and productive processes.

In the next chapter, Berger is concerned with understanding the psychological processes underlying the development of interpersonal relationships. He proposes that initial stages of a relationship are concerned with uncertainty reduction. When two people meet their 'uncertainty levels' are considered high; each is dubious about what attitudes and behaviours the other holds and what behaviour they should appropriately display themselves. Berger sees the development of a relationship then as a progressive move to make the other more predictable until a decision can be made as regards the desirability of further interactions. He suggests that one way of reducing uncertainty about others is to make (proactive) attributions about their backgrounds, personalities, and social attitudes from such cues as speech style.

It could be proposed that studies reported in section one are to a certain extent socially unreal, as many involve listeners attributing qualities to a person who is not actually talking *to them*. Indeed, a number of workers have pointed to the different attribution processes involved in decoding a person who is talking to another as compared with decoding the same speech acts addressed to them (Storms, 1973). Nevertheless, in Berger's system, the decoding of speech not directly addressed to listeners personally has great theoretical significance. He proposes that one of the passive strategies people often adopt in reducing uncertainty about others is to interpret their behaviour when talking to salient or significant *others*; indeed, listeners sometimes actively engineer such encounters. This 'eavesdropping' may even make us seek or avoid the target person in future interactions. The encoding feature of Berger's chapter, however, is in terms of the tactics speakers use to gain more information from (and hence understanding of) others. Therefore, speakers might question people initially on certain topics to elicit demographic information from them. Later, in order to ascertain more intimate statements, speakers might self-disclose some personal information about themselves in order to glean reciprocal details from their listeners.

In terms of Berger's uncertainty theory, we are portrayed as active in attempting to understand others by means of decoding and encoding strategies. This perspective provides us with the important notion that interactions have a temporal component, highlighting the fact that our goals, perceptions and attributions are continually being modified during the course of an interpersonal encounter. The recent work of Siegman (1977) can be considered as extending this framework by suggesting that not only do we encode our speech so as to monitor the behaviour of our interlocutor, we also sometimes monitor our own speech so as to safe-guard the impression we present to others. Siegman argues that in the interview context such self-monitoring has linguistic consequences, particularly with regard to temporal aspects of speech. He presents evidence suggesting that when interviewees perceive an interviewer who is apparently reserved towards them or has higher status, their speech patterns contain significantly more silent pauses than when the interviewer is perceived as warm or of equal status. This activity is considered to be a reflection of self-monitoring as under the former conditions the speaker feels the need to be more careful about what he or she says and therefore expends considerable cognitive energy in so doing. When, however, the interviewer is perceived as an equal, warm, or attractive, the need for self-monitoring is thought to be much reduced, and a decreased use of silent pausing is in fact evident. Under these conditions, interviewees also self-disclose more and, interestingly in view of the previous chapter, Siegman considers this to be a reflection of a concomitant increase in other-monitoring.

Chapter 6, then, points to cognitive aspects of self- and other-monitoring during the encoding process. The remaining chapters in this section focus more on affective components of speech production and acquisition. In Chapter 7, Ryan questions why, given the types of pressures militating against social advancement for non-standard speakers reported in the early chapters of the book, non-prestige language forms have survived today. In reviewing the literature, she points to the importance of distinctive language varieties as symbols of social identity especially for subordinate ethnic minorities across the world. Ryan discusses the tendency for people who possess strong ingroup loyalty, particularly the young, to mark this in their speech by means of a distinctive dialect or set of phonological features. Such varieties, as illustrated amongst the Mexican–Americans she has studied, is not only a symbol of group solidarity allowing group members to favourably differentiate themselves from competing outgroups, but is functional in an intragroup context for expressing valued feelings, attitudes and loyalties not amenable to representation in an outgroup code.

Bourhis, Giles, Leyens and Tajfel in the next chapter are concerned not only with noting the persistence of low prestige ethnic speech styles, but with determining the conditions under which group members would *accentuate* their distinctive varieties in interaction with a relevant outgroup. Using notions derived from a current theory of the role of language in ethnic relations, these authors asked Flemish students in Belgium to interact with a Francophone speaker who asked them sequentially ethnically-neutral and threatening questions in English. It was found that under conditions where the Francophone speaker was known prior to the encounter to be antithetical to Flemish ethnolinguistic aims, and the interaction itself was defined in intergroup terms, 50 per cent of Flemish students switched from English into Flemish when he verbally threatened their identity. The amount of English-to-Flemish divergence increased to almost 100 per cent of the sample in a follow-up study when the threatening speaker under the same conditions switched first into French.

These two chapters suggest that speakers encode their speech styles often to maintain, and sometimes to emphasize, their ingroup identity. Naturally, such contrastive patterns of speech are dependent on the speaker's definition of the situation and his or her ingroup loyalties as at other times (see Chapter 3) a speaker may wish to attenuate speech differences and accommodate to another. These intergroup processes, as Ryan points out, have educational significance in multi-ethnic societies, and therefore in the final chapters we return full circle to an educational perspective.

In chapter 9, Lambert argues that when children value their own group membership and its language variety, particularly if it has low status in an inter-ethnic context, it is possible that acquisition of an outgroup's language may result in feelings of 'subtraction' from their own group identity. Moreover, he suggests that learning one's school curricula at an early age via an outgroup language with all of its affective connotations will not facilitate ethnic pride and could well be a strong factor contributing to the low educational attainment of ethnic minority children. To bolster his position, Lambert then points to his research with certain groups of Franco-American children in Maine who are taught their school curricular first in French and move later into English. He finds that such children have more positive attitudes to ingroup speakers and out-perform children who are matched in all other ways except for the fact that their schooling is entirely in English.

The final chapter, by Gardner, continues in this vein, paying particular attention to the roles of attitudes and motivation in learning another language. He presents a theoretical model suggesting that attitudes (positive or negative) can determine to a large extent motivations (strong or weak) for acquiring a second language, and that these factors under certain conditions can be more predictive of language learning success than a 'natural' aptitude for languages. Moreover, the data he has collected on Anglo-Canadians' acquisition of French firmly supports the notion that motivation is important in this respect although the learners' beliefs, values and expectations are important intervening variables. Gardner shows that in mono- and bilingual contexts the attitude structures for learning a second language are quite different, and that individual difference variables, such as aptitude, are less important in the latter than the former context. He shows that the complex interactions of attitudes, motivations and social context in determining the success of second language acquisition are also dependent on the nature of the language learning experience and the particular dimensions of outcomes investigated.

Part Two shows that encoding, whether it be one's own native variety or an outgroup speech style, involves a complex array of social psychological operations. The subsequent speech patterns can reflect, and in fact are reflected by, the differing functions the spoken word can have. We have shown here that speech involves other- and self-monitoring devices and can express affective relationships with one's own and other groups. In all cases, the encoded speech is mediated by the speaker's role and socio-ethnic characteristics and their expectations, perceptions and interpretations of the ongoing situation.

SOME PSYCHOLOGICAL AND SOCIOLOGICAL CONSIDERATIONS

The book, then, explores the phenomenological world of speakers and hearers, and as such shows that social psychological concepts such as attitudes, motivations, intentions, expectations, and personalities are important aspects of the decoding and encoding processes. The authors have spent considerable time attempting to explain their findings by means of social psychological analyses in a manner that would have been inappropriate to have expounded upon here. Suffice it to say that a large number of social psychological theories are propounded in the succeeding chapters. Before returning explicitly to the question posed at the outset of this chapter as to what social psychology can offer sociolinguistics, it would seem useful to highlight those theories afforded greatest prominence in this volume, namely, cognitive uncertainty, attribution, similarity-attraction, gain-loss and intergroup identity.

These psychological theories depict us as being active in our attempts to understand and adapt to our social environments. Cognitive uncertainty theory (Chapters 3 and 6) proposes that when we meet others initially, we strategically attempt to make them predictable in such a way as to guide our own behaviour appropriately. The theory is concerned with making explicit in different situations the dimensions we seek to reduce uncertainty about in others, and the tactics we adopt for so doing at different phases in the development of a relationship. Causal attribution theory (Chapters 3, 4 and 6) has also been concerned with our assessments of other people and proposes that when we observe their behaviour we attribute motives and intentions to it. Workers from this perspective have been involved in determining the factors (amongst others) which influence whether that behaviour was guided by stable, internal dispositions of the individual (e.g., temperament, ability) or by transitory external factors operating at that time on the situation. Similarity-attraction theory (Chapters 3 and 6) or affective-reinforcement theory suggests that our attraction towards others is dependent on the extent to which we share important attitudes and beliefs in common. It is thought that perceived congruence on salient dimensions is positively rewarding for the individual as it consensually validates his or her actions and view of the world. The theory is concerned with determining those dimensions along which we seek similarities with (and dissimilarities from) others. Gain-loss theory (Chapter 3) focuses upon the tendency people have for being attracted most towards those whose admiration and respect they are gaining. It is thought that not only do people generally like the rewarding experience of others' attraction, but they enjoy most *increments* in others' liking for them. Workers from this perspective, then, are concerned with determining the nature of these increments and under what conditions they are operative. Finally, intergroup identity theory (Chapter 3, 7 and 8) suggests that we are not only concerned with attaining inter-individual rewards and a positive self-esteem, but that we also desire a favourable *group* identity. This theory is concerned with exploring the conditions under which group members will attempt to search for, and even create, dimensions in which they are psychologically distinct from other groups.

Forearmed then with a synopsis of some of the empirical findings and theoretical frameworks found in this book, it would seem appropriate now to make explicit the value of social psychology to sociolinguisitics both theoretically and methodologically. As regards the former, let us return to the two issues around which social psychology was deemed to have explanatory power; why we use speech variables for assessing others and why we modify our speech patterns from situation to situation. The answers to these questions will necessarily not be exhaustive but are determined by the research reported herein and hopefully will lead to a greater sophistication in the marriage of social psychology and sociolinguistics.

It would seem that language variables are used for assessing others because of their information value in at least two overlapping spheres; task-related and socio-emotional concerns (cf. Bales and Slater, 1955; Halliday, 1970). The purpose of many dyadic interactions is often task-related for one or both members. With reference to the chapters in this volume, the purpose can relate to assessing the worth of a witness's testimony, forecasting a pupil's scholastic potential, and so on. Speech cues (as well as nonverbal visual ones noted by von Raffler-Engel, 1977), given their association with social variables from people's experience, are thought to be fairly reliable indicators of a person's ethnic group (Chapters 7 and 8), social class (Chapter 2), control of the situation (Chapter 4) and personality attributes (Chapter 5). Inferences about a speaker's background, group membership and social attitudes from language cues can then be an economical process for eliciting further stereotypes which make others more predictable and our own actions more appropriate. Moreover, attributional principles suggest that when speech behaviour deviates from expected norms the salience of these cues is given particular significance by the decoder. Different speech variables are of course associated with different inferential structures and hence the salience of any one, or different combinations, of them depends on the cognitive uncertainty required to be reduced by the listener at that particular time.

Although sometimes a secondary aspect of the interaction, socio-emotional concerns operationalized in terms of the perceived attractiveness of the other can be a central feature of the encounter. It would seem that people like others who display, or make an attempt to display, and optimal linguistic similarity to their styles of speaking and mode of expressing themselves (Chapter 3). Such congruence may also be perceived as important in validating that person's way of expressing himself or herself and similarity in speech rate, perhaps one aspect of body rhythm (von Raffler Engel, 1977), seems quite important in this respect. In addition, people also make attributions of whether the other admires or respects them on the basis of expectations of typical speech behaviour and paralinguistic features of voice (Siegman, 1977) which can in themselves facilitate attraction. We enjoy the experience of others' liking for us and we often reward them for it. At the same time, however, we often seem more attracted to those whose admiration we are gaining rather than to those whose liking we have already secured. Such increments in perceived attraction can be gauged from the others' speech behaviours.

It seems useful to employ the notions of cognitive and affective concerns for explicating a speaker's tendency towards speech shifts from context to context. Regarding cognitive concerns, speakers often structure their conversations by apt use of probing questions and self-disclosures to discover more about the other (Chapter 6). In addition, the cognitive demands of monitoring one's own speech in formal or anxiety-provoking situations, whether it be a higher status other or a cognitively-demanding or emotional topic, affects temporal aspects of speech behaviour (Siegman, 1977). On the affective side, speakers may, depending on how they construe the situation, wish to integrate with another and secure his or her social approval and thereby converge towards the other's speech style (Chapter 3). In contrast, however, if the speakers possess strong ingroup loyalty and the situation is defined in intergroup terms, they may wish to maintain this identity by preserving their native language variety and nonverbal patterns of behaviour (Chapter 7). In still other situations, speakers may wish to emphasize their speech style and group allegiance, particularly when their identity is being threatened (Chapter 8) and actively resist learning the outgroup language to the extent of native-like proficiency (Chapters 9 and 10). In short, the underlying causes of speech style shifts are manifold and complex, yet they seem to arise from a speaker's desire to impart and process information as well as to present an appropriate self- or group-image, all of which are mediated again by the individual's definition of the situation.

Methodologically too, social psychology has significance for sociolinguistics, not only in its rigorous control and ingenious manipulation of many social variables. It has the methodological tools to deal with measuring complex psychological states of the hearer and speaker whether it be in terms of their ideologies, personality, temperament, prior expectations, attributions, or interpretations of the ongoing situation. In addition, these methodologies allow one to go beyond objective analyses (acoustic or linguistic) of speech differences and to determine the extent to which naïve listeners (and speakers) can detect them. In this way, we can more fully appreciate the real social meaning of language behaviour. Finally, sophisticated statistical techniques are a hallmark of social psychological methods, although this is not the only domain for them in the social sciences. Authors in this book have made an attempt to render their statistical reports more palatable than usual for the layperson. Hence, it is hoped that if at certain junctures readers become overawed, rather than deterring them from continuing, our efforts will stimulate an interest in exploring the mechanics and merits of statistics for sociolinguistic research more fully.

The pertinence of social psychological methodology may be of even more relevance to sociolinguistics if a current plea by some workers to research linguistically rather than sociologically determined groups receives impetus (e.g. Berdan, 1973; Fasold *et al.*, 1975). That is, classifying speakers according to speech communalities and determining their social characteristics rather than starting with large-scale, often quite heterogeneous, sociological dimensions (e.g., social classes) and reflecting their average use of certain linguistic features. The measurement of such social psychological states as aspiration levels, desires for achievement and approval, etc., may be salient variables in the formation of linguistically-determined groups. Moreover, social psychological work might benefit from a similar type of reorientation. Rather than working with sociologically or psychologically-determined groups and determining their average evaluations of speech variables, it might be fruitful to work with attitudinally-determined groups and discover their salient social characteristics.

As mentioned at the outset, it is somewhat surprising that language behaviour has not become a part of mainstream social psychology. It is hoped that this volume may intrigue the social psychologist, particularly given that authors have been cautious about over-glorifying the role of language variables in social behaviour. However, I shall not belabour the explicit usefulness of language behaviour to the social psychologist, as much of it is implicit in the preceding discussion, yet four important points about the relationship between language and social behaviour will be highlighted.

First, language is not a homogeneous, static system. It is multi-channelled, multi-variable and capable of vast modifications from context to context by the speaker, slight differences of which are often detected by listeners and afforded social significance. Second, a social or ethnic group's past, current mode of looking at the world, and aspirations for the future are intricately linked to language, and hence it is often a salient dimension of their identity. People like to emphasize their ingroup identity and psychological distinctiveness from others by language in some situations, while in others they desire acceptance and attenuate their distinct modes of expression. Third, with this association between language variables and societal structure, people use speech behaviour as cues to group categorizations and subsequent inferences for evaluation in important social contexts. Inferences are made about speakers' cognitive capacities, control of the situation, and psychopathological state from language behaviour, as well as those variables affecting the perceived quality of the message, its impact and persuasiveness. Fourth, the specific manner in which a speaker encodes language behaviour can be a subtle, indirect yet crucial indicant of how he or she defines the situation and or the other. In this way, as suggested by Siegman (1977), we can move away from pencil-and-paper tests of subjective reality, which are so prone to social desirability and other biases, to quite important objective tests of a person's psychological state.

FUTURE PERSPECTIVES

This book, then, shows explicitly some of the interrelationships between social psychology and sociolinguistics in a range of applied social contexts. Naturally, there is not room to have included in the discussion many linguistic indices studied by social psychologists, for example, address forms and pronoun usage (Brown and Gilman,

1960) and nominal-verbal styles (Fielding and Fraser, in press), as well as other social processes such as equity (Berkowitz and Walster, 1976) and group structure (Cartwright and Zander, 1968); these can be taken up elsewhere (Scherer and Giles, in press). This leads to the question of what type of research should have priority for the future. One important feature of the chapters in this book is that authors adequately answer this question at length for *specific* research areas. Indeed, if these ideas were taken up they would fill books and journals for many years to come. The present book as a whole, however, exhibits certain biases besides the omissions mentioned just previously, and it would be worthwhile to state them here.

First, it would appear that much empirical research and theory is concerned with one-to-one interactions (cf. however, Chapter 5) and more attention should be afforded *within-group* encounters. Second, much of the work in Part One emphasized reactions of the *dominant* member of a dyad to their subordinate partner's speech. Given that many contributors mentioned self-fulfilling prophecies in their discussions, more empirical attention could be given to the reverse process, that is, how defendants and schoolchildren, for instance, perceive their lawyers and teachers respectively. This would provide us with a more dynamic approach. Third, despite the sophisticated acoustical analyses reported in Chapter 5, the speech samples evaluated and produced were somewhat naïvely described linguistically. Obviously, linguists and phoneticians would be a welcome, if not essential, addition to this kind of research.

This leads to the question of what type of research venture is being proposed for the future. Ideally, it would be useful to engineer joint research projects between sociolinguists and social psychologists as ultimately any *complete* theory of language behaviour can emerge only at this level. Nevertheless, the pragmatics of such a proposal are enormous, and I feel that it is beneficial to have joint work on a problem from several perspectives; yet it is also important to have detailed analyses at specific levels as well. In other words, it seems useful to wed the two disciplines wherever and whenever possible with the co-operation of sociolinguistics' more traditional bedfellows, sociology and social anthropology.

But what then of 'the social psychology of language'? Besides the specific suggestions made by the authors themselves and the comments above, it seems that there is one important priority for workers in this field. Part One deals primarily with the encoding process and the social psychological factors that mediate between listening to speech and the elicitation of social judgements. Little empirical attention was directed towards determining how these attitudinal responses or intentions would be translated into *behavioural* acts by the listener (Giles and Bourhis, 1976a), and more particularly, as to how they would influence the listener's verbal response to the speaker. Part Two deals mostly with the social psychological factors mediating the encoding process. Little empirical attention was afforded as to how this was mediated by prior knowledge and evaluation of the listener and how this would affect his or her responses. In other words, the research tends to be understandably static in its empirical operations by dealing with the encoding and decoding processes as separate entities; however, it should be a priority for the future to deal interactively with both.

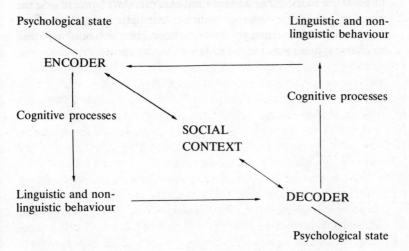

Figure 1.1 *Towards a model of the interactive process*

Figure 1.1 schematically presents in simplistic form an interactive, dynamic approach. The cognitive units here are, of course, crucial to the social psychological approach in language research. These processes, by taking account of expectancies, prior knowledge, attribution of what the other is intending to communicate, etc., mediate one's reaction and subsequent speech towards the other that is being continually monitored over time. In this regard, it also seems important to follow up the theoretical leads of Berger and Scherer (Chapters 6 and 5) as regards manipulating our language variables. Rather than stressing the relevance of one speech variable over another, let us ask the question—what is the hearer looking for at a particular time in the interaction, and how is this information marked in the speaker's speech? In addition, what is the speaker intending to convey and how is this constrained by situational and cognitive demands by means of appropriate verbal and nonverbal variables? A move in this interactive direction with explorations over time from both decoding and encoding perspectives within the same empirical investigation should produce important insights if coupled with the posing of theoretically relevant questions such as those just suggested.

Although both social sciences are undergoing critical appraisal currently, each has made valuable contributions that can be of direct importance to the other and may aid in future developments. At the moment, we are far removed from any adequate integration of the two conceptual systems; yet it is to be hoped that this book will lead to exciting prospects for development in the future.

PART ONE

The Decoding Process

2

Judgements and Confidence in Reactions to Disadvantaged Speech[1]

JOHN R. EDWARDS

Disadvantaged children are those whose home background and early socialization are such as to make the transition from home to school difficult. Thus Passow (1970) points out that:

> A child is at a disadvantage if, because of social or cultural characteristics . . . he comes into the school system with knowledge, skills, and attitudes which impede learning and contribute to a cumulative academic deficit . . . restricting later economic and social opportunities (p. 16).

Passow's view of disadvantage—generally known as the *difference* position—is by and large the one currently most prevalent. Here, although not merely a euphemism for poverty, the term *disadvantage* certainly encompasses such things as of material environment, family instability, unemployment, etc. An earlier view, although not without contemporary adherents, is that termed the *deficit* position; in this conception of disadvantage, children from lower-class environments are seen as cognitively deficient and culturally deprived with respect to their middle-class counterparts (see, e.g. Bereiter and Engelmann, 1966). The supporters of the *difference* viewpoint seized upon differences among subgroups in society, and that comparison among them which purport to show substantive intellectual deficiences proceed from a middle-class bias (see Keddie, 1973). Deficit cannot be deduced from comparisons of groups whose environments and lifestyles are unlike each other, most importantly in patterns of early socialization. Anthropological evidence citing wide differences among societies, and the seeming impossibility of constructing culture-free tests, bolster the *difference* position. There is currently, therefore, an increasing acceptance of a viewpoint which regards social subgroups as different from one another but not necessarily more or less capable in their own context. The term *disadvantage* remains, however, because although basic cognitive difficulties may not exist for children from certain groups, there are certainly strong social disabilities confronting them—especially in the context of school which generally reflects middle-class values quite unlike those assimilated by the disadvantaged child at home (Edwards, 1976a).

Of all the characteristics which contribute to, or reflect, disadvantage, one of the most important (and certainly the most discussed in the literature) is language. It was, in fact, largely through the exertions of linguists studying disadvantaged speech that the *difference* viewpoint was firmly established. Labov (1969), for example, showed that Black American speech is not a slipshod and inaccurate form of English, as was supposed by many. It is rather an internally-consistent and rule-governed dialect—nonstandard perhaps, but not substandard. The focus of language, however, clearly demonstrated the difference between cognitive and social problems. It is one thing to recognize that language varieties and dialects are of equal communicative validity for their users; it is quite another to assume that dissemination of this fact will rapidly remove social barriers among languages, dialects and accents. Within society-at-large, disadvantaged children will doubtless find the way they speak a hindrance in many situations for some time to come. And, within the educational context which gives definition to the term *disadvantage*, one finds teachers whose views on 'correctness' imply negative evaluation of the way many children talk (Edwards, 1977).

Earlier work attesting to such negative evaluation (e.g. Arthur, Farrar and Bradford, 1974; Baratz, 1972; Gumperz and Hernandez-Chavez, 1972) derives much of its importance from the possibility that unfavourable reactions by teachers may unfairly hinder pupils' progress. That is, children's speech, which may reflect little or nothing of their academic potential, may cause teachers to hold lower and essentially unjustified expectations of their performance. It is then argued that children of whom less is expected will come to feel that they have, in fact, less to contribute—a vicious circle which Rist (1970) has referred to as a self-fulfilling prophecy (see also Brophy and Good, 1974). While this reasoning may be unduly pessimistic—teachers interacting with children presumably come to have access to a variety of information about them, of which speech is but one aspect (Fleming and Anttonen, 1971)—there can be no denying that the way people *sound* is of considerable importance even when one has additional information about them (Giles and Powesland, 1975; Seligman, Tucker and Lambert, 1972; Williams, 1970).

In the present study, one objective was to further research on reactions to speech within a new geographical context. Earlier work has suggested that there are negative evaluations of disadvantaged speech in Ireland (Edwards, in press—a); it was considered important to amplify these previous findings and test their generality. This task takes on greater interest in the light of the current high level of concern about problems affecting disadvantaged children in Ireland (Edwards, 1974, 1976b; Kellaghan, 1972; Kellaghan and Brugha, 1972; Kellaghan and Greaney, 1973).

A second aim of this study involved asking speech raters how confident they were in their judgements of children's speech. The reasoning behind this was that, in rating tasks, subjects almost always comply with requests to fill in all the scales provided, even though they may feel that some are less appropriate than others. Their confidence, or lack of it, in such ratings is thus of some importance in the interpretation of results. Williams (1974) has also noted that respondents are willing to make judgements after only brief exposure to a stimulus, and describes a method by which raters can indicate the latitude of their estimates in making scale judgements of voice samples. Compared with simply making one mark on a scale after listening to a relatively short tape-recorded speech sample, a technique which incorporates a latitude of response would seem more realistic, and hence worthy of some attention (see also Abu-Sayf and Diamond, 1976, on the relationship between confidence in answers and test-descriptive statistics).

A third aspect of the present study was the investigation of judgemental differences attributable to the sex of the speaker and, especially, the sex of the rater. Previous studies, such as those of Seligman *et al.* (1972) and Williams (1970) have dealt mainly with female teacher-raters. This, of course, reflects the fact that in North America most primary school teachers, especially in the very early years, are women. Since in Ireland about one-third of elementary teachers are male,[2] it seemed both appropriate and potentially instructive to consider the sex-of-rater variable in this study. Recent interest in the effects of sex upon psychological tasks is exemplified by the work of Mazanec and McCall (1976) which found females to be more sensitive than males in inter-personal relationships, especially with regard to verbal style (for a pertinent review, see Thorne and Henley, 1975).

METHOD

Subjects

Children Taped speech samples were provided by 40 children—twenty of these were pupils at an inner-city Dublin school serving an area characterized by poor housing, low income and high unemployment. By any set of criteria these were disadvantaged children.[3] The other 20 children were from adjoining boys' and girls' schools situated in a settled middle-class area having none of the characteristics noted above. Within each group of children were ten of each sex. The average age of the disadvantaged group was 9 years and 11 months (SD = 10 months); for the nondisadvantaged group the mean age was 10 years 1 month (SD = 4 months). All the children were described by the teachers as average students.

Information was collected for all children on family socioeconomic status and family size. These data showed clear differences between the disadvantaged and nondisadvantaged groups. Socioeconomic status, determined by an adaptation from the British Census classification of occupations (see Edwards, 1974), is shown in Figure 2.1, in which it can be seen that 12 of the 20 disadvantaged families fall into the lowest classification (category 6—unskilled workers). By contrast, only one nondisadvantaged group family fall in this category, with the majority in categories 2 and 4 (businessmen and skilled workers, respectively). The family size data also differentiated the two groups. For the disadvantaged families, average number of children was 6.06 (SD = 2.65) while for the nondisadvantaged group it was 3.90 (SD = 1.41).

No specifically linguistic comparison was made here of the two groups of children, since they were drawn from similar populations as subjects in an earlier study (Edwards, in press—a). This previous investigation showed that, like their counterparts elsewhere, disadvantaged Dublin children produce fewer words and fewer grammatically complex sentences than middle-class children, at least within the formal context of the school (see Francis, 1974; Houstan, 1970). Within a *difference* viewpoint of disadvantage, such findings say nothing of the within-group adequacy of children's language; they do illustrate, however, the sort of differences obtaining between disadvantaged and nondisadvantaged speech, differences which may well prove a social deficit. In the present study, the major aim was to consider judges' reactions to disadvantaged speech, and on some of the scales provided (see below) reactions made reveal perceived speech differences (e.g. vocabulary, fluency, pronunciation) between the two groups of children.

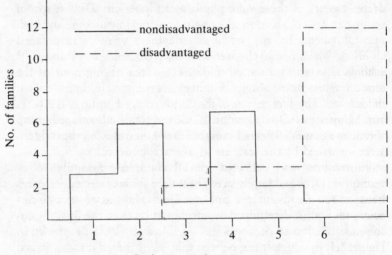

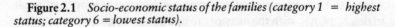

Figure 2.1 *Socio-economic status of the families (category 1 = highest status; category 6 = lowest status).*

Judges. The raters in this study, who were to listen to the children's taped voices and judge them along various dimensions, were 14 teachers-in-training at a Dublin college. All were second-year students and had had experience in the classroom. There were seven male and seven female judges, the ages ranging from 18 years 10 months to 23 years 2 months, with an average age of 19 years 10 months.

A note about why student teachers were asked to be judges is perhaps appropriate here. Information gained *from* beginning teachers allows examination of reactions to disadvantaged children prior to any large degree of involvement with them (see Cooper,

Baron and Lowe, 1975). The encouragement of flexibility in teachers' interactions with pupils, especially with respect to patterns of communication, is better approached through a knowledge of the views teachers bring with them to the classroom in the first place, rather than through views resulting from extensive experience, probably within an implicitly-held *deficit* framework. Similarly, information supplied *to* beginning teachers, on the subject of disadvantaged and nonstandard speech, is more likely, perhaps, to have useful results than if given to teachers already set in their ways (Harries, 1972; Williams, Whitehead and Miller, 1972).

Procedure

Each child was seen individually by the investigator who had spent considerable time in the schools and was a familiar figure to the children. Consequently, the pupils were, without exception, comfortable and willing to do the small task requested of them . The lack of reticence among working-class children noted in a recent study by A. Edwards (1976), in contrast to the experience of earlier studies, was also found here. All children read the same passage—a 99-word description of two children at school—which was selected with the assistance of the children's teachers. Each child read the passage twice; the first reading was a practice run in which children were helped if they stumbled over a word or if they made lengthy pauses. The second reading was tape-recorded. The 40 taped passages were then recorded in a randomized order for presentation to the judges.

Since the intention here was to study judgements of speech directly relevant to the school context, a reading passage (with suitable opportunity, in a practice trial, for removing gross errors) was considered to be the most appropriate sample on which to compare the two groups of pupils. In an earlier study (Edwards, in press—a), a more spontaneous speech sample was employed, but there is no evidence to suggest that greater freedom of speech leads to more favourable judgements of disadvantaged children. In general, however, the choice of sample is debatable; in the present study, the choice was determined by the wish to look directly at a form of speech common to all children at school. Again, it is worth emphasizing that results should not be seen as valid comments upon the general communicative adequacy of children's language, but rather as comments upon the perceptions of speech, within a relatively formal context, by middle-class judges (see also Frender and Lambert, 1972).

Since the judges listened to all forty children, the task was split into three sessions held on successive days. The judges were told that their job was to listen to, and form impressions of, each child along the dimensions provided. Seventeen seven-point scales were employed for this purpose (see Table 2.1) and the judges were instructed in the manner of using them. Scoring of the judges' responses was by assignment of a number from one to seven, each number corresponding to one of the seven choices available.

Selection of the particular seventeen scales used here was based upon dimensions employed in earlier studies of reactions to disadvantaged speech (e.g., Seligman *et al.*, 1972; Williams, 1970). In general, the scales were of two sorts: those which were more or less directly related to speech (e.g, those concerning vocabularly, fluency and reading ability), and those requiring more inference on the part of the judges (e.g., scales dealing with intelligence, writing and family background).

In addition to making these ratings, judges were also asked to indicate their degree of confidence in each judgement. For this purpose each of the seventeen scales was immediately followed, on the response sheets provided to each rater, by a further scale, thus:

Very confident : : : : : : Very unconfident

Scoring of these confidence scales ranged from one (very unconfident) to seven (very confident). As mentioned in the introduction, the confidence scales were intended to give judges the opportunity to show how certain they felt about the ratings made on each of the substantive dimensions.

The final part of the study was an individual interview with each judge in which he or she was asked about the experiment itself, and about their knowledge and opinions of disadvantage, and language and social context. The actual structure of these interviews will be apparent when the results are presented in the next section. Questioning of the subjects in experiments, although often leading to unquantifiable information, is a useful tool for increasing understanding. The data may not be sufficiently strong to stand alone but they inform the investigation as a whole and are a valuable adjunct to it (see Edwards, in press—b).

Table 2.1 *The rating scales*

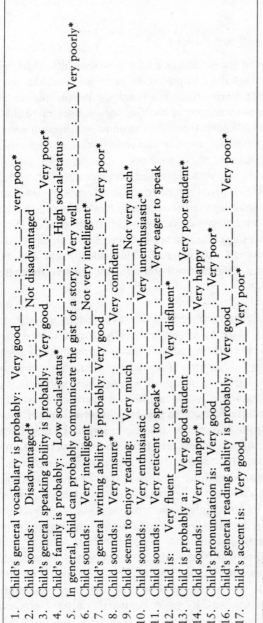

1. Child's general vocabulary is probably: Very good __:__:__:__:__:__: very poor*
2. Child sounds: Disadvantaged* __:__:__:__:__: Not disadvantaged
3. Child's general speaking ability is probably: Very good __:__:__:__:__: Very poor*
4. Child's family is probably: Low social-status* __:__:__:__:__: High social-status
5. In general, child can probably communicate the gist of a story: Very well __:__:__:__:__: Very poorly*
6. Child sounds: Very intelligent __:__:__:__: Not very intelligent*
7. Child's general writing ability is probably: Very good __:__:__:__:__: Very poor*
8. Child sounds: Very unsure* __:__:__:__: Very confident
9. Child seems to enjoy reading: Very much __:__:__:__: Not very much*
10. Child sounds: Very enthusiastic __:__:__:__: Very unenthusiastic*
11. Child sounds: Very reticent to speak* __:__:__:__: Very eager to speak
12. Child is: Very fluent __:__:__:__: Very disfluent*
13. Child is probably a: Very good student __:__:__:__: Very poor student*
14. Child sounds: Very unhappy* __:__:__:__: Very happy
15. Child's pronunciation is: Very good __:__:__:__: Very poor*
16. Child's general reading ability is probably: Very good __:__:__:__:__: Very poor*
17. Child's accent is: Very good __:__:__:__:__: Very poor*

*The end of the scale given a value of 1 in the scoring procedure.

RESULTS

The Substantive Ratings

For each of the seventeen scales, a school (disadvantaged and non-disadvantaged) by pupil-sex by rater-sex analysis of variance was performed. In this three-way analysis, the last measure was a replicated one since each of the fourteen judges rated all of the forty children—thus, each child received two ratings on every dimension, each representing the average score given by seven judges.

The results of these analyses are summarized in Table 2.2. On every scale the disadvantaged children received significantly less favourable ratings than their nondisadvantaged counterparts. Likewise, girls always received more favourable ratings than boys, the differences being significant on thirteen scales. The sex-of-rater effect was significant on six of the scales, with males making higher ratings overall than females. This tendency was seen in most of the remaining scales as well, though not to a statistically significant degree.

Significant interactions between disadvantage/nondisadvantage and pupil sex were found on ten scales. Inspection of the cell means revealed that although disadvantaged girls and boys were not, in the main, rated differently from one another, there were differences in the ratings given to nondisadvantaged boys and girls, with the latter always receiving more favourable ratings.[4] This illuminates the overall main effect due to pupil sex, in as much as it appears that the more favourable ratings accorded to girls are largely due to differences occurring in respect of the non-disadvantaged group.

Interactions between disadvantage/nondisadvantage and sex of judges proved significant on six scales. They showed that there were no large differences between male and female judges' ratings of disadvantaged children, but that nondisadvantaged children rated by male judges received more favourable ratings than those received from female judges.

In addition to the analysis of variance on each scale, a factor analysis was performed on the average ratings given by the fourteen judges. It was apparent, however, that no more than one factor would be produced by any of the usual criteria. The eigenvalue of the second factor, for example, was only 0.377. Supporting evidence of a one-factor structure was found in the correlation matrix, in which the smallest correlation within the set of seventeen scales was 0.839. This one-factor structure was the case not only for judges' ratings overall, but also for factor analyses of male and female judges' ratings considered separately.

The Confidence Ratings

As with the substantive ratings, separate analyses of variance were performed on each of the seventeen scales. These results are summarized in Table 2.3. On all scales the nondisadvantaged children were rated significantly more confidently than were their disadvantaged peers. Girls were rated with greater certainty than boys on all scales as well, the differences being statistically significant on nine dimensions. Female judges made more confident ratings than males on all scales—on twelve of the dimensions, significantly so.

Significant interactions between disadvantage/nondisadvantage and pupil sex were found on nine scales. The cell means for these showed that although there were no large differences between disadvantaged boys and girls in terms of the confidence ratings they elicited from judges, nondisadvantaged girls were rated with considerably greater certainty than were the nondisadvantaged boys (see Note 4).

A further analysis was performed on the confidence-rating data; this was to determine if there were any differences, over all the raters, in the degree of confidence associated with each of the seventeen scales—thus, the analysis was one-way, with the forty children as subjects and the seventeen ratings as replicated measures. The summary of this operation can be found in Table 2.4. Following the significant F-ratio ($F = 37.41$, $df = 16,624$) produced by this analysis, Newman-Keuls tests were carried out for each pair of scales to ascertain among which of them differences existed. The results of these tests are depicted in Figure 2.2.

It is apparent that raters were less confident about rating happiness and family socio-economic status than they were for any of the other scales. The patterns among these remaining fifteen scales reveals that confidence in the ratings made generally decreases as one moves further away from those dimensions most closely related to the speech sample itself. For example, vocabulary, fluency and reading ability were all rated with greater certainty than were the scales

Table 2.2   *Summary of analyses of variance for each rating scale*

	vocabulary 1	dis/nondis. 2	speaking 3	family SES 4	communication 5	intelligence 6	writing 7	confidence 8	enjoy reading 9
Disadvantaged/nondis. (A)									
disadv. mean	3.55	3.54	3.69	2.98	3.62	3.58	3.29	2.99	3.18
nondisadv. mean	5.88	5.97	5.94	5.37	5.97	5.75	5.65	5.80	5.51
F (df: 1, 36)	93.84*	153.34*	101.86*	152.83*	107.24*	72.72*	89.87*	74.41*	69.74*
Pupil sex (B)									
male mean	4.45	4.42	4.54	3.79	4.60	4.39	4.21	4.12	3.98
female mean	4.98	5.09	5.09	4.56	4.98	4.94	4.72	4.67	4.72
F (df: 1, 36)	4.90†	11.72*	6.11†	16.19*	2.80	4.74†	4.24†	2.83	7.15†
Sex of rater (C)									
male mean	4.89	4.86	4.89	4.43	4.88	4.70	4.53	4.40	4.39
female mean	4.54	4.66	4.74	3.92	4.71	4.63	4.41	4.39	4.31
F (df: 1, 36)	20.09*	9.29*	3.08	38.78*	6.24†	1.30	2.99	0.12	1.04
A × B F=	3.98	1.16	4.44†	2.51	6.01†	5.57†	4.70†	10.36*	8.43*
A × C F=	2.85	30.77*	0.19	34.19*	4.22†	2.19	6.43†	2.85	0.55
B × C F=	0.05	0.21	0.66	0.03	0.89	5.38†	0.38	0.06	1.21
A × B × C F=	6.50†	3.10	0.50	2.31	1.60	5.43†	1.14	0.61	0.32

*p<.01   †p<.05

Table 2.2 (cont'd.) Summary of analyses of variance for each rating scale

		10 enthusiasm	11 reticence	12 fluency	13 good student	14 happiness	15 pronunciation	16 reading ability	17 accent
Disadvantaged/nondis. (A)									
disadv. mean		3.37	3.70	3.15	3.57	3.87	3.64	3.12	3.54
nondisadv. mean		5.44	5.61	5.91	5.67	5.11	5.96	5.86	5.82
F (df: 1, 36)		55.47*	48.88*	73.70*	71.61*	46.60*	86.58*	76.95*	152.96*
Pupil sex (B)									
male mean		4.06	4.30	4.28	4.30	4.18	4.50	4.20	4.28
female mean		4.75	5.01	4.78	4.95	4.80	5.10	4.79	5.08
F (df: 1, 36)		6.22†	6.83†	2.50	6.82†	11.92*	5.68†	3.56	18.89*
Sex of rater (C)									
male mean		4.48	4.64	4.50	4.70	4.44	4.74	4.56	4.80
female mean		4.34	4.67	4.56	4.54	4.54	4.86	4.43	4.57
F (df: 1, 36)		1.87	0.21	0.53	4.53†	1.46	2.02	3.03	7.66*
A × B	F =	6.20†	4.35†	5.36†	3.80	9.28*	2.38	3.99	2.15
A × C	F =	2.15	8.59*	0.07	3.83	0.13	0.68	0.05	5.65†
B × C	F =	0.50	0.34	0.10	0.09	1.17	0.08	0.12	0.73
A × B × C	F =	0.17	1.06	0.22	0.30	0.54	0.16	0.12	0.49

*p<.01   †p<.05

Table 2.3 Summary of analyses of variance for confidence ratings associated with each scale

		vocabulary 1	dis/nondis. 2	speaking 3	family SES: 4	communication 5	intelligence 6	writing 7	confidence: 8	enjoy reading 9
Disadvantaged/nondis. (A)										
disadv. mean		5.86	5.68	5.75	5.48	5.75	5.64	5.61	6.01	5.71
nondisadv. mean		6.26	6.25	6.33	5.75	6.22	6.23	5.96	6.22	5.99
F (df: 1, 36)		22.64*	65.65*	70.77*	13.03*	39.35*	44.78*	16.22*	8.12*	12.81*
Pupil sex (B)										
male mean		5.97	5.89	5.93	5.58	5.92	5.88	5.73	6.03	5.75
female mean		6.16	6.04	6.15	5.66	6.05	5.99	5.85	6.20	5.95
F (df: 1, 36)		5.65†	5.32†	10.57*	1.47	3.46	1.95	2.20	5.66†	6.04†
Sex of rater (C)										
male mean		6.00	5.73	5.97	5.28	5.84	5.86	5.56	6.01	5.71
female mean		6.13	6.20	6.11	5.96	6.13	6.00	6.02	6.22	5.99
F (df: 1, 36)		7.61*	28.93*	3.82	68.52*	21.04*	3.47	41.92*	21.36*	18.57*
A × B	F=	1.79	6.82†	2.60	21.32*	2.11	2.09	8.86*	11.78*	4.02
A × C	F=	0.49	1.53	0.71	3.93	4.40†	0.45	2.43	1.01	1.46
B × C	F=	0.98	0.95	0.35	0.35	0.37	0.35	0.39	0.98	1.20
A × B × C	F=	1.03	2.78	0.89	0.50	1.56	4.18†	2.06	1.88	1.71

*p<01   †p<.05

Table 2.3 (cont'd.) Summary of analyses of variance for confidence ratings associated with each scale

	enthusiasm	reticence	fluency	good student	happiness	pronunciation	reading ability	accent
	10	11	12	13	14	15	16	17
Disadvantaged/nondis. (A)								
disadv. mean	5.77	5.60	5.88	5.50	4.95	5.82	5.84	5.62
nondisadv. mean	6.10	6.07	6.22	5.93	5.58	6.23	6.23	6.02
F (df: 1, 36)	18.88*	35.13*	17.33*	18.44*	43.94*	34.27*	18.55*	39.98*
Pupil sex (B)								
male mean	5.86	5.76	5.95	5.64	5.20	5.94	5.97	5.72
female mean	6.01	5.91	6.15	5.79	5.33	6.11	6.10	5.93
F (df: 1, 36)	4.38†	3.54	6.17†	2.62	1.91	5.89†	2.48	11.73*
Sex of rater (C)								
male mean	5.90	5.78	5.97	5.53	5.06	5.95	6.00	5.60
female mean	5.97	5.89	6.14	5.90	5.47	6.10	6.07	6.05
F (df: 1, 36)	3.61	2.55	10.39*	22.38*	28.57*	17.91*	2.97	55.56*
A × B F=	2.95	10.06*	1.26	4.50†	6.47†	0.37	12.29*	16.81*
A × C F=	0.91	0.20	0.66	0.08	2.69	3.58	0.84	7.50*
B × C F=	0.66	0.04	0.90	0.28	3.73	1.86	0.28	0.97
A × B × C F=	1.04	0.40	7.36*	2.08	0.39	2.86	2.30	0.56

p<.01   †p<.05

Table 2.4 *Summary of analysis of variance of confidence ratings given on each of the 17 scales**

Source	SS	df	MS	F
Between subjects	565840	39	14508.717	
Within subjects	581376	640	908.400	
Scales	284624	16	17789.000	37.406*
Residual	296752	624	475.564	
Total	1147216	679		

*All scores input to the analysis multiplied by 100 *p<.01

dealing with the child's general school performance and his writing ability.

The Interviews with the Judges

All fourteen judges were interviewed individually during the two days following completion of the rating task.[5] The interviews were structured with information elicited from each respondent on three broad areas of interest—the experiment itself, the importance of speech and speech cues, and disadvantage. In the interest of brevity, only general trends of response are reported here.

One question dealing with the experimental procedure asked about the making of ratings, and the time given to do so. Here, most agreed that the time was sufficient for the formation of an impression of the child; 'confidence', 'general fluency' and 'whether the child seemed to understand what he/she was reading' were commonly reported as important in the making of ratings. The smooth and understanding rendering of the passage was obviously of great consequence in the formation of an impression of the child. Accent was mentioned specificially by only four of the judges.

A second set of questions dealt with respondents' views of the importance of speech in general. All agreed that one's way of speaking was very important in terms of the clues it afforded to other aspects of personality. Some of the judges had reservations, however, about the making of firm judgements on the basis of speech alone, and four of them specifically felt that intelligence could be difficult to assess from speech. Seven of the fourteen judges stated that although there did exist, in their opinion, a social stigma attached to certain speech styles, this *should* not be so. Eight of the judges considered

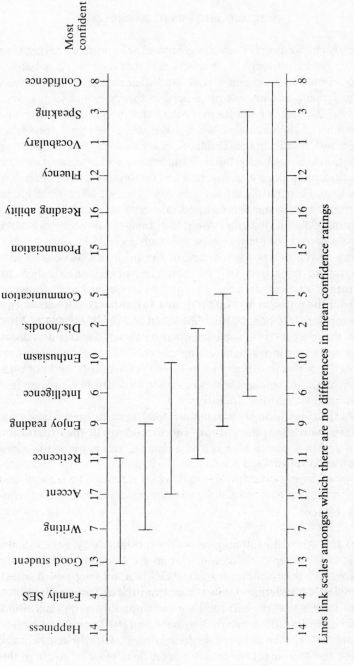
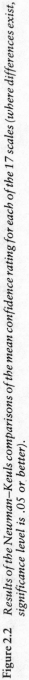

Figure 2.2 Results of the Newman–Keuls comparisons of the mean confidence rating for each of the 17 scales (where differences exist, significance level is .05 or better).

Lines link scales amongst which there are no differences in mean confidence ratings

that teachers especially attach a great deal of importance to the way a child speaks, although three others said that once teachers become accustomed to divergent accents and dialects they can effectively ignore them, and are not prejudiced in their views of such styles.

The third set of questions probed the judges' knowledge and opinions of disadvantage. When asked what the terms 'disadvantage' and 'disadvantaged children' meant to them, every respondent mentioned home background. Within this broad category, common specifics mentioned were low parental interest and attention, lack of books and generally low socio-economic status. Eleven of the judges agreed that language was an important factor in disadvantage. Concerning possible remedies for disadvantage, seven persons mentioned pre-school programmes, although several of these as well as some of the others were aware of the problems associated with pre-school education and, in particular, of the often ephemeral nature of gains made there. Four judges mentioned teacher awareness of the problem and saw the issue as one best dealt with within the regular classroom by more informed and flexible teachers. Most said that they received some information about language and disadvantage in their teacher-training courses, although several mentioned that this information was often very academic and not especially useful to teachers who were going to confront disadvantaged children in a real-life situation.

At the conclusion of the interview, each respondent was given full information about the purpose and procedures of the experiment, and within a month all received a detailed summary of the initial analyses of results.

DISCUSSION

The analyses of the ratings given on the substantive dimensions show that disadvantaged children in Dublin are evidently perceived less favourably than nondisadvantaged children, on the basis of speech samples. Considering disadvantage from the *difference* viewpoint, this implies that the self-fulfilling (and possibly quite unjustified) teacher expectations referred to by Rist (1970) and Brophy and Good (1974) may occur in the Irish context. Clearly, teachers and those responsible for the training of teachers must be aware of this possibility.

Another familiar finding supported here is that girls are rated more favourably than boys. It is interesting to note that the large number of studies (many reviewed by Brophy and Good, 1974) demonstrating more favourable teacher expectations for girls come mainly from America where most primary school teachers are female (e.g., Stevenson, Parker, Wilkinson, Hegion and Fish, 1976). It has been suggested that in countries where this situation is not so prevalent, patterns might be different; however, the evidence is not clear (Brophy and Good, 1974). An Irish study conducted by Kellaghan, Macnamara and Neuman (1969) found that there were no differences in teachers' assessments of the scholastic progress of boys and girls. The present findings, which appear to agree with the bulk of previous (American) research, indicate therefore an interesting avenue for further work in the Irish context, in which there are many male primary school teachers.

A further aspect of the present findings related to pupil sex is the interaction between the latter and disadvantage/nondisadvantage. Where differential ratings were given to boys and girls, these seemed mainly confined to nondisadvantaged children. This may be due to the fact that the raters, being middle class themselves, were more sensitive to sex differences among the middle-class children's speech, and less so towards differences in a speech style with which they were less familiar.

On six of the seventeen scales, significant interactions between raters' sex and disadvantage/nondisadvantage revealed that male raters gave more favourable ratings to disadvantaged children than did female raters. This is difficult to interpret, although it is related to the tendency for male judges to make more polarized ratings overall than females—i.e., examination of the main effect due to sex of rater showed that on most scales males' ratings were more favourable than those made by female judges. I shall return to this point again.

The factor analysis of the ratings given over all seventeen scales was obviously intended to reduce the variables to a smaller and more easily manageable data-set. As reported in the preceding section, however, all scales were highly correlated with one another and only one factor emerged—one which might simply be termed *disadvantage/nondisadvantage*. It is interesting to compare this outcome with that of Williams's study (1970) in which a factor analysis of twenty-two scales relating to disadvantage in an American context produced two major factors—one which Williams termed 'confidence-eagerness' and another, 'ethnicity-nonstandardness'. In his study, Williams had equal numbers of black and white children and scales related to the racial dimension clearly provided the high factor loadings for the 'ethnicity-nonstandardness' factor (see also Williams and Whitehead, 1971; Williams *et al.*, 1972, 1976). In the Irish context, of course, this ethnic dualism does not apply; if ethnicity is not a salient fact of life, then perhaps it is not surprising that only one factor emerged here (for a similar result, see Sachs, 1975).

The one-factor outcome of the present study perhaps warrants some further discussion. Although one would not wish to imply that raters operate only unidimensionally in this context, there is evidence that judgements of speech samples are made on the basis of an elicited stereotype. Williams (1974), for example, speculated that a stereotyped reaction could serve as an anchor point for evaluating the characteristics of children who are perceived to fit the category of the stereotype (see also Sachs, 1975). Throughout the work of Williams and his colleagues (Williams, 1970, 1974; Williams and Whitehead, 1971; Williams *et al.*, 1972, 1976) teachers' judgements of children's speech in America have consistently followed a two-factor model (see above). In the present study, the ethnicity factor was not relevant, and only one factor emerged. Of course, other scales and other speech situations could well evoke other factors; but it may well be that in the context of the school, teachers' judgements of disadvantaged speech along dimensions relating to language and school ability derive from an overall stereotype for disadvantage (for a general discussion of teachers' holistic judgements—the so-called 'halo' effect—see Freijo and Jaeger, 1976; Jaeger and Freijo, 1975).

Turning to consider the confidence ratings, one finds some rather surprising results. For example, on the scales the non-disadvantaged children are judged with greater certainty than their disadvantaged peers. And again, girls are rated more confidently than boys, this being especially for the nondisadvantaged sample. An interesting difference between the substantive dimensional ratings and the confidence ratings presents itself, however. It will be recalled that, for the former, there was a general tendency for male raters to give higher scores than females. For the confidence ratings, on the other hand, the reverse is the case—i.e., on all scales the female judges were more certain in their ratings than were their male colleagues. Apart from suggesting that one is not dealing here with a simple response tendency for one sex to make higher or lower marks on a scale, these findings allow some speculation on male–female differences in this context.

To summarize the two sets of results, it appears that male judges give more favourable ratings but are less certain about them, while female raters give less favourable ratings but are more confident in their judgements. This may reflect a sex difference in terms of willingness to commit, or possibly overcommit, oneself in making a judgement (males) as opposed to greater caution (females). If this is the case, then it is not an unreasonable assumption that males might take the opportunity given by the confidence scales to, as it were, 'soften' their judgements. Females, having been more circumspect from the start, may not find this so necessary.

The one-way analysis of variance performed on the seventeen confidence scales to determine if some were rated with greater certainty than others also provokes some interesting observations. It has been seen that all scales were highly interrelated; in that sense, it would not make much difference which smaller subset were to be employed in future work. The one-way analysis (and subsequent Newman-Keuls tests) shows, however, that there are scales with which raters feel more confident. This is also supported by the comments received in the interviews (see preceding section and below). Thus, one could select scales which have greater face validity for the judges, ones with which they are more comfortable. In general terms, these scales are those more directly related to the speech sample itself (i.e., such dimensions as fluency, reading ability and pronunciation). Judges were clearly less at ease, in the present study, with scales dealing with such things as happiness and family socio-economic status.

Finally, the interview results can be considered, although these data were dealt with in the preceding section and require less discussion and interpretation than the rest. There was general agreement that the experimental procedure was adequate for the task at hand; some judges, quite rightly however, had reservations about how well impressions would stand up with the provision of further information and/or actual interaction with the children themselves. This should remind experimenters that they are almost always dealing with a small and isolated sample of behaviour. The implication is not that the results of studies based upon such samples necessarily have little value, but rather that they should be interpreted with caution.

Interviewees were also asked about disadvantage. On the basis of answers in this area, one can see that although the rigidity and lack of teacher awareness of the problems of disadvantage have perhaps abated, there is still a need for greater and more practical emphasis upon the whole issue of language and disadvantage in teacher-training programmes.

CONCLUSIONS

In light of the finding that negative evaluations of the speech of disadvantaged children appear to exist in Ireland as elsewhere, the first point to be made here is that teachers, and especially student teachers, must be given better and fuller information about language and disadvantage. For, on every one of seventeen dimensions, disadvantaged children received less favourable ratings than their non-disadvantaged counterparts.

This finding is of greater interest, considering that it reflects the reactions of student teachers. The importance of the views that teachers take with them when they first enter the classroom hardly needs emphasis, nor does the observation that changes in teachers' attitudes are more likely to occur before long exposure to the regular classroom has taken place. The interviews revealed that, although teachers today are better informed about disadvantage than has hitherto been the case, there is still much room for improvement in teacher training. Much of this could take the form of practical experience of children whose life-style and language is different from that of the teacher. Related to this would be the provision of recent linguistic and psychological evidence which bears upon language, dialect and disadvantage.

Further work is suggested by the judges' reactions with regard to the sex of the child. The more favourable ratings given to girls were, it will be recalled, confined largely to the nondisadvantaged group. With the disadvantaged children, sex differences did not play a part in the perceptions of the middle-class judges. Perhaps, since the ratings of disadvantaged children overall were low, the judges felt that there was less room for variation in the speech assessments. And, as mentioned previously, perhaps judges were more sensitive to differences among children whose speech patterns were more like their own. These speculations deserve further study.

The results also revealed that male judges made more extreme ratings, but were less certain of them, than female judges whose ratings were made with greater confidence but were less favourable. The influence of teacher sex upon the assignment of marks is a confused area of the literature (see Brophy and Good, 1974). The interaction, however, which is often found between teacher sex and pupil sex was not evident here (see Table 2.2), and the overall finding that male judges assigned more favourable ratings than females is in contrast to the results reported in a well-known study by Carter (1952). He found that grades assigned by women were higher than those given by men, although he also reported that, on the whole, teacher sex was less important a factor than pupil sex in the assignment of marks (i.e. boys tend to get lower marks than girls). The ratings in the present study are not, perhaps, directly analogous to the assignment of marks in a classroom; there is, however, further evidence from person perception literature that in general female judges tend to make more favourable responses than males (see, e.g., Warr and Knapper, 1968). The present findings appear to go against general trends, therefore, and thus point to further investigation.

It was seen that all the dimensions used in this study were highly interrelated and appeared to represent only one factor. Bearing in mind that different sorts of scales and different speech situations may bring other factors into play, this finding does suggest possible economies for future work, in terms of the number of scales presented to judges. The use of the confidence scales, however, showed that dimensions are treated with greater certainty the more directly related they are to the speech sample. This implies that some scales have greater face validity than others, and this too should be borne in mind in further work.

To conclude, it is perhaps worthwhile to point out generally how useful the topic of disadvantage can be in linking sociolinguistics with applied social psychological problems. For language, central in any discussion of disadvantage, is (as we have seen here) capable of evoking strong social stereotypes which may have serious effects upon the school life of certain children. In his recent book on sociolinguistics, Dittmar (1976) spends considerable time on the difference-deficit controversy and effectively shows the importance of sociolinguistic inquiry for the study of disadvantage. Similarly, Williams *et al.* (1976) present an overview of the linguistic attitudes of teachers towards disadvantaged and ethnic-minority pupils. In short, language and social psychology combine, in the area of disadvantage, to provide an important and challenging study for the student of sociolinguistics.

3

Accommodation Theory: Optimal Levels of Convergence[1]

HOWARD GILES AND PHILIP SMITH

Sociolinguistics emerged as a multidisciplinary endeavour in order to provide an understanding of language behaviour with due regard to the context in which it was spoken. Its growth was prompted by the apparent lack of concern shown by linguists and psycholinguists for the importance of social setting in influencing the language behaviour observed (see e.g., Slobin, 1971); it was as though they had largely considered social context to be a static given. This is somewhat surprising since most of us can recount instances during each day when our style of speech has changed. For example, we are aware how often our speech becomes grammatically less complex with our children, that we tend to speak more slowly for foreigners, and so forth. Indeed, the nature of the setting, the topic of the discourse, and the type of person with whom we are talking all interact to determine the way we speak in a particular situation (see Giles and Powesland, 1975).

Sociolinguistic research has, in large part, consisted of attempts to discover the societal rules and norms that are thought to govern varieties of language behaviour, often resulting in the formulation of grammars with surface rules for the appropriate use of speech in different social contexts (Ervin-Tripp, 1969; Berko-Gleason, 1973). It has made great strides in informing us when, how, and on what linguistic levels we modify our speech in a given social context (Ervin-Tripp, 1969; Hymes, 1972), and its explanatory power in this respect has been mainly in terms of norms and rules (Labov, 1970; Sudnow, 1972). In some situations, it appears that we *can* identify a few such rules that everyone knows and uses in the same way, especially in bi- and multicultural settings (Herman, 1961). Such thinking has also made a contribution to foreign language learning techniques as educators seem more aware that if people are to become really skilled in another language, they should know not only the grammatical rules for its use, but the social ones as well

(Segalowitz, 1976). Yet when such analyses appear to be the only ones available, they cast the role of the normal speaker as a kind of 'sociolinguistic automaton'.[2] What of people's moods, feelings, motives and loyalties—surely these elements figure prominently in the production and interpretation of our verbal output? Considerations such as these (see also Miller and Steinberg, 1975) have fuelled a number of publications aimed at directing sociolinguistics towards a theoretical base in social psychology, culminating in a model of speech diversity termed 'interpersonal accommodation theory' (Giles, Taylor and Bourhis, 1973; Giles and Powesland, 1975). Based on explicit models of neither the speaker nor the listener, accommodation theory has drawn on four social psychological theories to focus on the interactive aspects of interpersonal communication. In the present chapter, we will review the development of accommodation theory, and consider new data which have led us to a conceptual framework highlighting its 'negotiative' character.

We started by attempting to explain a very important modification of speech in social interaction, that of 'convergence' (Giles, 1973b). The term *'convergence'* has been coined to refer to the processes whereby individuals shift their speech styles to become more like that of those with whom they are interacting. Such adaptation has been observed to occur on a number of descriptive levels, and in a manner that is not easily explicable in terms of traditional concepts of the normative demands of the situation. When two people meet, there is a tendency for them to become more alike in their language (Giles, Taylor and Bourhis, 1973), pronunciation (Giles, 1973b), speech rates (Webb, 1970), pause and utterance lengths (Jaffe and Feldstein, 1970; Matarazzo, 1973), vocal intensities (Natalé, 1975) and in the intimacy of their self-disclosures (McAllister and Keisler, 1975). Moreover, Leiberman (1967) has observed children of about twelve months of age converging to the pitch patterns of their parents by lowering the fundamental frequency of their babbling in the presence of their father, and raising it with the mother (see also Dale, 1972). In the development of accommodation theory, the assumption has been made that in all these cases, speech style shifts have occurred so as to encourage further interaction and decrease the perceived discrepancies between the actors. The assumption then is that in such situations, the speaker and the listener have shared a common set of interpretative procedures which allow the speaker's intentions to be (i) encoded by the speaker, and (ii) correctly interpreted by the listener. In the cases described above, it is probably safe to assume that these shifts resulted in a favourable appraisal of the speaker, that is, they have created an impression that the speaker is trying to *accommodate* to his or her listener(s). In fact, many speech shifts traditionally viewed as rule-governed, for example, adult-to-child, young-to-old, male-to-female and speech to foreigner, can be subsumed under an accommodation rubric. In all these cases, people may be converging their speech to how they believe others in the situation would best receive it.

Let us now examine the development of accommodation theory as it has incorporated ideas from four socio-psychological theories: similarity-attraction; social exchange; causal attribution; and Tajfel's theory of intergroup distinctiveness.

SIMILARITY-ATTRACTION PROCESSES

In its simplest form, similarity-attraction theory proposes that the more similar our attitudes and beliefs are to certain others, the more likely it is we will be attracted to them (Byrne, 1969). Speech convergence is but *one* of the many devices a person may adopt in order to become more similar to another. Specifically, it involves the reduction of linguistic similarities between two people in terms of their languages, dialects, paralinguistic features, etc. Since increasing similarity between people along such an important dimension as communication is likely to increase attraction as well as intelligibility (Triandis, 1960) and predictability (Berger and Calabrese, 1975), convergence perhaps reflects a speaker's desire for his listener's social approval. In as much as we more often desire another's approval than not, it is reasonable to suggest that there may be a general tendency for people to converge to each other in many situations.[3] Many factors could affect the descriptive levels on which, and the extent to which, convergence occurred, including the range of the speaker's repertoire, the probability of future interaction with the listener, status relationships, and recollections of previous shifts made by the listener.

A corollary of the notion that convergence might result in increased approval is the idea that the greater one's need for approval, the greater will be one's tendency to converge. Natalé

(1975) has found that speakers with high needs for approval converge more to another's vocal intensity and pause length than those with low needs for approval.

Considering the *perception* or *decoding* of a speech style, a cognitive analogue to convergence has been demonstrated by Larsen, Martin and Giles (1977) who found that subjects who thought that a speaker was a prestigious, authoritative figure, and who anticipated future interaction with him, perceived his speech to sound more similar to their own than did subjects who were told nothing about the speaker. This difference in appraisal of the speaker between the two groups gives further, indirect support to the similarity-attraction model of convergence. It also leads to an explicit recognition that a given style of speech will be perceived differently by people in two different situations.

SOCIAL EXCHANGE PROCESSES

The similarity-attraction model tends to emphasize only the rewards attending a convergent act, that is, an increase in attraction and or approval. However, it is likely that certain *costs* would be involved too, such as the increased effort made to converge, a loss of perceived integrity and personal (and sometimes group) identity. Social exchange theory, again in its simplest form, states that prior to acting, we attempt to assess the rewards and costs of alternate courses of action (Homans, 1961). Thus, if we have the choice of doing (or saying) A or B, we tend to choose the alternative which maximizes the chances of a positive outcome, and minimizes the chance of an unpleasant one. Engaging in convergent speech acts should then incur more potential rewards for the speaker than costs.

The notion of rewards attending the use of a certain speech style is problematic, but attempts have been made to specify what they might constitute in empirical terms. Moreover, it can be suggested that the specific rewards that may accrue from convergence may depend on the particular level (or levels) on which it takes place (cf. Taylor and Altman, 1975; Miller and Steinberg, 1975). Let us consider accent usage, and imagine the context of a job interview in which a male applicant has a less prestigious accent than his interviewer. One would predict that the prospective employee would shift his accent more in the direction of the interviewer than vice-versa, because of their relative needs for each other's approval. Studies in many cultures have shown that the more prestigious the accent you possess the more favourably you will be perceived on certain dimensions (Giles and Powesland, 1975). This is particularly true in England where 'Received-Pronunciation' (RP) speakers are viewed as far more intelligent, self-confident, industrious and determined than regional accented speakers, even by the latter themselves (Giles, 1971b). In addition, what one has to say will often be considered more persuasive and of a better quality, and also more likely to gain the co-operation of others than had it been voiced in a less standardized accent (Giles, 1973a; Powesland and Giles, 1975; Giles, Baker and Fielding, 1975).[4] Hence, in England, the *rewards* for our applicant's converging to the interviewer (a shift termed *upward* convergence) would not only include being more comprehensible to, and liked by, the interviewer. What he appeared to be and what he actually said also would be more favourably looked upon. Indeed, there is empirical evidence in a number of cultural contexts that supports the notion that people react favourably to those who converge towards them in terms of language, dialect or accent (Feldman, 1968; Harris and Baudin, 1973; Giles, Taylor and Bourhis, 1973; Simard, Taylor and Giles, 1976).

The rewards just suggested for accent convergence in England have, however, been based on *male* data (cf. Kramer, in press). A recent study investigating people's reactions to English female accented speech suggests that there may be additional rewards for women (Elyan, Smith, Giles and Bourhis, 1978). It was found that not only are RP-accented women stereotyped as more competent than their regional accented counterparts, they are also perceived as less weak, more independent, adventurous and feminine. In other words, upward convergence for women may glean a greater array of rewards than the same speech strategy adopted by a male. These findings have shed some light on the reasons why women in the United States and Britain adopt more prestigious sounding speech than men (Labov, 1966; Trudgill, 1974).

One could also imagine situations—such as an industrial dispute in a small family-owned firm—where there might be a greater need on the part of the *employer* to win his workers' social approval than vice-versa. In this case, the employer might be more prone (within the realistic limits of his repertoire) to shift his accent in the direction of his workers than they would to him (that is, to *downwardly* converge). More generally, a shift like this is undertaken to reduce embarrassment between people of differing status and to prepare a common basis for the communication of ideas and feelings. Indeed, mutual convergence can occur where upward convergence from one person is complemented by downward convergence for the other—if they both desire social integration. Thus far, it has been argued that speech convergence from another is favourably perceived. However, work on accommodation theory in a bilingual context (Québec) suggests that this is far too simplistic a process to operate under all conditions, and an elaboration of the theory is necessary. Since accommodation theory includes the possibility of convergence to less as well as to more prestigious speech styles and includes notions of rewards and costs to both speaker and listener, this leads us from an attempt to explain convergence merely in terms of the observable characteristics of the interacting pair to a consideration of the role played by the phenomenal worlds of the participants involved using notions derived from causal attribution theory.

CAUSAL ATTRIBUTION PROCESSES

Research on causal attribution theory (Heider, 1958; Jones and Davis, 1965; Kelley, 1973) suggests that we interpret other people's behaviour, and evaluate the persons themselves, in terms of the motives and intentions that we attribute as the cause of their behaviour. For example, we do not just observe a man donating money to a charity and automatically evaluate him as kind and generous. We often consider, as best we can, his motives first. In this case, an attribution of a motive of personal gain from this act might lead us to temper our evaluative enthusiasm, or even to assess him somewhat negatively as machiavellian and untrustworthy. We might expect that such processes operate in the perception of speech convergence as well (cf. Siebold, 1975). For instance, it has been shown that when French Canadian listeners attributed an English Canadian's convergence to French as due to a desire to break down cultural barriers, the shift was viewed very favourably. However, when this same behaviour was attributed to pressures in the situation *forcing* the other to converge, positive feelings were not so strongly evoked (Simard, Taylor and Giles, 1976). Similarly, it was shown that when non-convergence (the use of English by the English Canadian, in this case) was attributed to situational pressures demanding own-group language from the speaker, negative attitudes were not so pronounced as when the behaviour was attributed by French Canadian listeners to a lack of effort on his part.

Although interpersonal convergence is generally favourably, and non-convergence generally unfavourably, received, the extent to which this holds true will undoubtedly be influenced by the listener's attributions of the speaker's intent. Consider the situation in which one is interacting with a member of an outgroup hostile to one's own group. In such cases, valid and reliable information is often lacking about the other's true intentions, and attributions may be based on unfavourable stereotypes about the outgroup. For instance, we may be more ready to attribute convergence by outgroup members to unspecified situational pressures, or to deviousness, than to acknowledge a sincere desire on their part to reduce tension. In the same way, we may be more ready to attribute their non-convergence to a lack of effort than to consider the possibility that they do not possess the necessary linguistic skills, or that there were strong cultural pressures forcing them to use their native speech style.

Considering the interpersonal context of the present discussion, it is clear that an understanding of attribution processes as they operate in both the speaker and the listener will be necessary to an explanation of variations in speech style. From the point of view of the speaker, convergent acts will not always be intentionally *active*, and non-convergence intentionally *passive* responses—nor will they always be perceived as such by interlocutors. Non-convergence might act as a powerful symbol whereby members of an ethnic group would display their intention of maintaining their identity and cultural distinctiveness. This was exemplified a little while ago, when for the first time the Arab nations issued an oil communiqué to the world not in English, but in Arabic. Likewise, one bears witness to the efforts being made by many of the world's cultural minorities to maintain their own languages and dialects, as expressions of their cultural pride (Fishman *et al.*, 1966; Giles, 1977a). It may well be that in certain situations, people not only want to maintain their own speech style, but wish to emphasize it in interaction with others (Bourhis, Giles and Lambert, 1975; Doise, Sinclair and Bourhis, 1976). In these cases, speakers may wish to accentuate the differences between themselves and others (cf. Wolff, 1959; Tajfel and Wilkes, 1963; Tajfel, 1972), perhaps because of the other's outgroup membership, undesirable attitudes, habits, or appearance. Speech shifts *away* from the interlocutor's style, occurring with whatever intentions have been termed 'speech divergence' (Giles, 1973b). The incorporation of ideas from Tajfel's (1974) theory of intergroup relations and social change provides an appropriate context in which to consider divergent shifts more generally (cf. Peng, 1974; Lukens, 1976).

PROCESSES OF INTERGROUP DISTINCTIVENESS

In the very simplest of terms, Tajfel proposes that when members of different groups are in contact, they compare themselves on dimensions which are important to them, such as personal attributes, abilities, material possessions and so forth. He suggests that these 'intergroup social comparisons' will lead individuals to search for, and even create, dimensions on which they can make themselves positively distinct from the outgroup. The perception of such a positive distinctiveness by the ingroup will ensure that they have an adequate social identity. In other words, people experience satisfaction in the knowledge that they belong to groups which enjoy some superiority over others.[5] Given that speech style is, for many people, an important subjective and objective clue to social group membership (Giles, Taylor and Bourhis, 1977; Giles, Taylor, Lambert and Albert, 1976), it can be argued that in situations when group membership is a salient issue, speech divergence may be an important strategy for making oneself psychologically and favourably distinct from outgroup members. In a recent study in Wales, Bourhis and Giles (1977) examined divergence in a language laboratory setting where people who valued their national group membership and its language highly were learning Welsh. During one of their weekly sessions, Welshmen were asked to help in a survey concerned with second language learning techniques. The questions in the survey were verbally presented to them in their individual booths by an English (RP-sounding) speaker who at one point arrogantly challenged their reasons for learning what he called a 'dying language which had a dismal future'. As might be expected, a torrent of divergence ensued, in the sense that the informants significantly broadened their Welsh accents to him in reply. In addition, some informants introduced Welsh words, while others used a very aggressive tone of voice. In one case, a woman did not reply for a while, and then was heard instead to conjugate Welsh verbs very gently into the microphone. In a more recent Belgian study, a somewhat similar situation was set up which provoked Flemish informants to diverge from a Walloon (French) speaker by means of an actual language shift (see Chapter 8).

To summarize, we have noted that interpersonal speech style shifts do occur, and we have discussed, in terms of four social psychological theories, some of the reasons why speakers might make such shifts, and how they might be interpreted by listeners. The emphasis has been on moving closer to the interactive interface between speaker and listener, and arriving at the conception of the procedures employed by them in the production and interpretation of speech style shifts. Given the great variety of speech behaviours available to most individuals in terms of accent, dialect, and language (not to mention such paralinguistic behaviours as speech rate, pauses, pitch range, and so on), it is not unreasonable to ask whether there will not be, in a given specific situation, some combinations of speech features perceived as *optimally* accommodating by a listener (Giles and Powesland, 1975:169–70). This raises the possibility that *maximal* convergence by a speaker will not always be appreciated as the most accommodative of strategies by an audience. The demonstration of a non-linear relationship between convergence and attraction would locate the accommodation model firmly as a *psychological* theory, and reserve the terms 'convergence' and 'divergence' as descriptive socio-linguistic labels (though not devoid of psychological interest, as we shall see).[6]

OPTIMAL CONVERGENCE—AN EXPLORATORY INVESTIGATION

The research demonstrating a positive relationship between convergence and interpersonal attraction has focused more on aspects of *how* the message was spoken (e.g. the language or accent adopted) rather than on *what* was being said (cf. Argyle, Alkema and Gilmour, 1971). When two people converse, convergence between them can also occur in terms of the content of what they say. By taking account of the knowledge that they believe the listener possesses, speakers can both defer to the listener and increase mutual intelligibility. For example, it has been shown that people tend to use less jargonized and technical language with those who do not share their expertise on a topic being discussed (Moscovici, 1967). Moreover, a lack of what shall be termed 'content convergence', can often pose the listener with many critical problems in decoding the other's message (Flavell *et al.*, 1968; Krauss and Glucksberg, 1969). This raises some rather interesting questions about what we mean by speech *style*. In the context of the social evaluation of a speaker, should we in fact make a hard and fast distinction between *what* we say and *how* we say it? It suggested herein that we should not, and we take the opportunity afforded by this investigation to experiment with content convergence and to compare its effects with convergence on two other descriptive levels (those of pronunciation and speech rate). The explicit comparison of convergence on one level with convergence on other levels is in itself an innovation (cf. Bourhis and Giles, 1977). Although it is intuitively obvious that we can simultaneously change several aspects of our style of speech, the effects of doing so have never been explicitly examined.

Among the more obvious intralingual convergences that could take place would be those of pronunciation, speech rate and message content. That is, people can attempt to make themselves more similar and intelligible to others by attenuating their distinctive accents, slowing down their speech, and by presenting the substance of their message in a manner that would take account of their listener's familiarity with the topic under discussion. One aim of this study was to examine the evaluative significance of various combinations of content, pronunciation and speech rate convergences. It would be interesting to see which of these variables accounts for most of the favourable response made to converging speakers.

Thus far, the theory would suggest that the more a speaker converged towards another the more positively he would be evaluated by his recipients. Therefore, a speaker who converges on all three of the levels mentioned above should be more highly evaluated than one who converges on only one or two levels. However, this ignores the possibility that an increase in convergence may not be attributed to a positive intent on behalf of the speaker, but seen instead as patronizing, condescending, threatening, or ingratiating (cf. Jones and Jones, 1964). For instance, one could imagine an American visitor in the presence of British listeners, adopting what he considered to be a typically English mode of self-presentation. If the convergent shifts were very marked, the audience might be disposed to think that the American considers them (from his accent) in terms of an outdated cultural stereotype, and (from the content of his message) grossly ignorant about certain commonly debated matters. It could be suggested that in many situations, the underlying reason for negative reactions to large convergent shifts might be that listeners perceive speakers projecting an image of themselves that they find uncomplimentary or too simplistic a caricature. Fanon (1961) has talked about the patronizing speech whites sometimes adopt with blacks. He says that often it approaches what he calls 'pidgin-nigger-talk' leaving blacks feeling that they have been considered childlike or even subhuman (see also Shuy, 1977; Lukens, 1976). A second aim of this study was to determine whether a speaker is most positively assessed when making the most convergence.

In the present study, a Canadian male tape-recorded eight versions of the same short message for an English audience in Britain. One of these, a non-converging version, was a message in which the speaker did not converge towards the audience from a standard version on any of the three linguistic descriptive dimensions. The remaining seven versions represented all possible combinations of pronunciations, speech rate, and content convergence/non-convergence, completing a $2 \times 2 \times 2$ repeated measure design. The English listeners were required to rate each version separately on five evaluative rating scales. This investigation aimed to discover the most salient accommodative variable as perceived by the listeners, and to determine if the most convergent strategy would be the most attractive and highly evaluated.

METHOD

Subjects

Twenty-eight qualified teachers (half of each sex) attending a polytechnic in London, England,[7] on a part-time basis volunteered as subjects (Ss) for the investigation. They were all British-born aged between twenty-five and forty years. Matched for sex, they were randomly divided into two groups of fourteen Ss each.

Materials

The materials consisted of two versions of a stimulus tape and a subject questionnaire. On the last page of the questionnaire was printed the standard (no content convergence) version of a 120-word message describing the educational system in Ontario, Canada. This topic was chosen as it afforded many opportunities to converge or not to converge to listeners who had experienced a totally different educational system.

Two stimulus tapes were constructed in order to counteract the possible effects of evaluative fatigue. There were nine versions on each stimulus tape but the order of presentation differed between them. The first two on each tape were, however, identical, and consisted of a Canadian male in his early twenties reading the standard message in his normal, yet relatively fast, speech rate (approximately 145 words per minute). The first guise was prefaced on the tape by the apparent aside:

> All right Richard, let's try the Take for the North American audience.

This version was meant to be a basis for comparison with the eight versions which would follow. In other words, this message reflected how the speaker would address members of his own cultural group on this topic. Ss could then contrast the succeeding messages with this baseline to determine to what extent the speaker had adopted any linguistically accommodating strategies. The second message, identical to the first, was prefaced on tape by the aside:

> All right Richard, let's try Take One for the English audience.

This version represented the first stimulus voice that listeners were required to evaluate, and depicted absolutely no convergence in terms of message content (C), pronunciation (P) or speech rate (SR). The tape for one group consisted of these two versions plus the remaining seven in the following randomized order (where a + prefix indicated convergence and a − prefix indicates no convergence): −C +P +SR; +C +P +SR; +C +P −SR; +C −P −SR; −C +P −SR; +C −P +SR; −C −P +SR. The stimulus tape for the other group had these last seven messages appearing in the reverse order. Each voice on the two tapes was prefixed by the above aside but with the appropriate 'Take' number.

Ss were presented with questionnaire booklets which required them to rate the eight stimulus guises on nine-point rating scales in terms of: the effectiveness of the speaker's communication; the effort the speaker made in accommodating to his audience; how willing they would be to co-operate with this speaker later; how complimentary a view of his audience the speaker had; and how likeable the speaker seemed to them.

In the content convergence conditions, the speaker added eighty-five words in order to elaborate on items with which an English audience might not be familiar. For example, the speaker commented on the meaning of 'course credits', 'grade six' and so forth in the +C conditions. The speech rate in the +SR conditions was slowed down to about 100 words per minute as compared to 145 words in the −SR conditions. In the +P conditions, the speaker assumed a mild Received Pronunciation (RP) accent (that is, a standard BBC-like variant) which included for example the absence of postvocalic /r/ and the use of /o/ instead of the presence of postvocalic /r/ and /ɔ/ respectively in the −P conditions. The +P guises were not meant to be an accurate imitation of an Englishman with an RP accent, but rather, the assumption of a few phonological changes in this direction; they were independently judged by English nationals to be natural and realistic.

Procedure.

Two groups of Ss in the polytechnic evening classes were invited by a visiting psychologist from another college in England to help in a supposed research programme concerned with determining the most effective ways for foreigners to communicate with Britishers. They were told that a North American was about to embark upon a lecturing tour of Britain in which he was going to talk about Canadian Education. This lecturer has asked the psychologist's advice above the best manner in which to address an English audience. Ss were told that the psychologist had invited him to send examples of some of the possible ways he thought he might present himself to Englishmen together with an example of how he normally talked to a North American audience on an educational issue. The psychologist told Ss that they would listen to and evaluate these tape-recordings in due course.

Ss were then familiarized with the rating scales and their use and provided with a questionnaire booklet containing them together with a typewritten message about the educational system in Ontario. They were asked to read through this extract a number of times as this was the essence of the message they would hear from the Canadian lecturer. No mention was made to Ss about the nature of the variables they would hear on tape. Having familiarized themselves thoroughly with this message, Ss were told that they would first hear this extract delivered by the lecturer as he would address it to other North Americans. When they had heard this twice, Ss were told that they would now hear a further eight versions of this same extract with the Canadian trying out different styles of presentation for an English audience. After they heard each extract separately, they were to rate it on the questionnaire by means of the five scales provided.

At the conclusion of the procedure which lasted about twenty-five minutes, the investigator invited their comments in discussion and told them the nature of the empirical problems being investigated. It was evident from this discussion, and from unsolicited comments written on the questionnaire forms, that Ss had been able to detect the exact ways in which the speaker had varied his voice characteristics and message on tape.

RESULTS

The data for both groups of Ss were pooled and separate 2 × 2 × 2 ANOVAs for the factors of pronunciation, speech rate and content computed for listeners' ratings on each of the five rating scales. The effect of speech rate convergence was statistically significant beyond the 1 per cent level on four of the five dependent measures, content convergence on only one scale and pronunciation convergence on none.

The mean ratings afforded the eight versions of the message on the 'perceived effort made to accommodate' scale are arranged in ascending order in Table 3.1. Correlated tests were computed between these means to discover those versions perceived as similarly-accommodating. As can be seen from the table,
+C −P +SR and +C +P +SR were viewed as the most accommodat-

Table 3.1 *Means ratings[1] given to each message version on the "effort made to accommodate" scale, and the results of t-tests between the means*

Message version	Mean rating	t	t
+C−P+SR	2.82		
		1.68ns	
+C+P+SR	3.53		6.07**
		2.65**	
−C−P+SR	4.64		
		0.81ns	
−C+P+SR	4.96		2.10*
		1.59ns	
+C+P−SR	5.68		1.64ns
		0.33ns	
+C−P−SR	5.75		
		2.14*	
−C+P−SR	6.50		
		2.50*	
−C−P−SR	7.43		

[1]The lower the mean rating, the greater the effort the speaker was perceived to have made
*p<.05; **p<.01

ing guises with versions −C −P +SR and −C +P +SR rated lower, and versions −C+P +SR, +C +P −SR and +C −P −SR forming a cluster perceived as quite unaccommodating. Versions −C +P −SR and −C −P −SR each stood alone as the least accommodative. The ANOVA for this scale showed main effects due to speech rate (F= 116.68; d.f. = 1,216; p < 0.001), and content (F = 43.72; p < 0.01). Although there was no main effect for pronunciation convergence on this scale, it is interesting to observe from Table 3.1 that when it is the only variable being converged (i.e., −C +P −SR), it is perceived as significantly more accommodating than −C −P −SR.

A main effect for speech rate emerged on three of the other scales as well. When the speaker accommodated his speech rate by slowing it down, he seemed a more likeable person (F = 9.58; p < 0.01), Ss were more willing to co-operate with him (F = 20.63; p < 0.01) and his message was perceived to be more effective (F = 58.23; p < 0.005).

Significant three-way interaction effects emerged on two scales; how likeable the speaker seemed (F = 4.44; p < 0.05), and how complimentary a view of his audience the speaker was perceived to have (F = 8.30; p < 0.01). These effects can be most parsimoniously interpreted as follows: when the speaker was not making any content convergence, he was rated most favourably on the above two scales when he converged *both* his speech rate and pronunciation. However, when he did not converge in content, the speaker was accorded the most favourable ratings when he converged his speech rate *only*. In other words, when there was content plus speech rate convergence, the addition of pronunciation convergence was relatively poorly perceived. It was, nevertheless, more favourably perceived than the least converging strategies. These data support the notion of an optimal level of speech convergence, in that the speaker was more favourably rated in the +C −P +SR condition than when he converged the most (i.e. +C +P +SR).

DISCUSSION

With regard to the aims of the present study, two achievements have emerged. Firstly, this is the only study in which the interaction of several speech variables has been considered within the accommodation framework, and of these, speech rate has been found to be the most salient convergence variable. Interestingly, a number of writers (see Siegman and Feldstein, in press) have argued for the fundamental importance of *temporal* aspects of conversational features in an interpretation of dyadic encounters. Secondly, and perhaps more importantly in the context of the preceding discussion, we have demonstrated a non-linear relationship between convergence and attraction. Consideration of these results will help to clarify the conceptual framework of accommodation theory, and will point to some interesting directions for further research.

The fact that speech rate convergence was reacted to more favourably overall than either content or pronunciation convergence is perhaps surprising, and deserving of further empirical attention. Previous research has shown the facilitative effect of pronunciation convergence on listener evaluations of the speaker (e.g. Bourhis, Giles and Lambert, 1975; Doise, Sinclair and Bourhis, 1976), yet in the present study, it had a very limited positive effect on subjects' ratings. In view of the fact that the North American speaker would have been seen as a representative of an outgroup whose accent is positively evaluated by Britishers (Giles, 1970), pronunciation shifts may not have been expected. Had the speaker, however, represented an outgroup which had a low social and accent prestige, or was in conflict with the listener's own group, pronunciation convergence (often the marker of group membership, see Bouchard Ryan's chapter) might have been perceived as more of a concession to the audience, and had a correspondingly more positive effect. However, it appears that pronunciation convergence can lose its potency in combination with convergence at other levels.

The fact that content convergence influenced ratings to a lesser extent then the speaker's shift in speech rate is also perhaps surprising. It may have been that the listeners (who were teachers) were more sophisticated in transatlantic educational differences than we anticipated; post-experimental discussion with them, however, did not support such a contention. Alternatively, it could be that the serial comparison nature of the evaluative task detracted from the salience of content convergence. That is, once the content of the message had been elaborated in one Take, content convergence in subsequent Takes would have lost its initial salience. Nevertheless, some informants spontaneously and accurately wrote down on their questionnaire the modification in style that the speaker had made, thus appearing able to cognize the speech strategies that he was employing. One would also expect that if a 'saturation' effect was responsible for the low salience of the content convergence, it would also have operated with respect to speech rate convergence. To avoid the possibility of such confounding effects in future, independent samples of listeners should be employed to assess one version of the message each, and in an interactive situation which would enable us to examine their verbal behaviour in response to the speaker (Giles and Bourhis, 1976a). Certainly, we have gained only rudimentary knowledge about what constitutes an effective convergent strategy, even in this restricted situation. Even so, the usefulness of incorporating notions of content convergence into empirical studies of interpersonal accommodation has been demonstrated.

In the present study, the effect of adding pronunciation convergence to content and speech rate convergences was to attenuate the favourableness of the ratings. According to the listeners, they thought that the speaker had a very uncomplimentary view of them when he converged on all three linguistic levels. The addition of pronunciation shifts could have been perceived as patronizing or ingratiating. Alternatively, or in combination, pronunciation shifts plus the other convergences may have been perceived as threatening. According to Tajfel's theory outlined earlier, English listeners may have felt that they were losing their cultural distinctiveness as the Canadian adopted perhaps the most distinguishing linguistic attributes of their group identity—a 'British' accent. In this way, the speaker may have been perceived as stripping them of the veil of their group distinctiveness, while at the same time displaying how easy it was to take account of their characteristics by content and speech rate convergences. In further research, it will be interesting to determine whether optimal levels of convergence in different social situations (e.g. between-sex and intergenerational encounters) have the same linguistic features in common. It is our guess that they would not and furthermore that the underlying explanations of 'over-accommodation' might also be context-specific.

Besides optimal magnitudes of convergence, it is interesting to speculate that there might also be optimal *rates* of convergence. Aronson's (1972) 'gain-loss' theory of attraction proposes that we like more those people whose respect we are *acquiring* rather than those whose admiration we already possess. It could be suggested then that convergence is more effective when it takes place slowly enough so that the change is perceived in stages (or by degrees), rather than all at once. The latter strategy might perhaps imply to the listener that the speaker's respect was secure from the outset. Interestingly, it has been found that people naturally converge more to each other on subsequent occasions, appearing to converse convergent acts for use as bargaining tools or 'aces-in-the-hole', as gain-loss theory would predict (Lennard and Bernstein, 1960; Welkowitz and Feldstein, 1970; Natalé, 1975). In this sense, the 'negotiative' character of speech convergence can be understood. Aronson also proposes that we *dislike* most those whose respect we appear to be losing, rather than those who have never held us in high esteem. It may well be that gradual divergence is seen to be more of a symbol of dissociation from others than immediate, large-scale divergence. Gradual divergence may be attributed by listeners as a more meaningful and a considered reflection of the speaker's orientation towards them than a seemingly more impulsive and pre-ordained divergence encoded fully all at once.

Just as we have discussed the non-linear relationship between convergence and perceived attraction, we should also consider that a degree of *divergence* in some situations might be more positively evaluated than hitherto believed. In certain intergroup encounters, members of opposing or competing groups may expect nothing less than some linguistic divergence (rather than convergence) if only to remind themselves that they indeed have a dispute or difference (cf. Doise, Sinclair and Bourhis, 1976). Failure to confirm these expectations might indicate that something was 'wrong', that the intergroup situation had changed somehow without one party being aware of it. In this sense then, one can talk of optimal levels of divergence. Indeed, one can imagine situations in which the 'right' amount of divergence might elicit co-operation where convergence would not. Take the case of a stranger entering a foreign city. By diverging to the extent of making one's speech distinct from that of the local inhabitants', the speaker might be making him- or herself appear more interesting than by attempting to mask one's origins by converging. As Aboud and Taylor (1973) have shown in a series of studies on information seeking, a little difference is often more appealing and interesting than no difference at all, or too much of it.

To the extent that listeners interpret speech styles directed at them as, at least partially, a reflection of the speaker's evaluations of *them* as individuals, it makes sense to consider the range of all possible speech styles as points along an evaluative continuum. There will probably be more than a single convergent behaviour regarded by the listeners as reflecting an acceptable image of themselves. Such a notion is reminiscent of Sherif's 'latitude of acceptance' in social judgement research (cf. Sherif, Sherif and Nebergall, 1965). In this work, people are asked to categorize a large number of statements ranging from extremely positive to extremely negative pertaining to some attitude object (a person or an issue, for example). They will use a number of categories in judging these statements including a 'best estimate' category of their own position, a category containing statements which are acceptable to them, a category containing uncertain or non-committal statements, and one containing statements which are extreme and unacceptable. Furthermore, the relative 'widths' of the latitudes of acceptance, rejection and non-commitment of these evaluative items are thought to reflect the degree to which the individual is involved with the person or issue at hand. In the present context, the attitude objects can be considered

the listeners themselves, who are categorizing speech styles as reflecting acceptable or unacceptable evaluations of themselves, and
responding accordingly. Individuals and groups will undoubtedly
vary as to their range of tolerance, or latitude or acceptance, according to how they read the situation. Further exploration along these
lines would probably lead to some interesting and testable predictions (cf. Williams, 1974; Kelley, 1975).

However, the notion that speech styles lie on a unidimensional
continuum may be too simplistic. We have already pointed out that
convergence–divergence may take place on more than one descriptive dimension simultaneously, and that listeners can identify dis-
creet levels of convergence. This raises the possibility that a speaker
might, with a mind to being intentionally ambiguous, attempt to
converge on one level (that of speech rate, for example), while not
converging, or even *diverging* on another level (e.g. accent). The
effect might be even more subtle than intimated here, if one considers
(as do Bourhis and Giles, 1977) that shifts in speech style may occur
on two levels simultaneously, one for the benefit of the group, and
another (not even perceived by the outgroup) for the benefit of
members of the ingroup as a covert expression of solidarity.

There is another way in which the idea of a one-dimensional
evaluative continuum may be too simplistic. 'Similarity' is not the
only criterion for the evaluation of a speech style, as we have indicated. The purposes of inter-personal communication are as varied
as the contexts in which they occur, and we can expect that the
dimensions salient to the evaluation of speech styles will be context-
dependent. Thus we might expect in one teenager's evaluation of
another on the basis of speech, dimensions such as 'with-it/not
with-it', and 'old-fashioned/modern' might be important, while a
diplomat in conference with a foreign emissary might be more concerned how 'rigid-flexible', or 'integral-easily manipulated' her
partner sounded. This implies that a given speech style may get
different, and sometimes contradictory evaluations, when comparing its meaning in different evaluative domains.[8]

Just as the field of developmental psychology has moved away
from considering children as mere victims of their environments to
thinking of them as reactive beings often capable of selecting their
own input and negotiating their status with other children and
adults, so too should sociolinguistics reconsider its view of speech
behaviour as if it were a blob of clay moulded by situational con-

straints. The perspective adopted in accommodation theory is aimed at correcting the lop-sided reliance in sociolinguistics upon descriptive sociological methods in understanding spoken behaviour, and at indicating the contributions that can be made by social psychology, and by theories of 'naïve' psychology (attribution theory, for example). To understand why individuals speak the way they do, we must know something not only about their descriptive characteristics, but also about the manner in which they interpret 'the situation', and the procedures they use to act on those interpretations. We must also remember that speakers are also listeners (cf. Pellowe *et al.*, 1972) and that the same knowledge will be required about listeners as about speakers, in order to understand how they evaluate speech styles. Discussion about the most profitable point of intersection of the social scientist into this 'problematic', as we shall call it, must be left for another place. But we argue here that the interactive interface between speaker-listeners, i.e., 'the situation', is not a bad place to begin, and that is where accommodation theory has its roots. One useful feature of this theory as demonstrated in the present chapter is that it is amenable to a wide variety of conceptual extensions which suggests that it may be robust and powerful. The stage is now set for the development of a more systematic theory of speech accommodation, not only in explaining interpersonal phenomena but in providing clues to the dynamics of processes operating both within and between groups as they strive to cooperate or plot to remain distinct.

4

The Social Significance of Speech in the Courtroom

E. ALLAN LIND AND WILLIAM M. O'BARR

To anyone who has observed the trial of a civil or criminal law case, one of the most obvious characteristics of this social institution is the great amount of spoken communication which goes into the generation of the final verdict. Although much of the pre-trial development and much of the post-trial resolution of a case are realized through written documents, in the trial itself the case is quite literally 'heard'. In American courts, for example, the positions of the parties to a legal dispute are presented in spoken statements by attorneys and are supported by the spoken testimony of witnesses. In most instances even non-spoken evidence—documents, photographs, and other physical proof—must be introduced through the spoken testimony of a witness. The statement of the law itself, in a jury trial, is contained in oral instructions delivered by the judge.

In view of the importance of speech in legal trials, it is of interest to investigate empirically the social processes which govern the way in which those involved in trials express themselves. Equally important are the effects of variations in the manner of speech on those to whom it is directed. Considering the example of oral testimony, there are many ways in which the same facts can be communicated, and it seems reasonable to suppose that different 'manners' of testimony may have differing effects on the reactions of the jurors who must evaluate the testimony. The social and psychological processes involved in the generation and reception of court speech may be studied through the application of methods developed in sociolinguistics, political anthropology, and social psychology for the investigation of just such phenomena as those addressed here. We describe below a number of studies of court speech, emphasizing, in line with the focus of this volume, those which used the techniques of experimental social psychology. (We will present the results of anthropological and sociolinguistic studies where they are of importance, however.)

If we imagine ourselves in the position of a judge or juror hearing testimony in a trial, we may gain some insight into the possible psychological issues involved in the reception of court speech. Perhaps the most immediate decision we would have to reach in such a situation is whether we believe that the testimony of a particular witness is true. That is, to what degree do we wish to incorporate the information contained in the testimony in our understanding of the events involved in the case and, ultimately, in our judgement about the proper disposition of the case? Social psychological theory and research has long recognized the importance of this issue of 'credibility' in the reception of social communications (cf., Bersheid and Walster, 1969; Giffin, 1967; McGuire, 1969). From this work we know that the acceptance of a communication (in non-legal contexts, at least) is often influenced by judgements concerning the communicator's competence (his or her ability to make valid statements) and by judgements concerning the communicator's trustworthiness (his or her intention to convey only statements which he or she considers truthful; Hovland, Janis, and Kelley, 1953). Social psychological studies and theories have pointed also to the influence of such factors as the attractiveness and the social dynamism[1] of a communicator in the psychological acceptance of a communication (e.g., Giffin, 1967; Kelman, 1958). If we are correct in our assumption that credibility judgements are a major psychological process involved in the reception of court speech, we would expect that considerable social evaluation occurs in the courtroom, with judges or jurors attempting to assess witnesses on dimensions such as competence, trustworthiness, attractiveness, and social dynamism.

There is a growing collection of studies in social psychology that demonstrate that individuals use information from the manner in which an oral communication is spoken to evaluate the speaker. Giles and Powesland (1975) review and discuss a large number of studies which show that evaluations of speakers on such personal qualities as competence and social attractiveness vary as a result of characteristics of the speech heard by the evaluators. Most of these studies have involved presenting individuals with one of several speeches in which the same speaker presents the same information with different accents (e.g., in English or French). Those listening are then asked to indicate on rating scales their evaluations and impressions of the speaker, with the most frequent result being that there are considerable differences in the evaluations engendered by the different speeches. Although, as just noted, the majority of these studies have examined differences between various accents or various languages, similar results have been observed in studies investigating the effects of other speech differences. For example, a recent experiment has demonstrated that a communicator is seen as more competent and his or her communication is more persuasive when the communicator speaks rapidly than when he or she speaks slowly (Miller, Maruyama, Beaber and Valone, 1976).

Thus there exists in previous theory and research in social psychology considerable justification for supposing that an important part of the process by which court speech is received is the social evaluation of the speaker, and that the evaluation of the speaker may be influenced by the manner in which he presents his communication. Before we begin to discuss our own studies testing these suppositions, however, it is necessary to consider in more detail the social context of court speech. Our working assumption in these studies was that a major aspect of the use and effect of various styles of speech in the courtroom is the implication of each style for issues of social control and power. In explaining the results of our social psychological studies of court speech we will make use of these concepts.

SOCIAL CONTROL, SOCIAL POWER, AND COURT SPEECH

The ultimate purpose of a trial in a court of law is the resolution of a dispute existing either between two parties, as in the civil justice system, or between society and one or more of its members, as in the criminal justice system. This dispute resolution is accomplished through the binding decision of one or several (supposedly) impartial decision makers. Since the interests of those at trial are usually in extreme conflict, it is to be expected that many of the behaviours occurring in court trials are attempts to influence the judges or jury to reach particular decisions, and that these attempts at influence are often themselves conflicting, originating as they do from parties desiring very different resolutions of the case. The properties of trials—the imposition of a decision by societal agents and the exposure of these agents to influence attempts by those involved in a conflict—suggest that one way to attempt to understand the social processes involved in trials is to examine closely the implications of trial events for the distribution and use of social power and control over the final decision. It seems likely that those who watch and participate in trials are aware of the importance of social power and control issues in the legal system and that they base many of their own behaviours and their interpretations of trial events on these factors. This supposition is similar to those of Thibaut and Walker (1975) who, in an analysis of the social psychology of reactions to judicial procedures, present considerable evidence that perceptions of the fairness of procedural rules are dependent on the perceived consequences of the rules for issues of control. It is our belief, supported by the studies we report below, that those involved in trials are influenced in their choice of various ways of expressing themselves and in their interpretation of the social meaning of others' speech by power and control considerations.

Although all legal systems include this characteristic of conflicting attempts to exert social control over the legal decision makers, some systems are more explicit in providing procedures for such attempts than others. The general acceptance in Anglo-American law of the 'adversary system' of criminal and civil procedure is a familiar example of explicit recognition of social influence attempts as a part of the trial process. The adversary system has given rise to legal procedures and norms which provide that the judge, who has final immediate authority over most trial behaviour, should delegate control over the presentation of evidence and arguments concerning the case to attorneys who are partisan advocates of the conflicting viewpoints in the legal dispute (see Thibaut and Walker, 1975, for a more complete discussion of the procedural and psychological consequences of the adversary model). The attorneys are given great freedom in how they exercise this control, but it is generally assumed that a major part of their trial behaviour involves attempts to present the position of their clients in the most effective verbal expression.

We have digressed to this brief discussion of power and control relations in courts because there are many studies in social psychology which reveal that responses to influence attempts are affected by beliefs concerning the motivations and social situation of those attempting the influence (e.g., Mills, 1966; Mills and Jellison, 1967). Given the court social structure we have just noted, we expect social interpretations and responses to court speech to be especially dependent on beliefs about the position of the speaker with regard to the distribution of power and control in the court. It is certainly reasonable that this should be so, for, as we describe below, many of the actual variations in court speech seem to be patterned by power, control, and status relations in the court and in the society within which the court functions.

OBSERVATIONS OF COURT SPEECH

We report in this chapter several social psychological experiments in which we examined the effects of various manners of delivering testimony. These experiments were preceded by an extensive study of the speech actually used in a criminal trial courtroom.[2] With the permission of the court, all criminal trials in a North Carolina Superior Court were observed and tape recorded. These trials involved cases on a wide variety of charges and individuals from a variety of economic, social, and ethnic backgrounds. More than 150 hours of taped court speech were obtained with corresponding observations noting the social and legal situations within which each sample of speech occurred. These data were analysed by a team of investigators trained in linguistics, anthropology, and the law.

These observations and analyses served to identify common dimensions of variation in court speech. Several speech variables were manipulated in the experiment reported below in order to assess the consequences of the speech variables for the impressions and evaluations of those hearing the speech. The experiments focused on speech variables in testimony and their effects on individuals who were asked to assume the role of jurors in legal cases. The observation and analysis of the actual court speech also identified the social factors which were associated with various manners of delivering testimony. An additional benefit of the tape recording of the trials was that it provided samples of testimony which could be edited, transformed, and re-recorded to provide the stimulus speech used in the experiments. Thus the experiments we describe here were based on speech variables and speech samples which actually occurred in trial courts.

Many of the most common and important dimensions of variation in court speech seemed to carry information about the power, status, and control of the speakers. We will turn now to detailed considerations of three such variables. The first speech dimension on which we will comment is associated with the speaker's general societal status and prestige.

'POWER' AND 'POWERLESS' SPEECH

Among the speech variables examined in the sociolinguistic analysis mentioned above was a cluster of features which had been postulated to show sex differences in their frequence of use in American English. Lakoff (1973, 1975) suggests that there is a specific mode of speech which is used more frequently by females than by males. According to Lakoff, this mode of speech involves frequent use of *intensifiers* ('so', 'very', 'too', as in 'I like him *so* much'), *empty adjectives* ('divine', 'charming', 'cute', etc.), *hyper-correct grammar* (bookish grammatical forms), *polite forms, gestures, hedges* ('well', 'you know', 'kinda', 'I guess', etc.), and *rising intonation* and *a wider range of intonational patterns* (e.g., the use of rising, question intonation in declarative contexts). Lakoff contends that women who do not use this mode of speech are seen as less feminine than those who do and are negatively evaluated, but that those who use this mode of speech do so at the cost of reducing considerably the convincingness of their statements.

The sociolinguistic analysis of speech in the criminal court revealed that many female witnesses do indeed use the mode of speech described by Lakoff. However, frequent use of the features described above was by no means observed in the speech of all female witnesses, nor was the use of these features confined to the speech of female witnesses. Rather than being consistently related to the sex of the witness, the mode of speech we are considering seemed to depend on the social position of the witness *vis-à-vis* the court. For example, male and female physicians, parole officers, and other professionals giving testimony tended to show a lower frequency of use of the features mentioned above. In contrast, male and female witnesses who had little social prestige, who were unemployed or of low status, used these features more often. In light of this social patterning of the speech modes we are considering here, we term frequent use of the features described above the 'powerless' speech mode and infrequent use of these features the 'power' mode.

Once those two modes of speech had been identified, it was of interest to determine the effects of testimony delivered in each mode on social evaluations of the witness. To accomplish this an experiment was conducted in which the same substantive evidence was presented in either power or powerless speech. As a first step to conducting the experiment, we located in the recorded testimony an instance of a female witness using powerless speech. Using actors to play the parts of the (male) attorney and the (female) witness, this example of powerless mode of testimony was re-recorded, preserving the linguistic features by changing the names, dates, and locations mentioned and omitting some discussion of legal technicalities present in the original tape. A second recording of the testimony was made, using the same actors and presenting the same facts, but omitting most of the features characteristic of powerless speech. In order to assess the effects of power and powerless speech on evaluations of male as well as female witnesses, two other tapes were made in which a male actor spoke the part of the witness using either power or powerless speech features.[3]

Subjects in the experiment heard one of these four tapes after being asked to imagine themselves in the role of a juror and after being given a description of the case from which the testimony was taken. They then answered a number of ratings-scale questions about their reactions to the testimony, to the witness, and to those involved in the case. Some of the results of the experiment are presented in Table 4.1, which shows the mean ratings of the witness on a number of social evaluation dimensions.[4]

As may be seen from the table, there are striking differences in the social evaluations produced by the power and powerless testimony. For both the male and the female witnesses, the power speech testimony produced perceptions that the witness was more competent, attractive, trustworthy, dynamic, and convincing than did the powerless speech testimony. In light of Lakoff's hypothesis about the cost to women of not using the powerless features, it is interesting to note that in this experiment the female witness was not seen as less feminine when she used the powerless mode ($p < 0.005$).[5]

These findings confirm that variation in the manner chosen by a witness for verbal expression may have strong effects on how those hearing the testimony evaluate the witness. In this experiment subjects' acceptance of the testimony, as indicated by their ratings about the issue at trial, reached only marginal levels of statistical significance (<0.13 for the female witness, and $p < 0.17$ for the male witness). However, since witnesses using power and powerless

Table 4.1 *Mean ratings of witnesses using power and powerless speech*

Female witness:

Evaluation dimension	Power testimony	Powerless testimony
Competence	2.38	0.72
Social attractiveness	2.48	0.54
Trustworthiness	3.04	1.65
Social dynamism	0.67	−0.67
Convincingness	3.35	1.77

Male witness:

Evaluation dimension	Power testimony	Powerless testimony
Competence	1.77	0.11
Social attractiveness	2.52	1.23
Trustworthiness	3.48	2.00
Social dynamism	0.83	−0.98
Convincingness	3.89	2.48

Note: Higher values indicate more favourable ratings on the evaluation dimension. For all comparisons of speech conditions within each sex of witness the difference in ratings is significant, $p < .05$. See Note 4 for an explanation of the variables.

speech were perceived differently on a number of social evaluation dimensions which have been found in other social psychological studies to influence acceptance of a communication, we suggest that this speech variable could affect the outcome of trials in which a crucial witness used the power or powerless mode of speech.

The results of this experiment demonstrate that social evaluations are indeed affected by the use of power and powerless speech, but these data do not in themselves explain the psychological processes involved in this effect. There is, however, some evidence in the present data which suggest that the strongest effects of the speech variable are on basic social evaluations of the witness rather than on the perception of the information the witness presented. In view of the findings of the sociolinguistic study with regard to the natural use of power and powerless speech, it seems likely that the subjects in the experiment had learned from their past experience with those using the two modes of speech to associate the power speech mode with generally high social power individuals and the powerless mode with speakers having low social power. The common belief that individuals with high social power obtain that power from their considerable control over a variety of tasks (and, thus, have high competence) and that such individuals can deliver social rewards (making them more attractive) may explain the evaluation effects observed. That is, the use of power or powerless speech may provide cues which are interpreted as identifying the speaker as a particular type of individual and this identification may have certain connotations for the judgement of personal qualities.

NARRATIVE AND FRAGMENTED TESTIMONY

The experiment just described dealt with a speech variable which the sociolinguistic analysis identified with general social prestige. There are, however, other aspects of social power and control which may be reflected in the speech used in testimony. We describe in this section and the next two experiments speech variables related to the distribution of control over the testimony between the witness and the lawyer conducting the interrogation in court.

Our observations of court speech suggested that a major variable in testimony speech was the length of a witness' response to the lawyer's questions. It was apparent that in some of the observed testimony the witness responded at length to the lawyer's questions while in other testimony the witness gave a relatively brief answer to each question. As might be expected, relatively fewer questions were usually needed to elicit the same amount of information in the former, 'narrative' type of testimony than in the latter, 'fragmented' type of testimony. Legal scholars writing on trial tactics often consider these two types of testimony (cf. Keaton, 1973; Morrill, 1971). Lawyers are generally advised by the authors of trial tactics manuals to allow their own witnesses some leeway for the use of narrative answers and to restrict opposition witnesses to brief answers as much as possible. This advice seems to be based on the implicit hypothesis that narrative answers are better received than fragmented answers.

There are social psychological reasons also for our examination of the narrative/fragmented distinction. We noted above the principle in Anglo-American legal procedure that most of the control over the substance and form of testimony is delegated to the interrogating attorney. Since this principle of attorney control is widely known, it seemed likely that narrative testimony would be seen by jurors as an instance of voluntary, partial transfer from the attorney to the witness of control over evidence presentation. That is, in permitting a witness to respond at length, the attorney may be seen as surrendering to the witness some of his control over the testimony. A group of social psychological models—termed attribution theory—suggests that the type of testimony heard would be interpreted as carrying information about the attorney's perceptions of the witness.

Attribution theory (cf. Jones and Davis, 1965; Kelley, 1967) is based on the assumption that individuals analyse the behaviour of others in search of the underlying causes of their behaviour. In the situation considered here, the theory suggests that if our earlier supposition is correct, jurors would seek a causal explanation for the transfer of control involved in narrative testimony. Such an explanation is available in the attribution that the attorney in a narrative testimony situation has generally favourable impressions of the witness and believes that the witness is capable of presenting evidence without constant prompting. Attributions of this sort, if they do indeed occur, might influence the juror's own social evaluations of the witness, as would happen if the jurors accepted the apparent evaluation of the witness by a liked attorney. The attribution process posited here would suggest that, if the jurors accepted the attorney's apparent evaluation of that witness, they would react more favourably to narrative testimony than to fragmented testimony.

The attribution theory analysis suggests another factor which may influence reactions to narrative and fragmented testimony. Social psychological studies of the attribution process have shown that attributions concerning others' beliefs and evaluations are strongest when the observed behaviour is contrary to the behaviour expected from social norms (cf. Jones and Davis, 1965; Jones, Davis and Gergen, 1961). Several writers have suggested that current norms call for men to be more assertive in their speech than women (Key, 1975; Lakoff, 1973, 1975; Thorne and Henley, 1975). Since the use of narrative answers may be viewed as a form of linguistic assertiveness, those hearing narrative testimony delivered by a female witness, or fragmented testimony delivered by a male witness, might view such speech behaviour as non-normative and, according to attribution theory, as particularly indicative of the attorney-witness relationship. We might expect that the combination of a female witness and narrative testimony would result in the attribution that the attorney has an especially low evaluation of the witness.

A third possible factor in reactions to narrative and fragmented testimony was examined in the study. Although we have devoted many of our remarks to the reactions of jurors, many legal cases are tried by judges sitting without juries. In such cases an essential question in trial tactics is how a judge, rather than a juror, will react to the testimony. We were not able to examine directly differences in the reactions of judges and jurors, but we were able to investigate one aspect of these different classes of listeners—the degree to which they have been trained in the law. By conducting the study both with lay listeners and with listeners trained in the law, we could examine some of the differences which might arise between the reactions of judges and the reactions of jurors to the two types of testimony.

The effects of narrative and fragmented testimony on social perceptions were examined in a study similar to that used to investigate the effects of power and powerless speech. Again basing the experimental testimony on actual court speech, we used actors to record segments of testimony in which the same substantive evidence was presented in narrative answers and in fragmented answers.[6] Tapes of the narrative and fragmented testimony were made both with a female and with a male actor as the witnesses. (On all four tapes, as in the preceeding study, the lawyer's part was spoken by a male actor.) Groups of subjects with and without legal training (law students and undergraduate psychology students, respectively) listened to one of the four testimony tapes and then answered a questionnaire about their reactions to the testimony. The questionnaire solicited ratings of the subject's reactions to the case, ratings of the subject's impressions of the witness and the lawyer, and, because of possible importance of social attributions concerning the lawyer's evaluation of the witness, ratings of how the subject thought the lawyer perceived the witness.[7]

Table 4.2 presents some of the major results of the experiment. As may be seen from the table, for undergraduates hearing the male witness and for law students hearing the female witness the narrative testimony produced higher ratings on each dimension than did the fragmented testimony.

For each rating dimension reported in the table these differences were statistically significant. No significant differences in ratings of the narrative and fragmented testimony were observed for undergraduates hearing the female witness or for law students hearing the male witness.

Table 4.2 Mean ratings — Narrative and fragmented testimony

Rating dimension	Sex of witness	Subjects' legal training			
		No legal training		Legal training	
		Narrative Testimony	Fragmented Testimony	Narrative Testimony	Fragmented Testimony
Attribution of lawyer's impression of witness' competence	Male	1.11	-1.55	-0.55	0.23
	Female	0.63	0.50	2.80	-0.05
Attribution of lawyer's impression of witness' social dynamism	Male	0.84	-1.74	-0.32	-0.41
	Female	0.21	-0.16	2.15	-1.23
Subject's own impression of witness' competence	Male	0.55	-1.10	-0.73	-0.64
	Female	0.29	0.50	2.05	-0.68
Subject's own impression of witness' social dynamism	Male	-0.42	-1.52	-1.14	-0.82
	Female	0.26	-0.43	2.10	-1.82

Note: Higher values indicate more favorable ratings. For each rating dimension the Narrative vs. Fragmented X Legal Training X Sex of witness interaction is significant, $p < .01$. See Note 6 for an explanation of the variables.

Closer examination of the mean values in Table 4.2 reveals that the narrative/fragmented differences are due to the particularly low ratings of the male witness-fragmented tape by the undergraduates and to the particularly high ratings of the female witness-fragmented testimony tape by the law students. That is, for the undergraduates the male witness-fragmented testimony tape produced lower ratings on each measure than did the male-narrative, female-fragmented, and female-narrative tapes, all of which produced approximately equal ratings. For the law-trained subjects, the female witness-narrative testimony tape produced ratings on each measure which were consistently higher than the ratings produced by the female-fragmented, male-narrative, and male-fragmented tapes; again the last three tapes mentioned did not differ significantly in the ratings they produced. Measures of the witness' convincingness and of the subject's beliefs concerning the guilt of the defendant against whom the witness testified showed the same pattern of effects, but statistical tests on these measures fell short of significance ($p < 0.12$ for the three-way interaction for both measures).

A speculative explanation of these results may be advanced using the attribution theory ideas introduced earlier. We assume that the implications of the narrative/fragmented distinction for testimony control are as posited above, that the subjects held traditional expectations concerning sex-related difference in speech assertiveness, and that the subjects with legal training expected the lawyer to maintain greater control over the witness' verbal behaviour than did the subjects without legal training. Let us consider first the subjects who had been trained in the law. These subjects might expect the attorney to maintain overall control of the testimony, but might not expect this control to be carried to the extreme of suppressing the normative assertiveness of the male witness. When such suppressions of expected assertiveness did occur, as was the case on the male witness-fragmented tape, the subjects saw the testimony as unusual and particularly indicative of the lawyer's evaluation of the witness. Stated slightly differently, the lay subjects might have believed that only if the lawyer disliked the male witness would he deny the witness an opportunity to exercise male assertiveness through delivering narrative testimony. The male witness-narrative and female witness-narrative tapes, according to this line of reasoning, were not seen as distinctive (and, hence, did not produce distinctive ratings) because these subjects expected only a moderate level of lawyer control and saw nothing unusual in the lawyer's permitting a witness of either sex to speak at length. The female witness-fragmented testimony was not contrary to the subjects' sex stereotypes for linguistic assertiveness and, thus, was not unexpected behaviour and did not produce distinctive ratings.

In contrast to the lay subjects, the law-trained subjects, perhaps by virtue of their schooling in the theory and practice of the adversary system, may have expected the lawyer to maintain very strict control over the witness' speech behaviour. If this is so, the male witness-fragmented testimony would not be seen as exceptional by these subjects, since the law-trained subjects would not expect male assertiveness norms to 'override' the strict lawyer control. What would be unexpected by these subjects is the lawyer's allowing narrative testimony by a witness who is originally expected to be non-assertive—the situation which arose in the female witness-narrative testimony. Again following social attribution theory notions, only this unexpected combination of stereotypes and speech behaviour would be viewed as particularly indicative of the lawyer's impressions of the witness, in this case suggesting that the lawer held high evaluations of the female witness when she was permitted to deliver narrative testimony.

The effects observed on subjects' own impressions of the witness may be explained by assuming that the subjects accepted the lawyer's apparent evaluation of the witness. This seems reasonable since ratings of the lawyer by the subjects were generally on the positive side of the rating scales, indicating that he was evaluated favourably. In addition, since the testimony used in the experiments was from the direct examination of the witness (i.e., the lawyer was heard questioning a witness he had called to testify) the lawyer might have been thought to be well acquainted with the witness, leading subjects to believe that the lawyer's (perceived) evaluation of the witness is accurate.[8]

The explanation above of the results of this experiment is admittedly highly speculative, and additional research will be needed to verify the psychological processes we propose. It is clear, however, that when differences do occur in reactions to narrative and fragmented testimony they are in the direction of more favourable evaluations of witnesses giving narrative answers. Further, that the testimony type affected not only evaluations of the witness but also perceptions of the attorney-witness relationship shows that listeners use court conversations to arrive at rather complex beliefs about those they hear.

PERSEVERANCE AND ACQUIESCENCE IN SIMULTANEOUS SPEECH

In most of the testimony we observed in our study of speech in the Superior Court, the attorney and the witness co-ordinated well the timing of their utterances. Whether the witness gave narrative or fragmented answers, for example, the witness usually did not begin a question before the attorney had finished the question and the attorney seldom began asking another question until the witness had finished speaking. There is, however, a class of testimony situation in which simultaneous speech by the attorney and the witness was frequent. Occasionally, a lawyer and a witness would become involved in a verbal clash which seemed to our observers to carry the connotation of considerable hostility between the two speakers. One of the most characteristic aspects of these hostile exchanges was the frequent occurrence of instances of simultaneous speech.

Because hostile exchanges between an attorney and a witness seemed to us to constitute one of the most serious challenges to the adversary norm of attorney control, we focused part of our analysis of the court tapes on such exchanges. This analysis revealed that in the most hostile of verbal clashes neither individual was wholly responsible for the simultaneous speech—the attorney interrupted the witness about as frequently as the witness interrupted the attorney. Simultaneous speech began both at 'turn relevance places', points in a sentence where the second speaker might have assumed that the first speaker would end an utterance (see Sacks, Schegloff and Jefferson, 1974), and at other points in sentences.

One interesting variable in simultaneous speech is who dominates in such instances. That is, given the occurrence of an instance of simultaneous speech, the attorney might persevere in an utterance while the witness acquiesces and stops, or the witness might persevere and the attorney stop. Over the large number of simultaneous speech instances found in hostile exchanges one individual might persevere more often than the other and might thus appear to dominate the exchange. Since speech variables related to control, such as the power/powerless and narrative/fragmented distinctions, had been found to influence social evaluations, we sought to determine whether the perseverance/acquiescence dimension, which seemed likely also to carry control implications, also produces differences in the evaluations of the speakers.

In order to examine the social evaluation effects of the perseverance/ acquiescence dimension, an experiment similar to those described above was conducted. Once again an example of the speech situation of interest—in this case an example of simultaneous speech instances in a hostile cross-examination—was located in the trial tapes and used as a basis of the experimental testimony. Using (male) actors to play the parts of the attorney and the witness, four different versions of the testimony were re-recorded. (We used only a male witness because the narrative/fragmented study had suggested that lay subjects are most sensitive to male attorney–male witness speech conflict.) The four tapes of the testimony included one version in which there were no instances of simultaneous speech. Reactions to this 'control' tape served as standards against which reactions to the other three tapes, each of which included a high degree of simultaneous speech, could be compared. The other three tapes were constructed to show varying degrees of attorney perseverance in simultaneous speech. On the high attorney perseverance tape the great majority of instances of simultaneous speech ended with the attorney persevering in his utterance while the witness acquiesced and stopped speaking. On the medium attorney perseverance tape the attorney persevered and the witness acquiesced in about half of the instances of simultaneous speech while the witness persevered and the attorney acquiesced in the other half of the instances of simultaneous speech. On the low attorney perseverance tape the attorney acquiesced and the witness persevered in the majority of simultaneous speech instances. (Of course, one might also call these tapes the low, medium, and high witness perseverance tapes, respectively.)[9]

In this experiment, as in those described above, subjects were given a description of the legal case within which the original testimony was given and were asked to assume the role of jurors in the trial.[10] The subjects then listened to one of the four tapes and responded to a questionnaire assessing their impressions of the witness, of the attorney, and of the defendant against whom the witness testified. Other questions asked the subjects to what extent they thought the witness had had the opportunity to present the evidence he wished, the degree to which the attorney controlled the testimony, the degree to which the witness controlled the testimony, and how fair the attorney had been to the witness.

Some of the results of the experiment are presented in Table 4.3. The first set of means presented in the table reveal that the attorney was seen as having less control relative to the witness when there was simultaneous speech (i.e., on the three experimental tapes) than when there was not simultaneous speech (i.e., on the 'control' tape). That is, the experiment showed that whether the attorney persevered or not, he was seen as having less control when both he and the witness spoke at the same time; there were no statistically significant differences between the simultaneous speech tapes on this measure.

The other major findings of the experiment arose from the statistical comparison of responses to the high attorney perseverance tape to responses to the low attorney perseverance tape. As may be seen from Table 4.3, subjects thought that the witness had less opportunity to present evidence, that the attorney was less fair to the witness, and that the attorney was less intelligent when the attorney persevered in simultaneous speech instances than when the attorney acquiesced in such instances. These differences were evident in the responses of both male and female subjects.

However, on four other measures male and female subjects differed in their responses to the high and low attorney perseverance tapes. (In the two studies described above there were no significant differences in the way female and male subjects reacted to the speech distinctions under study.) Male subjects in this experiment thought that the witness was more competent and more likeable, and that the attorney was more skilful when the attorney persevered than when he acquiesced. In contrast, the female subjects thought that the witness was less competent and less likeable, and that the attorney was less skilful when the attorney persevered than when the attorney acquiesced. The results observed on a measure assessing the degree to which the subjects accepted the witness' testimony (which stated that the defendant was an unreasonably aggressive person) were statistically significant and showed the same pattern of means as that observed on the evaluations of the witness. That is, for the male subjects, the high attorney perseverance tape produced higher ratings of the aggressiveness of the defendant than did the low attorney perseverance tape, while for the female subjects the high attorney perseverance tape produced lower ratings of the aggressiveness of the defendant than did the low attorney perseverance tape.

Table 4.3 *Mean Ratings — Perseverance-Acquiescence Study*

Comparison of "control" tape to simultaneous speech tapes:

Rating dimension	"Control" testimony	Simultaneous speech testimony
Attorney control–Witness control	5.90	3.52

Comparison of high attorney perseverance tape to low attorney perseverance tape:

Rating dimension	Sex of subject	High attorney perseverance	Low attorney perseverance
Witness had opportunity to present his evidence	Male *and* female	−0.09	1.50
Attorney was fair to witness	Male *and* female	0.41	2.00
Attorney was intelligent	Male *and* female	1.68	2.79
Witness was competent	Male	0.00	−1.22
	Female	−0.92	0.93
Witness was likeable	Male	0.20	−1.56
	Female	−1.17	0.33
Attorney was skilful	Male	1.70	0.11
	Female	−0.42	2.40
Defendent is aggressive (Agreement with witness)	Male	2.70	1.88
	Female	1.08	2.80

Note: For the "Attorney control–witness control" dimension, higher values indicate more control by the attorney relative to the witness. For all other dimensions, higher values indicate more agreement with the statement noted. All comparisons or interactions are significant. $p < .05$.

Some of the observed responses to the tapes are relatively easy to explain, while other of the results, especially those involving differential responses by males and females, are more difficult to interpret. The decrease in the control index in the simultaneous speech conditions relative to the condition in which no simultaneous speech occurred suggests that an attorney was expected to maintain his control over testimony without having to resort to overt clashes with witnesses. The results on the dimensions assessing the subjects' perceptions about the opportunity of the witness to present evidence, the fairness of the attorney in his treatment of the witness, and the intelligence of the attorney suggest further that, once the attorney had lost some of his social control by participating in an overt verbal clash with the witness, an attempt by the attorney to re-establish his dominance by 'overpowering' the witness verbally was viewed unfavourably. When, as was the case in the simultaneous speech conditions, the testimony is not congruent with the courtroom norm of high and uncontested attorney control, those hearing the testimony may expect the attorney, who might be seen as more responsible than the witness for restoring courtroom order and decorum, to avoid attempting to persevere in order to avoid escalating the verbal clash.

Explanations at this time of the effects observed on ratings of the attorney's skill and of the witness' competence and likeableness must be very tentative. As shown in Table 4.3, ratings on these dimensions depend on the sex of the subjects, and it is difficult to determine with confidence any single variable which might show sex differences and which might account for the different reactions to the high and low attorney perseverance tapes. With these cautions in mind, however, we may speculate about the processes involved.[11] Let us consider first the ratings of how skilful the attorney is. If it is assumed that the female subjects expected the attorney to exercise his verbal skills in an effort to appear fair and to avoid negative reactions to himself, it is congruent that the female subjects would rate the attorney as less skilful in the condition where this was not achieved—in the high attorney perseverance condition. The male subjects, in contrast, may have expected the attorney to devote his efforts to 'winning' the verbal conflict with the witness, and since he accomplished this end in the high attorney perseverance condition, the male subjects may have taken this as evidence of the attorney's skill. The sex differences we postulate in expectations about the verbal conflict are conjectural, but are congruent with research on the behaviour of women and men when they are themselves involved in interpersonal conflict. Previous research suggests that, where sex differences in conflict behaviour do occur, females seem more oriented to interpersonal relations and males seem more preoccupied with the outcome of the conflict (see Rubin and Brown, 1975:169–74, for a review and analysis of this research).

If these suppositions are correct, the effects observed on the ratings of the witness may be explained in the following manner. The male subjects, who are postulated to be focusing on the outcome of the interpersonal conflict between the attorney and the witness, may have felt that in view of the attorney's power in the court it was foolish for the witness to be too assertive, as he was in the low attorney perseverance tape. The perseverance witness in this condition may have been seen as pushing the conflict too far in the face of strong attorney-control norms and may have received lower evaluations as a result of this apparently brash action. The female subjects may have been more concerned with what they saw as the fair presentation of the evidence than with the outcome of the verbal clash and may have given the witness higher evaluations in the low attorney perseverance conditions since it was in this condition that the witness was seen as securing greater opportunity to present his information to the court. Whatever the psychological processes involved in the witness evaluations, the evaluations which did occur seem to have influenced subjects' reception of the testimony, since the highest ratings of the defendant's aggressiveness (which was the point the witness was trying to make in his testimony) occurred in the conditions where the witness was seen as most competent and most likeable.

CONCLUSIONS

The studies we have reported here confirm that the manner in which witnesses and attorneys speak in the presentation of testimony can affect social evaluations of them by those who hear the testimony. The first experiment described here demonstrated that a socially patterned variable in witness speech, the relative frequency of use of 'powerless' features, has strong effects on evaluations of the witness and on perceptions of the witness' credibility. The second and third experiments presented showed that speech dimensions in the form of the attorney/witness interaction, as exemplified by the narrative/ fragmented testimony distinction or the various conditions of simultaneous speech, also influence the social perceptions and evaluations engendered by testimony. These findings have, we believe, important implications for language studies, social psychology, and the law.

As is the case with most research projects, the investigation reported here raises many questions which can be answered only with additional research. The social psychological explanations we have suggested for our findings, although consistent with the data and with previous theory and research in social psychology, are admittedly speculative and will require additional studies to clarify the psychological processes involved in reactions to court speech. In addition, there are aspects of court speech other than those examined in this project which may have important consequences for the conduct of trials and which must be examined in other studies. We have not, for example, investigated the effects of a witness' accent or dialect—variables which are often seen in some courts and which have been shown to be important in social evaluations (cf. Giles and Powesland, 1975).

In addition to exploring further the social, linguistic, and psychological processes involved in court speech, future research and thought in this area must be directed to the appropriate response of the law to findings such as those presented here. At the present time American rules of evidence are concerned, for the most part, with questions about the content of testimony; for example, with such issues as 'hearsay' in testimony. As we noted earlier, the legal profession has shown considerable concern with speech variables—primarily in the context of tactical considerations in trial advocacy—but this concern has not been translated into procedural restrictions on the use of particular manners of court speech. The present studies suggest, however, that speech dimensions which are influenced by factors which are supposed to be irrelevant to judicial decisions may in some instances affect such decisions. For example, if our analyses of power and powerless speech are correct, social status factors may influence witnesses' credibility by affecting their speech. Given such findings, a number of applied questions arise, the answers to which may be important to future judicial decisions related to court speech. These applied questions are amenable to the same sort of analysis, investigation, and experimentation that we have applied here to the study of basic questions in the reception of court speech. It is possible, for example, to construct experiments which examine the capacity of judicial instructions to witnesses or jurors to moderate the 'biasing' effects of various speech characteristics in testimony.

With regard to directions for future research on court speech, there are certainly many theoretical orientations in the social sciences which may be relevant. It is our belief, based on the present studies, however, that investigators of court speech may find helpful concepts in considering the importance of social power, control, and status relations in the court. The results of these experiments, together with those of other investigations of the social psychology of legal issues (e.g., Thibaut and Walker, 1975), suggest that those involved in trials are remarkably sensitive to such relations in legal systems.

The social psychological study of court speech may also be expected to be of considerable value to the understanding of the social psychology of language in other situations. The courtroom provides a social context with definite and widely recognized social relations within which general speech may be studied. While studies will be needed to determine the accuracy of generalization from studies of court speech to other speech situations, there is no reason to think that such generalizations are not valid. For example, it may well be that the social psychological processes we posited in our explanation of the effects of narrative and fragmented testimony function in similar situations in everday conversations between individuals of unequal social power. If our explanation of the narrative/fragmented distinction is possible, it may be that speech cues provide a major source of 'data' for the social attributions used to understand and predict everyday relationships.

Although the research reported here constitutes a beginning to the understanding of the social, linguistic, and psychological processes involved in court speech, we believe that the most important result of this project has been the fact that the methods and theories of several social sciences have been combined effectively to investigate these processes. In a speech context as complex as the courtroom, the sociolinguistic, anthropological, and legal research which preceded our psychology experiments was necessary to ensure that we manipulated variables which had real relevance to court speech and to give us an understanding of the social determinants of the variables which we studied. Similarly, our investigations would have been incomplete without the social psychological research and analysis. The observational studies told us much about the use of various speech variables, but it was only through experimentation that we were able to make definite statements about the consequences of these speech variables, and only from the perspective of social psychological research and theories that suggestions could be made concerning the process by which court speech is interpreted.

5
Voice and Speech Correlates of Perceived Social Influence in Simulated Juries[1]

KLAUS R. SCHERER

It seems to be almost a matter of common knowledge that in order to 'win friends and influence people' words alone do not suffice. One of the most elementary social skills, which is apparently picked up rather early in the socialization process, is the ability to appropriately modify a whole gamut of nonverbal behaviours, vocal and nonvocal, in the attempt to influence another actor's attitudes or behaviour.[2] Both the young child's begging to stay up after hours as well as the defence attorney arguing for the acquittal of his client, in spite of the enormous difference between these two types of attempts at social influence, seem to be aware of the fact that their posture and facial expression and particularly the nature of the vocal delivery of their arguments, pitch and loudness of their voice, number and location of pauses as well as the nature of the intonation contours, are essential and powerful components of their argument.[3] Mastery of this important skill seems to be essential in all walks of life. The reason why many American citizens would not have wanted, and probably still don't want, to buy a car from Richard Nixon is not because of the things he said but because of the way he said them (Kraus, 1962; Harrison, 1974:172–5). Like many other important phenomena studied by social psychologists, the important role of the non-linguistic factors in persuasive speech has been discussed at length by Aristotle, whose distinction between the appeals to ethos, pathos, and logos have served as convenient chapter headings ever since (Andersen and Clevenger, 1963; McGuire, 1969).

Given that it is neither new nor surprising that nonlinguistic aspects of persuasive messages may be important prerequisites for successful social influence attempts, it is all the more surprising that so little systematic empirical research should have been conducted in this area. This deficit is obvious both in the nonverbal communication literature, even though there has been a publication explosion lately, and in the venerable classic field of attitude change research. In this comprehensive and authoritative handbook review on attitude change research, McGuire (1969) deals with message factors almost exclusively on the semantic level or on the level of arguments (fear appeals, inclusion-omission, order of presentation, etc.). In a passing reference to non-linguistic message factors, McGuire points out that practising some kind of 'cerebral hygiene' most social psychologists have successfully avoided becoming acquainted with the relevant research that has been conducted in speech and rhetoric departments. But even if one does cross disciplinary boundaries, as adventurous social psychologists are increasingly prone to do (cf. Giles and Powesland, 1975), it becomes painfully obvious that even the pooling of resources of several disciplines does not provide us with a clear or consistent, let alone definitive, body of knowledge concerning the persuasive impact of particular types of nonlinguistic, but speech-related, vocal and nonvocal communicative behaviours.

In a survey of relevant work, restricting our focus mostly to voice and speech cues, we can distinguish three major research strategies. Two of these present naïve receivers with standard persuasive messages that have been manipulated differentially for different groups of subjects and measure the effect of these messages, whereas the third attempts to analyse communicative cues in semi-natural influence situations, consisting mostly of discussions in dyads or groups.

SYSTEMATIC MANIPULATION OF VOICE AND SPEECH CUES

Adherents of this research strategy which we shall call 'cue manipulation approach', present speech samples, generally persuasive messages, to naïve listeners and obtain ratings on the source's personality and credibility (as well as, in some cases, attitude change scores). Different versions of these speech samples, in which individual voice or speech cues or characteristic patterns of such cues (sets of styles) are systematically varied in experimental designs, are presented to different groups of subjects.

This strategy has been most popular both in social psychology and in speech research. We can distinguish between approaches using more molar manipulations, where whole sets of vocal cues are manipulated (such as accents, dialects, or delivery styles) and more molecular manipulations where one or more classes of individual cues, such as voice quality or non-fluencies, are manipulated. Examples for the former are the matched-guise technique studies (Lambert *et al.*, 1960; Giles and Powesland, 1975) where speakers deliver the same text in both standard accents and nonstandard dialect versions, or studies in which the speaker adopts a dynamic versus a conversational style; conversational delivery involving 'a relatively smaller range of inflections, a greater consistency of rate and pitch, less volume and generally lower pitch levels' (Pearce and Conklin, 1971:237). On the molecular level, speech rate and number of non-fluencies in the rendering of a text (Miller and Hewgill, 1964; Sereno and Hawkins, 1967) as well as different voice qualities (Addington, 1971; Brown *et al.*, 1973, 1974) have been manipulated.

The dependent variables used in these studies are mostly semantic differential type ratings on a number of scales which seem to belong to two major dimensions: competence, dominance and dynamism on the one hand, and likeability, benevolence and trustworthiness on the other. The results in these studies tend to show that standard accent (Giles, 1973a; Powesland and Giles, 1975), dynamic delivery (Schweizer, 1970; Pearce, 1971; Pearce and Conklin, 1971; Pearce and Brommel, 1972), fast speech rate (Brown *et al.*, 1973, 1974), relative lack of non-fluences such as pauses and repetitions (Miller and Hewgill, 1964; Sereno and Hawkins, 1967; McCroskey and Mehrley, 1969), and 'normal' voice quality (Addington, 1971) produce higher ratings on competence, dominance and dynamism. The results show inconsistent and rather weak relationships of these factors to the ratings of trustworthiness, likeability or benevolence.

Even though the differential cue manipulations in these studies did affect the perceived credibility of the source, effects on attitude change were rarely found and even though the listeners evaluated the speakers differently, they did not generally yield more to the competent, dynamic appearing speakers as compared to the less competent and less dynamic appearing one. There are many possible explanations for the fact that these speech style manipulations did not affect attitude change. One problem is the interaction between speech style manipulations and other characteristics of the source such as status or expertise ascribed to them in the experiment (e.g. government official versus sophomore; Pearce and Brommel, 1972) or the nature of the argument (e.g. left wing versus right wing stand; Powesland and Giles, 1975). Another possibility is that truly persuasive sources need to be seen as *both* competent *and* trustworthy. Since the personality evaluations have shown that a dynamic speech style may boost perceived competence but may be detrimental to perceived trustworthiness, an imbalance between these components of source credibility could be the result. If Giffin (1967) is correct in assuming that there are even more components of source credibility than the two mentioned above, the fairly gross speech manipulations created a lopsided impression and thus prevented an optimal combination of the valence of these components in terms of persuasive impact. This point will be taken up again later in this chapter since there is the intriguing possibility that the 'proper mix' of these source credibility components is dependent on the nature of the influence situation and the degree of ego involvement of the persuadee.

However, the reason for the lack of persuasive impact of the speech manipulations may also be sought in methodological factors. Though the cue manipulation research strategy has a number of advantages (it allows the assessment of differential effects of individual cues and cue combinations, it permits fairly clean experimental procedures with well defined independent variables and standardized context variables and, last but not least, it is fast, easy, and cheap to carry out), it does suffer from a large number of conceptual and methodological drawbacks. In most cue manipulation studies one speaker or several speakers are asked to produce several renderings of a standard speech varying certain more or less well defined cues from one rendering to the other. It is rather unlikely, even if extreme precaution is taken, that the second rendering of the standard speech will be different from the first *only* as far as the cues to be manipulated are concerned. We know from acoustic-phonetic studies that even the formant structure of vowels changes rather drastically from one rendering to the next. It cannot be ruled out, then, that concomitant changes occur which may be congruent or incongruent with the effects sought by the experimenter. This problem is made even more salient by the fact that the speaker or actor will have hypotheses of his own as to what types of personality traits covary with the voice and speech cues or speech styles he is supposed to portray and may systematically bias his portrayal in the direction of the results that he sees as intended by the experimenter. There are some possible solutions to this problem, as, for example, manipulating a standard tape recording electronically (Scherer *et al.*, 1972) or with the help of a digital computer (Brown *et al.*, 1973, 1974) or to use synthetic stimuli (Scherer, 1974b). However, these methods are still in the development stage and may not even be applicable in some cases. Moreover, they are very costly and time-consuming.

Aside from the standardization problem, however, one may ask whether the range within which cues are manipulated and the type of cue combination are ecologically representative (Brunswik, 1956). Decisions on the range of cue variation and cue combination in experimental designs are rarely based on prior information about the occurrence and the range of variability of these cues in social reality. There is a danger that the experimenter, in trying to produce stimuli that are sufficiently different, ends up with extremes that invite stereotypical perceptions. This problem is all the more serious since if there is one consistent finding in research on the judgement of personality from voice and speech, it is the existence of judgemental stereotypes on the part of naïve listener judges (Allport and Cantril, 1934; Kramer, 1963; Pearce, 1971). The major drawback of many studies in the cue manipulation research tradition is the blatant artificiality of the experimental situation and the obvious demand characteristics and other experimental artifacts (Rosenthal and Rosnow, 1969) that this situation entails. Even if decent experimental controls for demand characteristics, pre-test sensitization effects and other artifacts were used, which is not often done in most studies of this kind, the question remains to what kind of real-life situation this experimental paradigm can be generalized. The attitude change research paradigm of using a 'one-way one-shot' persuasive message in a laboratory experiment is an outdated relic from the hey-day of propaganda research in social psychology. This research paradigm is appropriate to mass communication research, where it started, but not to the study of social influence in face-to-face settings, where interactive discussions rather than monologic speeches are the rule. Even if one were to argue that in most of these studies the persuasiveness of the delivery of a communicator in a mass communication setting is to be explored, the potential generalizability of most research seems remote. The type of rhetorical persuasiveness appeal which is often used as a persuasive message is rather outdated since television, the 'cool medium' (McLuhan, 1964), has replaced radio as the major vehicle for propaganda and advertising. Persuasive messages of the kind used in the studies under scrutiny seem generalizable to little else except campaign speeches of politicians and exercises of debating societies. This point cannot be further elaborated here. There can be little doubt, however, that the cue manipulation research strategy could greatly benefit from a more clear-cut differentiation of studies designed to assess the persuasive impact of mass communication sources, which would require a thorough modernization of the research paradigm to current trends in television campaigning and advertising, and the study of persuasion and social influence in interpersonal face-to-face settings, which again requires a research design rather different from the one currently used.

ENCODING OF SPECIFIC SOURCE STATES VIA ROLE PLAYING

The second research strategy, the 'state encoding approach', requires naïve subjects or actors to role-play potential speaker or source states such as confidence, persuasive intent, or desire for approval by others, without being told about the communicative cues to use in this role-play situation. These portrayals can then both be analysed in terms of the cues used to encode different states and by presenting them to judges for ratings on the state portrayed. This research strategy has of course been vastly popular in studies on the expression of emotion (Kramer, 1963; Scherer, 1970a). Strangely enough, only a handful of studies have been conducted in which states relevant to the persuasive intent of the speaker have been manipulated. Mehrabian and Williams (1969) asked their subjects to be persuasive, Rosenfeld (1965, 1966) induced subjects to behave in such a way as to obtain approval from an interaction partner, and Scherer, London and Wolf (1973) asked a speaker to encode a standard text in terms of confidence and doubt. Approval induction, intended persuasiveness, and expressed confidence, which is seen by London (1973) as the major correlate of persuasive intent, are expressed by faster speech rate, more fluent speech with fewer pauses, higher volume and more variable intonation. In those cases where audience evaluations were obtained, these portrayals were also seen as more persuasive and more confident. The study by Scherer *et al.* (1973) provides further evidence that such 'dynamic' delivery is seen by naïve listeners as indicative of activity, energy, confidence and competence on the part of the speaker but unrelated to personal orientation, professionalism, or being businesslike.

It is interesting that the encoders in these experiments seem to aim more, or at least succeed more, at being perceived as competent, dominant and dynamic rather than being likeable and trustworthy. Either there are strong discrepancies between the expected and the actual effects of certain speech styles, or the encoders consider the credibility component of competence and dynamism as being more important in most influence settings and choose to be seen favourably on this component if they can influence only one component of the receiver's attribution. It is an intriguing possibility that attributions of different components of source credibility are caused by different and possibly incongruent verbal and nonverbal cues which, if they were to occur jointly (unless this is impossible due to the fact that different valences of the same cues affect these components) might produce the impression of insincerity.

The advantages of the state encoding strategy lie in the possibility of exploring in a fairly simple and straightforward research design which cues and which degree of variation of these cues are used by speakers under certain conditions. If the situation is realistic, this may provide at least a first glimpse at the ecological representativeness of certain cues and cue combinations. If both an objective measurement of the cues and an assessment of the audience evaluation is carried out, it is possible to assess the relationship between encoding and decoding of persuasion-relevant states. Even though these types of encoding experiments can be conducted in somewhat more realistic situations and thus suffer less from the criticism levelled against artificiality of experimental situations, they still suffer from similar disadvantages. The most serious drawback certainly is the requirement of role-playing by naïve subjects or professional actors. The fact that actors, and possibly also naïve encoders, may employ highly stylized or ritualized, traditional renderings for certain emotions or psychological states, has frequently been noted. Since one does not generally have a standard against which these portrayals can be measured, it is difficult to have complete faith in their ecological validity.

SEMI-NATURALISTIC STUDIES OF DYADIC INTERACTION OR GROUP PROCESSES

The third research strategy, which we will call 'interactional approach,' relies on discussion in dyads or groups which are organized in the laboratory in such a way as to allow social influence of one or several participants on others. Generally these interactions are audio-and video-taped to allow an objective analysis of the verbal and non-verbal behaviour of the group members. The auditory and the visual information can then be presented to naïve judges to check whether they are able to use behavioural cues to identify those participants who exerted influence successfully in the situation. Examples for this type of research approach are almost non-existent. One of the few studies directly relevant to persuasion research is the work by London and his collaborators (London, 1973; Timney and London, 1973) who have organized two-person juries and analysed the way in which one member of the dyad persuaded the other. Although conceived from a somewhat different methodological and conceptual angle, the studies on emergent leadership (Morris and Hackman, 1969; Stein, 1975; Stein et al., 1973) which ran leaderless task groups in the laboratory and analysed the way in which certain group members came to be recognized by the other group members as leaders, are also relevant in this context.

Analysing, the effect of vocal cues, London (1973) found that the more persuasive subjects in his two-person juries spoke with fewer filled and unfilled pauses and showed fewer repetitions. The results of the emergent leadership studies are not directly comparable to these jury studies since non-linguistic voice or speech cues were not analysed except for participation rate (extent of a group member's contribution to the discussion), and since the notion of group leadership is not quite the same as the notion of persuasion and social influence used in most other studies reviewed. Yet Stein's (1975) most recent work shows that observers seem to be able to identify leaders from both verbal and non-verbal cues, even with participation rate controlled, which so far, however, was generally found to be the major predictor of perceived leadership (Jones and Gerard, 1967; Morris and Hackman, 1969; Stein et al., 1973). These results imply that voice and speech cues, among others, differentiate leaders and non-leaders in these groups and thus provide an impetus for further studies to identify the nature of these cues.

The advantages of this interaction analysis research strategy are higher ecological representativeness and behavioural cues and psychological states under study as well as less need to worry about experimental artifacts, since it is possible to conduct these group discussions in seminaturalistic settings with tasks that bear strong resemblance to real-life objectives for group interaction. There are also quite a few disadvantages, of course, such as the lack of experimental control of the independent variables, which necessitates the use of a correlational approach and makes causal analysis virtually impossible. There is the further problem that the more naturalistic the group interaction is, the more difficult it is to obtain clear-cut differences in the persuasiveness or the social influence of the participants. Weak or inconclusive results are therefore highly probable. Even if all goes well in studies of this kind, the research, if done properly, is difficult, costly and time-consuming.

The disadvantages of the interaction analysis approach seem to be tolerable given the promise that the results in these types of studies may be more useful in the long run than those of other approaches. It seems desirable to invest research money and energy in this approach in order to find out what types of communicative cues and cue combinations command persuasive impact. If such preliminary information is available, a systematic programme of experimental research becomes feasible in which definite hypotheses about the effect of certain types of voice and speech cues and their combinations on source evaluation and attitude change are tested.

The remainder of this chapter describes a modest exploratory venture in this direction. Using 'surplus' data from a cross-cultural jury simulation study (cf. Scherer, 1972) not originally designed for this purpose, we will ask the following questions:

1. Which personality traits do group members in simulated jury discussions attribute to those individuals whom they credit with having strongly influenced the group discussion and the verdict?
2. Are there certain types of verbal and vocal cues (such as speech style and voice quality) which covary with the amount of social influence attributed to a participant?
3. Do group members with a high degree of perceived influence possess certain types of personality traits that distinguish them from non-influential group members?

4. Is it easier to judge the degree of influence a person has if one just hears him talk or if ones sees his face and watches him move, i.e., to what extent does the attribution of influentiality to a group member depend on verbal or vocal cues in the auditory channel as compared to cues such as physiognomy, facial expressions, gestures, and the like in the visual channel?

METHODS

Simulated Jury Discussion

The simulated jury discussion was chosen as a setting for semi-naturalistic group interactions under the assumption that this kind of situation would arouse sufficient interest to attract volunteers from different social strata and occupational groups and that it would provide a task intriguing enough to make the participants in this discussion forget that they were taking part in a study in the university laboratory. The study was originally planned to obtain interactive speech samples in semi-naturalistic settings to study the relationships between voice and personality. Since a detailed report on the procedures used is available in a publication on the results of the voice and personality study (Scherer, 1972) only a rough overview of the procedure is provided here.

The participants in this study discussed a case of manslaughter in simulated juries of six persons each. The case material presented to the jurors consisted of information about the circumstances of the crime, the statements of the prosecuting attorney and of the defence attorney, who claimed that the accused was not responsible for the act at the time that he has committed it, as well as expert opinions by psychiatrists, who contradicted each other. The jurors had to decide between the risk that a potentially dangerous man would walk the streets v. possibly condemning someone who was legally innocent. After being introduced to the case and their task by a senior law student, jurors were given one hour in which to reach consensus about their verdict.

Simulated jury discussions of this kind were run in Cambridge, Massachusetts and Cologne, Germany. Volunteers were recruited from local adult education centres to take part in a study advertised as concerning the role of personality in jury decision making. In each country a total of five sessions were run, with a total of thirty-one German jurors (one session had seven participants) and twenty-eight American jurors (one session had only four jurors). Each session was recorded on audio- and video-tape using high quality professional equipment. As had been expected, a lively discussion on the case ensued in each session; most jurors became very involved and seemed to completely forget the microphones and the fact that they were only role-playing a jury. At the conclusion of the session the jurors discussed the case as well as the purpose of the research project as a whole with the legal expert and the main investigator. Participants were adult males between twenty-five and fifty years of age.

Self and Other Juror Personality Ratings

Before the start of the discussion the jurors filled out a battery of personality tests and rating scales containing a Personality Research Inventory (PRI) consisting of modified scales from Jackson's and Eysenck's personality inventories (Jackson, 1967; Eysenck, 1959), the Adjective Check List (ACL) of Gough and Heilbrun (1965), a thirty-five item Personality Adjective Form (PAF) and a five dimension rating form (DIM) with detailed descriptions of five major personality dimensions (conscientiousness, emotional stability, extraversion, assertiveness, and agreeableness; cf. Scherer, 1970b, 1972). In addition, 'other juror' personality ratings were obtained by asking all participants to rate all other five members of their group on the Personality Adjective Form (PAF) after the 'verdict' had been passed.

Assessment of Perceived Influence

After the 'verdict' had been announced and each juror had given a summary of the proceedings in his own words, all participants were asked to fill out a juror evaluation form. In addition to some other questions about the performance of individual jurors, each juror was given the following task: 'Please rank-order the jurors, including yourself, in terms of how influential you think they have been in determining the final group verdict.' The mean rank for each juror, his ranking of his own performance excluded, was used as index of perceived influence. To check the degree of consensus in the rank ordering of the jurors, Kendal's Ws were computed. The results are shown in Table 5.1. The agreement on the rank ordering is significant on the 0.01 level in six groups and on the 0.05 level in one group. In two German groups there is only a tendency toward agreement, and in one American group fairly little agreement about the influentiality of the jurors was found. We can assume on the basis of these results that for the large majority of jurors a reasonably valid index of perceived influence was obtained.

Table 5.1 *Agreement between jurors on rank ordering each other according to degree of influence in each session (Kendall's W)*

Group number	American juries				German juries			
	W	P	K	N	W	P	K	N
1	0.34	<.20	5	6	0.30	~.10	6	7
2	0.93	<.01	4	4	0.77	<.01	6	6
3	0.58	<.01	6	6	0.52	<.05	5	6
4	0.56	<.01	6	6	0.54	<.01	6	6
5	0.95	<.01	6	6	0.38	~.10	5	6

Note: K = number of jurors judging, N = number of jurors judged.

Analysis of Voice Quality Parameters

For each speaker, a twenty-second excerpt from his contribution to the discussion was taken from the original audio recording and content-masked to render the verbal content unintelligible. This was done by cutting stretches of recording tape into little pieces and splicing them back together again in random order, a technique we have called 'randomized splicing' (Scherer, 1971). In addition to being content-free these speech samples are also largely free from suprasegmental speech variables such as intonation contours, pauses, rhythm, etc. Six American phoneticians, all with doctorates or advanced standing as graduate students in linguistics or speech communication, rated the voices of twenty-six American jurors and twenty-two German jurors on the following scales: Absolute pitch height (low, high), pitch range (narrow, wide), loudness or vocal effort (soft, loud), loudness range or dynamic contrast (little, much), preciseness of articulation (loose, precise), breathiness (none, breathy), creak (none, creaky), glottal tension (open, tight), nasality (none, nasal). More detailed descriptions of these voice quality parameters as well as details of the rating procedure and results on the reliability of the ratings and the intercorrelations of the parameters can be found elsewhere (Scherer, 1974c).[4] In addition, computer-based extraction of fundamental frequence of the voice (F_0) and F_0-variability using the Giessen Speech Analysis System was performed.[5]

Analysis of Speech Parameters

For the German speakers analyses were performed in three student theses on the relationship between personality and speech content (von Borstel, 1976), time and continuity aspects of speech (Herpel, 1976) and voice quality (Kühnen, 1976). The discussion tapes were first transcribed using a newly developed standardized transcription system.[6] These transcripts were then punched on cards for computer processing. A text analysis program was used to obtain number and relative frequency of different words in the corpus.

On the basis of the transcripts and the results of the computer text analysis, the following content variables were obtained: type-token ratio, certainty/uncertainty ratio, self-reference, verb-adjective-quotient, and mannerisms. The type-token ratio was computed on the basis of consecutive 100-word segments for each speaker and then averaged to obtain an index of linguistic expressions of certainty (such as 'without any doubt', 'evidently', etc., or expressions with 'cannot, must not, it is clear', etc.) by the number of expressions of uncertainty; criteria given by Busemann (1948) and Ertel (1973) were used. The mean reliability for three pairs of two raters each was Kappa = 0.76 (cf. Tinsley and Weiss, 1975). In addition, an uncertainty index consisting of the number of expressions of uncertainty divided by the total number of words was computed.

A self-reference index for each speaker was obtained by dividing the total number of references in the first person singular (I) and all inflections of the possessive pronoun (my) by the total number of words. In addition, an I/One quotient was obtained by dividing the references to the personal pronoun and the possessive pronoun in both the first person singular and the first person plural (I, we, our) by all occurrences of the impersonal pronoun (one) and the respective possessive pronouns. The verb-adjective-quotient was computed by taking every fifth punched card of the transcripts for each speaker and counting the number of actional and qualitative expressions following the rules formulated by Busemann (1925). Decisions on the type of expressions were determined by all three coders jointly, thus no reliability coefficient was computed. The number of actional expressions divided by the number of qualitative expressions resulted in a verb-adjective-quotient for each speaker. Mannerisms, such as the German equivalents of 'you know, well, I would think' were counted for each speaker in the respective transcript. The mean reliability for three pairs of two coders each reached Kappa = 0.85.

Time- and continuity-dependent indices of speech variation were grouped into three classes and obtained somewhat differently. The first two types, productivity and continuity-related variables, were obtained for the total contribution of each speaker. Productivity was defined simply as the total number of words spoken by each speaker. In addition, an index of average utterance length was obtained by dividing the total number of words of one of the jurors as well as a short comment.

The degree of speech discontinuity was determined by the speech disturbance ratio (essentially the 'non-Ah ratio' (cf. Mahl and Schulze, 1964) and the 'Ah ratio'. The latter is the number of filled pauses, which had been transcribed, punched onto the computer cards, counted automatically and divided by the total number of words (productivity). The speech disturbance ratio is the sum of the occurrences of tongue slips, omissions, sentence-incompletions, word incompletions, word repetitions, and repetitions of sentences or parts of sentences divided by the total number of words. The mean reliability coefficient for the coding of the speech disturbance categories was Kappa = 0.80.

Pause and rate phenomena were assessed both by computer extraction of silent periods and observer coding of silent hesitation pauses. For the former, only those parts of the contributions for each juror which had been digitalized for computer analysis (as described above) were subjected to this analysis. Using the facilities of the Giessen Speech Analysis System all silent segments exceeding 250 msec were counted as silent periods (cf. Boomer, 1965; Helfrich and Dahme, 1974; Goldmann-Eisler, 1968). The following parameters were obtained in this way: average pausing time (the duration of silent periods in msec divided by the total duration of the digitalized segment in msec), average pause length (silent period duration in msec divided by the number of silent periods), the variability of silent period duration in msec), rate of speech (duration of the digitalized speech segment divided by the number of syllables), rate of articulation (duration of articulation divided by the number of syllables). In addition, the average number of silent hesitation pauses was determined by observer coding of the number of silent pauses in the total transcript and dividing by the total duration of the speech segment.

In addition to these content and speech style oriented variables some indices connected with the interaction process were determined. These were the number of unsuccessful attempts to take the turn, the number of interruptions of other speakers, the number of interruptions by other speakers, the number of task oriented utterances, the number of utterances, expression agreement and the number of utterances expressing doubt. All of these values were standardized to the length of the contribution of each speaker by dividing by the number of total words or productivity for each speaker.

The same variables, except for the type-token ratio and all of the interaction process variables except number of interruptions of other speakers, were analysed for the speech samples of the American jurors using exactly the same procedures as in the German case.[7] The following mean reliability coefficients (Kappa) were obtained (using two pairs of two raters each): certainty/uncertainty ratio 0.66, verb/adjective quotient 0.79, mannerisms 0.75, speech disturbance ratio 0.79.

RESULTS

(1) Personality Traits Attributed to Participants Perceived as Influential.

The jurors, after having reached their verdict, rated each other both on the degree of influence and on the Personality Adjective Form (PAF). These variables, which may strongly reflect the implicit personality theories of the jurors, are probably not independent of each other. In this case, it is not possible to determine whether the jurors assigned a high influence rank to participants to whom they had attributed to proper kind of personality or whether, conversely, their assessment that this person had had a great deal of influence on the group decision determined their ratings of the personality traits.

There is a small chance of separating the cues upon which these influences are based by trying to find differential correlates with voice and speech behaviour. Unfortunately only a small portion of the behavioural cues available to the other jurors in the discussion can be assessed on the basis of the audiotapes of the discussion.[8]

In spite of these shortcomings, it is interesting to look at the correlational structure between the attributed personality traits and the perceived influence ranking. The correlations are shown in the 'Other Jurors' column in Table 5.2. As expected, most attributed personality traits correlate rather highly with the perceived influence score. The pattern of intercorrelations across personality traits is rather similar for the American and German jurors. A profile correlation between the two sets of correlation coefficients (treating the eight personality traits as observations) yields $r = 0.88$, $p < 0.005$. In both cultures the strongest correlations are found for task-ability, dominance, and sociability. Slightly weaker but still significant correlations are found for dependability, stability and likeability. Interestingly enough, there is no relationship with aggressiveness. This pattern of intercorrelations suggest that there are two dimensions which account for most of the variance in the personality and influence attributions to the jurors by each other.

The dimensions look roughly like the competence-dominance versus the likeability-benevolence factors which, as mentioned above, were frequently found in research in this area. Factor analyses of the

Table 5.2 *Correlations between perceived influence and self and other jurors' personality ratings*

| Personality rating scale | Perceived influence | | | |
| | American jurors (N = 28) | | German jurors (N = 31) | |
	Self	Other jurors	Self	Other jurors
Dependability	0.03	0.52**	−0.42*	0.33
Task ability	0.12	0.73***	0.22	0.72***
Neuroticism	0.24	−0.26	0.43*	−0.45*
Stability	0.09	0.75***	−0.28	0.40*
Sociability	0.33	0.56**	−0.32	0.79***
Dominance	0.40*	0.72***	−0.31	0.63***
Likeability	−0.27	0.43*	−0.31	0.46*
Aggressiveness	0.10	0.16	−0.07	0.25

*p <.05, **p <.01, ***p <.001

ratings support this interpretation. In both the German and the American cases the perceived influence score loads highly on the first factor which can be described as the competence-dominance factor. Except for the minor differences the factor structure is very similar in both cases. Apparently, then, the likeability-benevolence factor in this case is less important a component for source credibility compared to competence-dominance. As pointed out above, it is possible that the roles these components of source credibility play vary from situation to situation.

One possibility is that in situations in which there is a high degree of ego-involvement and self-interest, likeability or benevolence are more important aspects of a successful influence agent because of the direct relevance of the influence attempt on our own fate. In a jury discussion situation like the one described here, a juror is not affected personally by the verdict except for his desire to pass a just verdict. In this case the competence of an influence agent may be a more salient component of source credibility since it seems to guarantee more than likeability-benevolence that the 'right' decision is taken.

In a jury, each juror can assume that the other jurors do not have a personal interest in the matter. This de-emphasizes the importance of assessing trustworthiness, which, as we have seen above, may be part of the likeability-benevolence dimension or at least highly related to it. It is possible, then, to argue that a situational analysis of influence settings according to ego-involvement and self interest of the influences, availability of 'just' or 'correct' decisions, and potential self-interest of the influence agent may yield differential predictions as to the importance of the different components or source credibility in that situation.

(2) Covariation between Perceived Influence and Voice and Speech Cues.

Voice Quality The correlations between the phoneticians' voice ratings and the perceived influence score showed quite different results for the American and German groups of jurors. For the American jurors, there is a significant correlation for pitch range ($r = 0.49$, $p < 0.05$, $N = 26$) and a tendency for loudness ($r = 0.32$, $p = 0.11$, $N = 26$) indicating that jurors who were perceived as influential spoke with a more expressive voice, varying their intonation contours within a greater range, and with a somewhat louder voice. Correlations between these voice quality variables and the personality ratings by the other jurors show that jurors with high pitch range were perceived mainly on task ability ($r = 0.46$, $p < 0.05$, $N = 26$), whereas jurors with louder voices were perceived as more sociable ($r = 0.41$, $p < 0.05$, $n = 26$) and more likeable ($r = 0.54$, $p < 0.01$, $N = 26$). This seems to indicate that it is not a homogeneous group of jurors who spoke with a high pitch range *and* a louder voice and were therefore perceived as more influential, but that these two different voice qualities may be perceived as indicative of two different components of source credibility.

In contrast, there is little relationship between the voice qualities of the German jurors and perceived influence. The only variable which shows a tenuous covariation with perceived influence is dynamic range or loudness contrast which correlates negatively with perceived influence ($r = -0.34$, $p = 0.12$, $N = 22$). However, this variable does not correlate with any of the personality attributions by the other jurors. The only voice quality variable that does correlate with the personality attributions by the other jurors is precision of articulation. Jurors with a more precise articulation were rated as more task-able ($r = 0.56$, $p < 0.01$, $N = 22$) and more stable ($r = 0.42$, $p = 0.05$, $N = 22$). Given that the relationships between voice quality and perceived influence are very weak for the German sample, it is not possible to identify a particular set of voice qualities for the more influential jurors. The lack of relationship between perceived influence and voice quality might be due to the fact that the expert voice raters were American, although only objective, supposedly culture-free voice qualities were to be assessed. A more detailed discussion of the differences in the results found for the German and American groups will be deferred to a later part of this chapter.

Speech Characteristics The strongest predictor of perceived influence in both cultural groups seems to be participation rate, i.e., the total length of each juror's individual contribution to the discussion. Productivity, as measured by the total number of words spoken, correlates with perceived influence for both the German sample ($r = 0.54$, $p < 0.01$, $N = 29$) and the American sample ($r = 0.42$, $p < 0.05$, $N = 28$). Increased productivity can be due to either longer average duration of utterances or to a higher number of utterances. The results show that the *number* of utterances seems to be a more important parameter for productivity than average *duration* of utterances since the former correlates highly with both productivity (US: $r = 0.80$, $p < 0.001$, $N = 28$; GY: $r = 0.77$, $p < 0.001$, $N = 29$) and perceived influence (US: $r = 0.36$, $p < 0.06$, $N = 28$; GY: $r = 0.38$, $p < 0.05$, $N = 29$). Average length of utterances does not correlate highly with productivity or perceived influence. Thus, those jurors who took the floor more frequently but not for longer periods of time, tended to be perceived as more influential by their co-participants. These results strengthen the conclusion reached by earlier investigators that participation seems to be the single most important predictor of perceived influence or perceived leadership in small group discussions (cf. Morris and Hackman, 1969; Stein, 1975).

Productivity, although frequently dealt with under the heading of speech characteristics, is not truly a speech style variable. The studies on speech style and persuasion which were described in the introduction focus mostly on delivery style, such as conversational versus dynamic styles with emphasis on voice quality variations, and on speech style variables, such as hesitation and pausing, speech rate, etc. For the American jurors perceived influence correlates negatively with the number of silent pauses ($r = -0.44$, $p < 0.05$, $N = 28$) and positively with the number of speech disturbances (SDR, $r = 0.38$, $p < 0.05$, $N = 28$). The latter may seem somewhat surprising since one might expect a negative correlation between speech disturbances and perceived influence.

An independent analysis of the components of the speech disturbance ratio such as sentence incompletion, stuttering, tongue slips, omissions, etc., shows that only repetition correlates positively ($r = 0.50$, $p < 0.01$, $N = 28$), whereas other speech disturbance categories do not correlate at all or correlate negatively (but not significantly) with perceived influence. It is possible that the repetitions of words and parts of utterances scored by the coders in this category are of two different types, one indicating a speech disturbance (in the sense that the speaker does not know how to continue and therefore repeats a word or part of an utterance to gain time) and one which may be intended as an emphasis of what has been said. In the present study these two types of repetitions were not systematically differentiated. One could argue, therefore, that only those American jurors who frequently used repetitions of words or parts of utterances in order to emphasize particular points strongly were perceived as more influential. Further studies will have to explore this possibility systematically.

For the German jurors there are only some very weak correlations between speech style variables and perceived influence. German jurors perceived as more influential seem to speak with somewhat fewer filled pauses ($r = 0.34$, $p < 0.10$, $N = 29$) and with a somewhat higher rate of articulation ($r = 0.30$, $p = 0.11$, $N = 29$). There is a very slight tendency, then, for more fluent, faster speakers to be perceived as more influential. The respective correlation coefficients for the American sample do not reach significance.

An analysis of the content of utterances does not yield very strong results. For the German jurors there is a slightly negative correlation between perceived influence and the number of doubtful utterances ($r = -0.37$, $p < 0.05$, $N = 29$) and the number of utterances expressing agreement ($r = -0.32$, $p < 0.10$, $N = 29$). For the American jurors we find a tendency for expressions of uncertainty to correlate negatively with perceived influence ($r = -0.31$, $p = 0.11$, $N = 28$). It seems that neither expressions of agreement nor of doubt are very conducive to influence other group members in task groups. None of the other content variables correlate significantly with perceived influence in either sample.

Another aspect of verbal behaviour related to floor apportionment is the frequency with which a speaker interrupts other speakers, i.e., initiates simultaneous turns (Duncan, 1972). Here we find an interesting cross-cultural difference. Whereas number of interruptions correlates positively with perceived influence for the American jurors ($r = 0.38$, $p < 0.05$, $N = 28$) there is no such relationship for the German jurors. Interestingly enough, German jurors who frequently interrupt others are seen as not dependable ($r = 0.45$, $p < 0.05$, $N = 28$), not task-able ($r = -0.40$, $p < 0.05$, $N = 29$), and not stable ($r = -42$, $p < 0.05$, $N = 29$). These attributions are of course quite contrary to the traits attributed to the jurors who are seen as influential. For the American jurors number of interruptions correlates with attributed neuroticism ($r = 0.40$, $p < 0.05$, $N = 28$) and aggressiveness ($r = 0.41$, $p < 0.05$, $N = 28$). Again, these traits are not the ones which are generally attributed to jurors seen as influential in the American groups, but here the frequency of interrupting others still does seem to account for at least a small part of the variance in perceived influence. It is possible that the attributions of the lack of the very traits considered important for influential persons (as in the case of the German jurors) is more damaging than the attribution of somewhat negative traits, which, however, are relatively peripheral for the attribution of influence (as in the case of the American jurors). One possible explanation for this cross-cultural difference might be that there are more severe sanctions against interruptions in the German culture than in the American culture.

Prediction of Perceived Influence   Using multiple regression techniques we assessed what percentage of total variance in the perceived influence score could be predicted on the basis of the voice and speech variables for the jurors in both cultures. Using productivity, number of repetitions, number of interruptions, number of silent pauses, and pitch range as predictors in the American case, a multiple correlation coefficient $R = 0.78$ was obtained $(R^2 = 0.60, p < 0.001.$ df $= 5.22)$. For the German sample, using the variables of productivity, number of expressions of agreement, number of filled pauses, rate of articulation, and dynamic range, we obtained a multiple correlation coefficient of $R = 0.75$ $(R^2 = 0.56, p < 0.001,$ df $= 5.23)$. Thus, more than half of the variance in the perceived influence ratings can be predicted on the basis of these variables in both cultures.

It can be argued that productivity of a speaker in a discussion should be clearly differentiated from his delivery style as characterized by more strictly nonverbal behaviours. Since productivity accounts for a sizeable part of the variance in perceived influence (particularly in the German case), the elimination of productivity as a predictor in the regression equations could lead to a severe drop in the percentage of the variance accounted for by the variables under investigation. However, regressions in which productivity is dropped from the array of predictor variables show that the remaining variables still account for close to half of the variance (American sample: $R^2 = 0.50$, $p < 0.001$, df $= 4.23$; German sample: $R^2 = 0.48$, $p < 0.001$, df $= 4.24$). In the German case one might want to exclude expressions of agreement also, a variable belonging to the verbal rather than the nonverbal aspects of behaviour. Regressing perceived influence on number of filled pauses, rate of articulation, and dynamic range only, one obtains a multiple of correlation of $R = 0.60$ $(R^2 = 0.36, p < 0.05,$ df $= 3.25)$.

Although in both cultures about half of the variance of perceived influence can be predicted on the basis of vocal behaviour alone, the predictor variables differ markedly, except for productivity, between the American and German samples. Clearly, there is no interculturally valid cluster of types of vocal behaviour which characterizes speakers who are seen as influential. On the contrary, for some domains of vocal behaviour, particularly pitch- and loudness-related phenomena and interruptions, the signs of the correlation coefficients do not even point in the same direction. (Since most of these correlations did not reach significance, they are not reported here.)

How can these cross-cultural differences be explained? We can do little more than speculate at this point. As always in cross-cultural comparisons, methodological artifacts cannot be ruled out. Although great care was taken to standardize the jury situation in both cultures to such an extent that procedures were almost identical, there are still a large number of factors which could not be controlled due to the nature of the study itself. It is possible that visitors to adult education centres are different kinds of people in Germany and the United States, that volunteering for a jury simulation study is more characteristic of a particular type of person in one or the other culture, or that the nature of the case to be discussed is perceived differently in each culture. Also, as pointed out above, the voice ratings were made exclusively by American phoneticians who might not be as accurate on German voices as on American voices (even though the reliability on these expert ratings is almost equally high for the German voices as for the American voices; cf. Sherer, 1974c).

Given the relative importance of verbal predictor variables in the German case, and disregarding the possibility of methodological artifacts for a moment, one might wonder whether Germans are more verbally oriented than Americans are, and might attach more significance to the content of what is said as compared to how it is said (at least in the kind of task discussion groups that were studied here), since the jurors' consensus on the influence ranking must be based on some type of observable behaviour—verbal or non-verbal. The investigation of the intriguing possiblity of cultural differences in the importance assigned to certain communication channels requires a more comprehensive and systematic treatment than was possible with the present set of data. However, one possible explanation that can be checked using these data is the possibility that different types of persons were seen as influential in each of the two cultural groups and that these types of persons show characteristic voice and speech style.

(3) Personality Traits of Jurors Perceived as Influential

We can use the self ratings of personality to check the possibility that different types of jurors were seen as influential in the two samples. The correlations between self ratings of personality and perceived influence are given in the self rating column of Table 5.2. These results show rather striking differences between the American and the German samples in terms of the kind of personality traits that characterize influential jurors. Even though the correlations are not very strong, it looks as if American jurors perceived as influential see themselves as dominant, whereas influential German jurors see themselves as rather neurotic and *not* dependable.

Correlations with the subscales of other personality tests administered in this study strongly support this notion. For the American jurors there are high correlations of perceived influence with achievement (PRI: $R = 0.38$, $p < 0.05$, ACL: $r = 0.47$, $p < 0.05$, $N = 28$), and dominance (ACL: $r = 0.40$, $p < 0.05$, $N = 28$). For the German jurors the correlations of subscales of the Personality Research Inventory (PRI) and the Adjective Checklist (ACL) illustrate more clearly the nature of the self attributions of personality that characterize the influential jurors. Perceived influence correlates with the PRI-scales of impulsivity ($r = 0.36$, $p < 0.05$), order ($r = -0.43$, $p < 0.05$), neuroticism ($r = 0.51$, p. < 0.01) and the CAL scales of personal adjustment ($r = -0.53$, $p < 0.01$) achievement ($r = -0.38$, $p < 0.05$), dominance ($r = -0.44$, $p < 0.05$), endurance ($r = -0.45$, $p < 0.05$), nurturance ($r = -0.43$, $p < 0.05$), and affiliation ($r = -0.40$, $p < 0.05$). The picture of the influential German juror which emerges from these data is that of a highly non-conformist person who sees himself almost as a negative stereotype of German modal personality or national character as popular lore has it. These jurors seem to be very impulsive, autonomous and somewhat moody persons who do not attach themselves easily to others.

There is rather strong evidence, then, that different types of persons are seen as influential in the two cultures and that personality may play a major role in characterizing these types. The question that arises immediately is whether these types of persons do have characteristic voice and speech behaviours and whether these provide the cues that seem to affect the perception of influence by other group members.

In order to answer this question we have performed a number of path analyses following the procedure in Scherer (1974a, 1976). These path analyses are simply a series of regression analyses in which the order in which the predictors are entered in the prediction equation is determined by a theoretically derived causal model. In this case a modified Brunswikian lens model (Brunswik, 1956) is used, assuming that traits are reflected in distal cues (voice and speech characteristics in this case) and that these lead to attributions of the traits by the receiver (cf. Figures 5.1 and 5.2). Arrows with strong path coefficients support these causal assumptions for the variables entered into the specific model. Since one would like to find all behavioural cues that mediate the attribution of a trait, it is desirable that the path coefficient for the 'direct' arrow, bypassing the mediating behavioural cues, is as low as possible.

The path diagram for the American case is shown in Figure 5.1, for the German case in Figure 5.2. In both cases productivity, although an important predictor of perceived influence, is unrelated to personality. Most other predictors, however, do correlate highly with personality. An interesting difference between the German and the American cases is the fact that the correlation between dominance and perceived influence in the American case seems to be largely mediated through the behavioural characteristics entered into the regression equations, since the residual path from dominance to perceived influence is very low compared to the original correlation. This is not the case for the German sample, where the residual path is still fairly strong, indicating that neuroticism is likely to correlate with further cues relevant to the perception of influence which have not been entered into the regression equation. Given the explanatory nature of the present study, this type of analysis can only be illustrative of the approach that could be taken towards an in-depth analysis of the determinants of perceived social influence.

The present results clearly indicate that it is not sufficient to identify behavioural styles in different channels of communication which may have a persuasive impact on receivers. It seems essential to complement that type of analysis by introducing measures of stable and transitory characteristics of the source, such as personal-

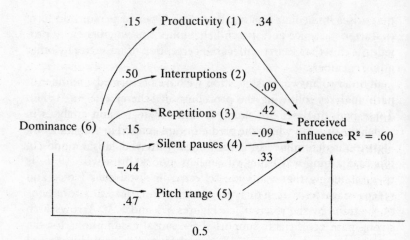

Note: Curvilinear arrows = Pearson r's
      Straight arrows = Standardized beta coefficients
      Numbers in parentheses = Order in which variables were entered
      into the regression equation

Figure 5.1 *American sample: Path diagram for regression of perceived influence on voice and speech variables and self rating of dominance*

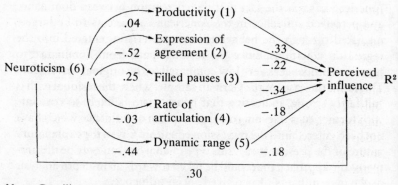

Note: Curvilinear arrows = Pearson r's
      Straight arrows = Standardized beta coefficients
      Numbers in parentheses = Order in which variables were entered
      into the regression equation

Figure 5.2 *German sample: Path diagram for regression of perceived influence on voice and speech variables and self rating of neuroticism*

ity and emotional states, as well as situational determinants. All of these may account for parts of the variance in the behaviour shown by the source in the communication situation, which in turn determines the attributions and reactions of the receiver(s). In addition, a more careful analysis of the source trait and state attributions made by receivers and the relationship of these attributions to perceived influence is called for.

One important requirement for progress in this respect is the ability to isolate the 'predictive power' of particular cues and cue combinations for personality attributions. We have advocated a 'breakdown and re-combination' method to separate clearly the effects of certain cue and cue combinations on receiver attributions (Scherer et al., 1977).

(4) The Importance of Auditory versus Visual Cues in Inferring Personality Traits Related to Perceived Influence

The results of our exploratory analyses seem to suggest that participants in group discussions base their attributions of perceived influence or leadership to some extent on verbal and non-verbal vocal voice and speech characteristics. As pointed out in the introduction, it would be interesting to find out whether non-vocal cues communicated in the visual channel, such as facial expressions, gestures, body movement, eye contact and possibly also static cues such as physiognomy are also used as cues in inferring perceived influence and whether they are more or less important. Unfortunately, the videotapes used to record jury sessions in Germany and the United States had to be erased due to shortage of funds long before detailed micro-analyses of non-vocal behaviours could be performed. The only visual records saved were video clips of about 15 to 20 seconds' duration for each of fifteen of the American jurors. This selection of video clips had been assembled early in this research to carry out a study on differential attribution of personality based on multi-channel presentation of verbal and non-verbal cues (Scherer et al., 1977).

In this study subjects made personality judgements of stimulus persons on the basis of auditory and visual cues presented in isolation and/or combination. In a 3 × 4 factorial design either no visual cues or photos or video clips were presented in the visual channel, whereas in the auditory channel either transcripts (content cues), or electronically filtered speech (sequence cues), or random-spliced speech (frequency cues) or normal speech samples were presented. Details on the preparation of the stimulus material and the rating procedures can be found in Scherer *et al.* (1977). Twelve groups of college student judges rated each of the fifteen stimulus persons on the basis of the respective exposure condition on five personality dimensions: conscientiousness, emotional stability, extroversion, assertiveness, and agreeableness.

We can regard the perceived influence rating as an external criterion and correlate the ratings in all of the above stimulus exposure conditions with the perceived influence ratings. High correlations can be interpreted as indicating that both the other jurors and the college student raters based their respective ratings on the same or similar cues, given the agreement of their respective inferences based on these cues.

There is no systematic pattern of correlation between perceived influence and the assertiveness and extroversion ratings in the multi-channel study. For conscientiousness, emotional stability and agreeableness, however, there are interesting differences in the size of the correlations in the different cue exposure conditions. The results, shown in Table 5.3, show that the naïve judges attribute conscientiousness and emotional stability to jurors with high perceived influence, if, and only if, they have access to speech and voice related cues. A comparison of the first column of Table 5.3 (script only) with the last column (normal speech) shows that the correlations are close to zero if only speech content information is present regardless of whether static physiognomic cues, as in the photo condition, or dynamic visual cues, as in the video condition, are available, whereas there are high correlations under all conditions where there is exposure to normal speech cues.

We strongly suspect on the basis of these findings that non-vocal visual cues have little effect on perceived influence by themselves although they may have an additive effect in combination with auditory cues. The latter can be demonstrated quite convincingly by comparing the first row of Table 5.3 (except for the script only conditions, where no speech or voice cues are available) with the third row (where both auditory and dynamic visual cues are provided). The addition of dynamic visual cues leads to an increase in the size of the correlations, particularly in the case where only partial auditory cues, as in the electronically filtered speech condition, are

Table 5.3 Correlations between perceived influence and naive judges' ratings on conscientiousness, agreeableness and emotional stability under different conditions of exposure to auditory and visual cues American jurors)

Visual cues	Auditory cues		Script only cues	Content-filtered speech	Random-spliced speech	Normal speech	Mean visual
None	CON		0.357	0.385	0.347	0.574*	0.42
	EMO		-0.034	0.265	0.553*	0.440	0.34
	AGR		-0.268	0.227	0.158	-0.223	-0.03
Photo	CON		0.135	0.123	0.049	0.533*	0.21
	EMO		-0.193	-0.341	-0.037	0.441	0.13
	AGR		-0.552*	-0.322	-0.605*	-0.510	-0.50
Video	CON		-0.043	0.542*	0.398	0.677**	0.39
	EMO		0.101	0.700**	0.417	0.618*	0.35
	AGR		-0.467	0.172	0.186	-0.171	-0.07
Mean Audio	CON		0.15	0.35	0.26	0.59	0.34
	EMO		0.02	0.28	0.23	0.54	0.27
	AGR		-0.43	0.03	-0.09	-0.30	-0.20

Note: *p <.05, **p<.01, N = 15
CON = conscientiousness, EMO = emotional stability, AGR = agreeableness

available. The absence of an increase in the size of the correlations for the random-spliced speech condition is probably due to the fact that the synchrony between the auditory and visual cues is destroyed by randomizing the sequence of the speech flow. It seems likely, then, that it is not just the joint presence of both auditory and visual cues that allows the inference of influence-related personality traits, but also the synchrony between these different communicative cues.

The data suggest further that neither sequence cues (content-filtered speech) nor voice frequency cues (random-spliced speech) by themselves provide a basis sufficient for inferring influence-related personality traits. As one might expect, a joint presence of all these cues in the normal speech condition yields the highest correlations between perceived influence and personality traits of conscientiousness and emotional stability. An analysis of variance without replications which was computed for the data in Table 5.3 yielded a significant linear trend component of the main effect for auditory cues for conscientiousness ($F = 6.59$, $p < 0.05$) and a tendency in the same direction for emotional stability ($F = 4.36$, $p < 0.10$), indicating a systematic increase in the size of correlations from the script only to the normal speech condition.

The results in the second row of Table 5.3, where the auditory cues are combined with static visual cues (photos), are interesting in themselves. The presence of static physiognomic cues seems to weaken the ability of the judges to infer influence-related personality traits such as conscientiousness and emotional stability. Even though the quadratic component of the visual cue main effect in the analysis of variance (photo conditions lower than no visual cues or video conditions) is not significant for the conscientiousness and emotional stability, the direction of the results and significant findings in the main multi-channel study (Scherer *et al.*, 1977) seem to indicate that photo cues may confuse judges and inhibit their ability to assess accurately certain personality traits.

The data for the agreeableness ratings may point to one possible cause for this effect. The respective data in Table 5.3 indicate that jurors who were perceived as very influential are seen as rather disagreeable on the basis of their photos. A strongly significant quadratic component of the visual cue main effect in the analysis of variance on the data in Table 5.3 for the agreeableness ratings ($F = 23.28$, $p < 0.001$) supports this interpretation. It is possible that physiognomic cues visible on photographs are very salient for the inference of agreeableness. Due to the implicit personality theories of the judges, disagreeable stimulus persons were also judged as lower on conscientiousness and emotional stability, which may account for the reduced size of the correlations between these traits and perceived influence in the photo conditions. Since an unattractive physiognomy (leading to ratings of disagreeableness) seems to be positively related to degree of perceived influence in the jury discussion (cf. Table 5.3), the accuracy of the inference of influence-related personality traits is severely reduced. Should these results be replicated in further studies, one would be forced to draw rather far-reaching conclusions. If inferences based on physiognomic cues are in fact detrimental to an accurate assessment of a person's potential for interpersonal influence, task ability and competence, it may be rather dysfunctional to ask for the inclusion of a photograph in job applications, applications for admission to graduate school, or other selected situations.

Of course, the findings that have been presented here must be treated with all due caution, given the case of an exploratory analysis with rather few observations (N = 15, in this case). It seems quite reasonable, however, to advance several hypotheses on the strength of the present findings which could be tested in further work. One hypothesis is that static physiognomic cues may be detrimental for the inference of the task ability or competence dimensions of source credibility or perceived influence. On the basis of the present data, no predictions can be made as far as the importance of such cues for the inference of the attractiveness or benevolence dimension is concerned. A second hypothesis is that both speech sequence and voice frequency cues, as well as the synchrony of these cues with simultaneous non-vocal visual cues, provide important information for the attribution of an actor's task ability or competence in group interactions.

EPILOGUE

We hope that the reader has safely emerged from this jungle of correlation coefficients and ex-post-facto explanations. For afficionados of clean-cut, experimental analysis of variance designs in social psychology this must have been a very arduous, if not positively frustrating, trip through unfamiliar country. Yet we hope, in spite of the obvious inadequacies of the present study (which are mostly due to the fact that it was really a side-product of a somewhat different research enterprise), that the case for careful analyses of vocal and non-vocal correlates of social influence processes in naturalistic situations has been made. Such analyses must be done before rigorous experimental tests become viable or promising. We hope to have shown in the introduction that most research in this area suffers from severe methodological shortcomings and from, in the Brunswikian sense, an almost total lack of representativeness. However, the results of the present study show that the phenomena under investigation in this area of research are important variables for a social-psychological analysis of social influence processes which were unduly neglected in the past.

Clearly, the central findings in this study is that about half of the variance in the influence attributions can be traced to the jurors' verbal and vocal behaviour in the jury discussions, indicating that voice quality and speech style are powerful tools, if not in winning friends, then certainly in influencing people.[9] However, the power of these persuasive tools seems to depend strongly on cultural context: whereas the influence-related speech variables of the American jurors suggest a determined, confident and somewhat aggressive style of verbal behaviour, the influential German jurors seem to be characterized mostly by verbal fluency and rather a lack of dramatic style. Even though these preliminary results need further replication, it seems quite obvious that simple dichotomies like conversational versus dynamic delivery are inadequate conceptualizations of the patterns of vocal cues observable in the behaviour of actors with different degrees of perceived social influence. Also, given the strong possibility of major cross-cultural differences in the persuasive impact of verbal-vocal behaviour, cross-cultural and cross-sex comparisons should be the rule rather than the exception in this area of research.[10]

A somewhat surprising and potentially very important finding in this study are the relatively strong correlations between personality traits and some aspects of vocal behaviour, on the one hand, and with perceived influence on the other. Personality may be a more important determinant of social behaviour than many situationists, who seem to throw out the baby with the bath water, would want to acknowledge. A speculative summary of the processes underlying the pattern of results in this study might run as follows: after evaluating the nature of the task requirements in the situation in which they are placed, the jurors form an impression of the characteristics of a potential influence agent that would help the problem solving activities of the group. Since the goal is to reach a just verdict, desirable characteristics might consist of certain personality traits such as intelligence, capacity for logical thinking, conscientiousness, autonomy, among others, of certain values, such as adherence to certain ethical standards, and of attitudes and intentions related to the task at hand. Each juror then tries to assess the presence of these characteristics in the other group participants by observing their verbal and nonverbal behaviour and inferring stable traits and transitory characteristics on the basis of certain behavioural cues. Those jurors credited with possession of characteristics beneficial to the group task are then described as influential, which may possibly be quite independent of the actual degree of influence that the arguments of these persons have had on the other group members. If the personality inferences based on behavioural cues have been accurate, i.e., if the target person actually possesses those traits which are attributed to him, one would expect a correlation between personality and perceived influence.

Admittedly, the basis for these speculations is small. It does seem promising, however, to approach the study of social influence processes by conceptualizing source credibility and influence potential in terms of the role traits and states for situation-specific task requirements. We have argued elsewhere (Scherer and Scherer, 1977) that personality traits and attitudes are more likely to determine behaviour than are situational factors, the more molecular (i.e., low spatio-temporal extension and low intenstiy), the more negotiable (i.e., subject to denial and reinterpretation) and the less task-relevant (in terms of the joint definition of the situation) the behavioural units are. Many of the voice and speech cues with which we have dealt in this chapter are prime examples of molecular, negotiable and task-irrelevant behavioural units. The assumption that these behavioural cues are rather strongly determined by personality traits, and possibly attitudes, is thus both consistent with theoretical formulations and some empirical findings. The results in this study, as well as other research, have shown that these behavioural cues are also important determinants of personality attributions and perceived influence or leadership. Under these circumstances, social psychologists can hardly justify further neglect of

these important variables in the analysis of social influence processes, particularly as further evidence of the importance of
behavioural style in social influence, as advocated by Moscovici and
his collaborators (Moscovici, 1976), becomes available.

PART TWO

The Encoding Process

6

Beyond Initial Interaction: Uncertainty, Understanding, and the Development of Interpersonal Relationships

CHARLES R. BERGER

In attempting to develop theoretical explanations for interpersonal communication phenomena, communication researchers have relied heavily upon theoretical frameworks from other disciplines. Exchange formulations from social psychology and sociology (Adams, 1965; Altman and Taylor, 1973, Homans, 1961; Thibaut and Kelley, 1959; and Walster, Berscheid and Walster, 1973) have been employed by communication scholars to explain developmental aspects of interpersonal relationships (Miller and Steinberg, 1975). The reinforcement-affect approach of Byrne (1971) and Clore and Byrne (1974) as well as the various attribution theories (Heider, 1958; Jones and Davis, 1965; and Kelley, 1967, 1973) have also stimulated considerable interpersonal communication research. To this list could be added the sociolinguistic approaches represented by such researchers as Gumperz (1964), Gumperz and Hymes (1972) and Hymes (1968).

While many of the above theoretical positions have served a valuable heuristic function for interpersonal communication researchers, their utility for explicating the development and disintegration of interpersonal relationships is limited in one way or another. The social-psychological theories of attribution, reinforcement-affect, and exchange do not explicitly deal with various issues concerning communicative behaviour. The sociolinguistic approaches are concerned with language choice and speech style, but they tend to focus on the interaction between language and social structure and the ways in which communicative behaviour is controlled by implicit and explicit rules. Giles (1977b) has pointed out that sociolinguistic approaches to the study of speech behaviour tend to treat man as a kind of social automaton whose behaviour is governed by norms and rules. A similar automatonistic model of man has been attributed to the radical behaviourists (Harré and Secord, 1972).

The present chapter takes the view that sometimes communicative behaviour is something which persons both endeavour to understand and something which they employ to gain knowledge and understanding of others. Attribution approaches (Heider, 1958; Jones and Davis, 1965; and Kelley, 1967, 1973) are directly relevant to the process of understanding one's own and others' communicative behaviour. And, although there has been considerable attention directed towards the way in which persons use communication to *control* each other in relationships (Marwell and Schmidt, 1967; Miller, Boster, Roloff and Seibold, 1976; Miller and Steinberg, 1975; Rodnick and Wood, 1973), relatively little attention has been paid to the ways in which communicative behaviour is employed to gain *knowledge* and *understanding* in relationships. In the present view, the communicative processes involved in knowledge generation and the development of understanding are central to the development and disintegration of most interpersonal relationships. Rather than viewing man as an object at the mercy of reinforcement contingencies or socially prescribed rules and norms, the present perspective sees man as an inquirer; attempting to understand himself and those with whom he has relationships. It is not claimed that persons are always preoccupied with such epistemological concerns; in fact, part of the present chapter will be devoted to an explanation of the conditions under which such concerns are likely to become salient.

UNCERTAINTY, KNOWLEDGE AND UNDERSTANDING

In a previous paper, Berger and Calabrese (1975) argued that when strangers meet, their primary concern is one of reducing uncertainty about each other. In their axiomatic theory, uncertainty was defined in a manner similar to the way in which the construct is viewed by information theorists (Shannon and Weaver, 1949). Specifically, it was argued that the problem in initial interactions is one of predicting the likely behaviours of the other person or persons in the situation so that one can select from his own behavioural repertoire those alternative modes of behaviour which are deemed most appropriate to the other person or persons in the situation. This view is similar, but not identical, to the repertoire selection thrust of sociolinguistic research (Grimshaw, 1973). While the social context itself may aid in the prediction-making linguistic-selection process, the motives, attitudes, and values attributed to each other in the situation also determine repertoire selection.

In addition to the prediction problem created by the number of alternative possible messages which might be sent in a situation, Berger and Calabrese (1975) point out that uncertainty is also dependent upon the extent to which persons have a limited number of plausible alternative explanations for their own and others' behaviour in the relationship. Thus, uncertainty is reduced by generating and confirming *predictions* and constructing and verifying *explanations* for the behaviour of one's self and the other. In subsequent research, Berger (1975) demonstrated how information obtained in the course of initial interaction is used to make predictions (proactive attributions) and how the same information is used to construct explanations (retroactive attributions). Speech style as well as speech content can be used as a basis for the formation of proactive and retroactive attributions. Several chapters in the present volume deal with these attribution processes.

One issue not dealt with by Berger and Calabrese (1975) concerns the possibility that uncertainty may occur on different levels. Specifically, these authors point out that when two persons meet for the first time, their levels of uncertainty about each other are relatively high; yet, several studies (Berger, 1973; Berger and Larimer, 1974; and Calabrese, 1975) have found that in initial interaction situations, the kinds of information asked for and given are fairly predictable. This apparent contradiction suggests that the uncertainty construct might fruitfully be viewed on at least two different levels. The Berger and Calabrese (1975) conception of uncertainty clearly refers to a *cognitive state*. This state can be differentiated from the uncertainty level of a given stream of discourse. Under some conditions, cognitive and linguistic uncertainty may covary; however, there are circumstances in which the level of uncertainty of verbal exchanges made in interaction may not be reflective of the underlying cognitive states of uncertainty of the interactants. Initial interaction situations are one example, but there are others. Many interactions involving strangers acting out formal roles may also involve a discrepancy between the two levels. Thus, what gets said and the way it gets said may be highly predictable in formal role situations; however, the cognitive states of the actors in such situations may remain highly uncertain.

The above analysis is consistent with Jones and Davis's (1965) correspondent inference theory. These theorists argue that observers will take the overt behaviours of actors to be reliable indicators of their underlying dispositions *when actors behave out of role*. When actors conform to rules and norms, observers tend not to be able to make highly confident inferences about actors' dispositions from observations of their behaviour. When actors conform to norms and rules, they are behaving like all other members of the social group which share these norms and rules. The actor is *not distinctive* and is thus not perceived as an individual with a unique personality. One point apparently overlooked by Jones and Davis is that in-role behaviour may be used to make inferences about 'normality' or 'mental health' of actors. Both Gardner (1976) and Schulman (1976) found that in-role communication behaviour gave rise to higher estimates of both general attractiveness and mental health.

In spite of the qualification cited above, the Jones and Davis (1965) position is significant because it suggests that communicative behaviours which are strongly constrained by social rules and norms and are highly predictable produce epistemological deficits in observers, when observers wish to know persons *as individuals*. Thus, while it is true that observers can use information disclosed in initial interactions as a basis for making proactive attributions for the purpose of reducing cognitive uncertainty, these proactive attributions are likely to be quite tentative in nature. It is not until the actors communicate in ways which are less constrained by social rules and norms that observers are likely to feel that they have reliable information about the persons *as individuals*. This line of argument highlights the utility of the distinction made between cognitive and behavioural uncertainty. Moreover, the cognitive-behavioural differentiation sensitizes us to the more general problem of making inferences about cognitive and affective states from analyses of communicative behaviour, a caution which has frequently been voiced about content analysis (e.g., Holsti, 1968).

Given the distinction made between cognitive and behavioural uncertainty, we can now proceed to relate cognitive uncertainty to the concepts of knowledge and understanding. In prior work, Berger, Gardner, Parks, Schulman, and Miller (1976) distinguished among various levels of knowledge and understanding. In their analysis, they posited three knowledge levels: descriptive, predictive, and explanatory. When persons make statements which describe the current behaviour, attitudes or dispositions of another, they are operating at the descriptive level. If they make inferences about the future behaviour, beliefs or dispositions the other is likely to display, they have moved to the predictive level. Finally, when observers can generate a limited number of plausible causal attributions for behaviour, they have achieved the explanatory level. Each level requires more complex cognitive operations than the preceding one and more cognitive effort is required to achieve each successive level. Thus, the explanatory level is reserved for relatively few relationships.

Certain kinds of knowledge can be generated without producing significant increases in understanding (Hamlyn, 1974). Thus, it may be reasonable to say 'I know him well but I do not understand him'. This condition may arise when one has descriptive and predictive knowledge about the other but has little in the way of explanatory knowledge. Understanding is most likely to occur when considerable knowledge has been generated and verified at the explanatory level and mutual understanding is likely to obtain when both parties in the relationship have accumulated and verified considerable explanatory knowledge. The levels of knowledge and the conception of understanding discussed here in Berger, Gardner, Parks, Schulman and Miller (1976) closely parallel the discussion of cognitive uncertainty presented above and in Berger and Calabrese (1975). In short, when cognitive uncertainty is decreased, persons are more likely to assert that they know and understand each other. The extent of their knowledge and understanding is determined by the level of knowledge reached and the opportunities available for verifying that knowledge.

Again, it should be noted that persons do not attempt to generate explanatory knowledge about the understanding of everyone they meet. Few of us have occasion to care *why* a sales person behaves the way he or she does on the job. In many routine everyday interactions, the level of specific descriptive knowledge about others, as individuals, necessary for 'successful' interaction is relatively low. However, when we wish to develop significant and long term relationships, failure to achieve higher levels of knowledge and understanding may be disastrous. In the sections which follow, we will consider the conditions set in motion in the quest for higher knowledge levels and ultimately mutual understanding, and the strategies, both active and passive, which persons employ to achieve higher levels of knowledge and understanding. It should be emphasized that no claim of exhaustiveness is made. The enumeration of antecedents and strategies presented here represents a tentative discussion in need of expansion and elaboration.

ANTECEDENTS TO INTERPERSONAL KNOWLEDGE GENERATION

It is assumed that when persons interact with each other, they do so at varying levels of *awareness*. At times, persons enact communication routines at very low levels of awareness; that is, if the persons are asked what they and the other persons actually said during the interaction, the persons attempting to recall would have considerable difficulty. At other times, persons very closely monitor what they say and what other persons in the interaction are saying and doing. It might be that communication routines which are highly ritualistic and constrained generally occur at low awareness levels and that less constrained interactions produce closer monitoring of both one's self and others. It is further assumed that in order to generate reliable knowledge and a high degree of understanding of others, close monitoring of their behaviour as well as the relationship between the others' behaviours and one's own is required. Routine interactions may be informative for assessments of 'normality' discussed above; however, in terms of developing higher levels of knowledge and understanding, non-routine communicative exchanges are probably more informative (Jones and Davis, 1965). Thus, an important step in the generation of knowledge and understanding is an increase in *awareness* about the *monitoring* of one's own and other's behaviour. In the discussion that follows, we will consider several antecedents to increases in awareness and monitoring. It is assumed that the various antecedents to increased monitoring of behaviour are not necessarily equally important.

Incentives

As was mentioned at the beginning of the present chapter, several social-psychological theories concerned with explaining relationship development have employed the constructs of reward and cost as central explanatory variables (Adams, 1965; Altman and Taylor, 1973; Homans, 1961; Miller and Steinberg, 1975; Thibaut and Kelley, 1959; and Walster, Berscheid and Walster, 1974). In addition, the reinforcement-affect theory of attraction (Clore and Byrne, 1974) accords the reinforcement value of perceived similarity a central role in explaining the development of attraction. The present formulation differs from some of the above positions by postulating a mediating mechanism between perceptions of the reward value of a particular stimulus person and the eventual development of attraction.

In the present view, when persons come to believe that others can satisfy certain needs, that is, the others have incentive value, we expect that efforts will be made to find out more about the person with high incentive value so that the perceiver can develop strategies for obtaining rewards from him. As perceived reward value of a person increases, the perceiver will increase his level of monitoring of the other's communicative behaviour and increase his level of monitoring of his own behaviour. This position is similar to the one proposed by Miller and Steinberg (1975) when they assert that frequently persons try to increase their ability to predict the behaviour of others in order to receive rewards from them. Furthermore, in their chapter in the present volume, Giles and Smith discuss the ways in which *speech convergence* is used as a strategy for obtaining desired rewards.

It is important to recognize that the kinds of rewards that can be dispensed by a particular target person may significantly influence the extent to which incentive levels affect monitoring levels. For example, in a job situation, a particular boss may have control over the salary levels of the employees who work under him. We might expect that an employee will want to get to know *enough* about his boss so that he can receive raises from him. However, it is unlikely that an employee will expend any more time and effort than is necessary to gain sufficient knowledge to insure himself of a raise. Of course, the boss may be able to offer rewards beyond those associated with salary increases. Under these conditions, a particular employee might spend more time intensely monitoring the boss's behaviour and his own.

A recent factor analytic study (Berger, Weber, Munley, and Dixon, 1976) dealing with dimensions of attractiveness found that the kinds of support target individuals were perceived to provide the respondent were the best discriminators among the various relationship levels of formal role, acquaintance, friend, close friend and lover. The types of support loading on the *supportiveness* factor were such things as understanding, reinforcement, loyalty, concern for welfare, liking, rapport, and help in reaching goals. Interestingly, liked persons in the Close Friend category were rated higher on this dimension than were persons designated as Lovers. In general, this study strongly suggests the importance of *perceived supportiveness* as an antecedent to attraction. Moreover, it is possible that when we speak of 'rewards' or 'incentives' we are actually referring to a more general set of behaviours which are seen as 'supportive'. Thus, when persons are seen as potential sources of support, those needing the support will increase their awareness of the other person's behaviour and their own behaviour.

Deviation

A second antecedent to increased awareness and monitoring is that of deviation from expectations, norms, and rules. Specifically, as observers in a particular social situation attend to the streams of behaviour (Barker, 1963) of others and the others deviate significantly from expectations, observers will monitor deviant behaviour more closely than they will monitor expected behaviour. Newtson (1973) has presented both theory and data relevant to this issue. He argues that one critical variable in the formation of attributions is that of *unit of perception*. As persons observe the actions of others, they can divide the others' behaviour sequences into perceptual units of varying widths. A series of acts performed by a person might be seen as a single 'episode' or 'pattern' of behaviour by one observer, whereas a second observer might 'chunk' the same sequence of acts into smaller units.

In a series of experiments, Newtson (1973) found that when persons were instructed to view sequences of behaviour employing either fine units or gross units of perception, those who used fine unit perception were more confident of their attributions of various traits to the actor. Also, Newtson found that when the actor behaved in ways which were unpredictable, there was also a tendency for persons viewing the deviant sequence to use finer perceptual units and to make more confident attributions. From this series of studies, Newtson concluded that when persons behave in unpredictable ways, observers of their behaviour employ finer perceptual units *to re-establish a higher level of predictability of their behaviour*. In addition, several studies reveal a strong tendency for unpredictable behaviour to be judged negatively (Gardner, 1976; Kiesler, Kiesler and Pallack, 1967; Kiesler, 1964; and Schulman, 1976).

The theory and evidence presented above give rise to an interesting paradox. On the one hand, we have noted that in-role behaviour is more attractive to others than is out-of-role or deviant behaviour. On the other hand, we have found, consistent with the Jones and Davis (1965) attribution analysis and the Newtson (1973) research, that out-of-role behaviour generates both closer monitoring of the behavioural stream (finer perceptual units) and more confident attributions. This paradox is neatly illustrated by data obtained in a pilot project of ours which indicated that as the number of compliments given by a person in an initial interaction increased, he was perceived to be progressively more friendly *but* progressively less sincere and honest by observers of his behaviour (See Note 1). Thus persons who communicate in socially desirable ways may indeed be judged to be more friendly, however, apparently observers of their behaviour suspect *ulterior motives* such as ingratiation for their behaviour and judge it to be less sincere and honest.

From the above discussion we can draw some important conclusions about the epistemological significance of routine and ritualized communication behaviour. First, the Jones and Davis (1965) theory and the Newtson (1973) findings suggest that when persons engage in highly constrained and ritualistic communication episodes, their levels of awareness, as indexed by fineness of perceptual unit processing, are likely to be relatively low. This lowering of monitoring intensity should, in turn, increase the epistemological deficit referred to earlier, however, the *affective* consequences of conformity to such communication routines should be positive. That is, close conformity to communicative conventions should increase the attractiveness level of the conformer. Second, deviation from communication rules should have negative impacts upon affect but lead to the generation of more reliable knowledge about the other.

A third possibility is that conformity to and deviation from communicative conventions have different impacts upon attraction and understanding depending upon the stage of relationship. For example, when two persons meet for the first time, close conformity to socially prescribed communication rules is essential for generating the positive affect necessary for continuance of the relationship. If deviations occur in the initial interaction, the negative affect generated might prevent the parties from interacting in the future. However, conformity to communicative routines may not be highly informative. As the relationship develops, deviations from socially prescribed rules are more acceptable and are probably *expected*. If they do *not* occur, persons in the relationship may conclude that there is little desire to move the relationship to a more informal and/or intimate level. Professors' spouses do not expect professors to communicate with them as they would with their students (although some do). In order for a relationship to grow beyond a formal level, persons have to behave in ways which distinguish them from all other members of the social system of which they are a part; that is, they must become unique individuals in each other's eyes. Deviation from certain communicative conventions is required for such individuation to take place.

Future Interaction

Another determinant of the degree to which persons will monitor their own communication outputs and the outputs of others is the probability that they will interact with each other in the future. A distinction should be made here between the desire to want to develop a relationship with someone because they have some kind of incentive value and knowing that certain circumstances will guarantee that one will come into contact with another. The desire to develop a relationship is most probably a product of the factors we considered under the topic of incentive determinants. In the present case, we are considering circumstances in which persons know that they will come into contact in the future whether or not they wish to do so. The general proposition here is that as the perceived probability of future interaction increases, persons will more closely monitor each other's behaviour and their own.

There is evidence to support the contention that when persons believe they will interact in the future, they will increase the amount of biographic and demographic information they exchange in an initial interaction (Calabrese, 1975). In his study, Calabrese (1975) asked strangers to 'get acquainted' and then unobtrusively recorded their conversations over a 13 minute period. Half the participants in the study were told that they would be talking with each other again at a later date, the other half were informed that they would not be interacting in the future. In his analyses of the distribution of various types of communication content through time, Calabrese (1975) found that exchanges of biographic-demographic information were significantly higher during the initial phase of the conversations in the group which believed they would be interacting in the future.

In addition to the above findings, Kiesler, Kiesler and Pallak (1967) found that commitment to future interaction had significant effects on evaluations of persons who violated social norms in an experimental situation. Consistent with their hypothesis, they found that commitment to future interaction increased the attractiveness of the person who conformed to social norms and decreased the attractiveness of persons who violated the social norms. Thus, if persons were led to believe that they would not see the norm violator again, their negative evaluations of the norm violators behaviour were significantly attenuated. Within the present framework, these findings support the view that probability of future interaction can exert strong effects on evaluations of persons' behaviour. Moreover, Kiesler (1969) has pointed out that commitment to future interaction may also exert considerable influence on overt behaviour. Specifically, when persons know they will be interacting in the future, they may supress certain behaviours for fear of being evaluated negatively.

One classic example of the influence of the future interaction variable on communicative choice is the 'stranger-on-the-plane' situation. Apparently, it is not uncommon for persons to receive highly intimate information from total strangers while on route to a far-away destination. The willingness of some persons to disclose highly intimate information to total strangers under such circumstances can at least be partially explained by the probability of future interaction variable; that is, the discloser has little to lose even if the disclosee develops a relatively negative evaluation of him or her. The chances are slim that the two will ever meet again.

The above example raises an interesting question regarding the relative contributions of perceived deviance and probability of future interaction to awareness levels in such a situation. We previously argued that when persons behave in deviant ways, observers of their behaviour are more likely to monitor their behaviour closely.

We have also asserted that as the perceived probability of future interaction increases, monitoring levels will also increase. The stranger-on-the-plane situation is at least somewhat deviant but at the same time low in probability of future interaction. Assuming that the two variables make about equal contributions to generating higher levels of awareness, we would expect moderate levels of monitoring in such situations.

Summary

In the preceding discussion we have considered three antecedents to the closeness with which observers monitor the behaviour of others in social interaction situations. Other variables were considered but not included because it was felt that they could be subsumed by the present set. For example, one might argue that high levels of *perceived threat* would produce increases in the closeness with which an observer monitors the behaviour of an actor. However, the kinds of behaviours which are likely to produce perceived threat are likely to be deviant ones. Most persons are not frequently faced in a situation where another is threatening them with a weapon. For most persons this is a 'deviant' current in the stream of another's behaviour. While threat may not be totally subsumed by the deviance construct, certainly there are deviant behaviours which are not very threatening. A person in a restaurant trying to consume soup with a fork is displaying deviant behaviour which is not threatening to observers. A restaurant owner being held up is both a deviant and a threatening situation for most observers. From these examples it seems that the perceived deviance construct is capable of subsuming more situations than is the threat construct; that is, deviant situations may be perceived to be novel and enjoyable as well as threatening. Thus, the deviance construct seems to be more abstract and more useful theoretically.

One might also suggest that when high and low status persons interact, the low status person will monitor the behaviour of the high status person more closely than the high will monitor the low. Here again, the status variable seems to be at a lower level of abstraction than the incentives construct discussed previously. That is, one reason the low status person is likely to pay more attention to the high status person's behaviour is simply that he wishes to receive the rewards the high status person can give.

STRATEGIES FOR DEALING WITH UNCERTAINTY

Now that some of the antecedents to increased awareness of behaviour have been explicated, we can ask what kinds of strategies persons use to generate knowledge once the salience of this concern has been raised by perceptions of incentive value, deviance, or probability of future interaction. In the present discussion, strategies are viewed as plans that persons develop in order to accomplish certain general goals. For example, a person may wish to form a friendship with another to reduce his feelings of isolation. His general goal is to reduce felt isolation and to accomplish this goal he must achieve the subgoal of forming a friendship. The next problem for our lonely person is to devise a strategy for forming a friendship with the target person. The particular set of strategies we are concerned with here are the ones that persons use *to find out things about others* in order to reduce their uncertainty about them.

Obviously, not all strategies for generating knowledge and understanding necessarily involve communication. Persons can learn a great deal about others by assuming the roles of unobtrusive observers. These kinds of strategies we shall refer to as 'passive strategies'. This is not to say that the process of observation is passive, however; here the notion of passivity refers to the lack of direct intervention by the observer. The observer has minimal effects upon the actor's behaviour. Another class of strategies we will call 'active strategies'. These strategies require the observer to exert some kind of effort in order to find out something about the target person. However, they do not involve direct contact between the actor and the observer. A third class of strategies will be referred to as 'interactive strategies'. In these cases, the actor and the participant-observer engage in direct symbolic exchange. The passive strategies emphasize decoding processes, while the active and interactive strategies require both encoding and decoding for their successful implementation. An exhaustive listing of strategies within the three categories cannot be done at present; some possibilities will be considered under each category.

Passive Strategy I: Reactivity Search

Gaining information about another by being an unobtrusive observer has certain limitations. If the observer desires to remain unobtrusive, it is obvious that it will be extremely difficult for him to make observations in situations where there are relatively few other persons present or in private situations. Even with these limitations, the observer has a range of choice of observational contexts in which to collect data about the unknown other. One of the situational dimensions along which the observer can choose is that of *reactivity*. By reactivity we mean the extent to which the social situation in which the actor is present demands that he communicate with and react to others.

At one end of the reactivity continuum are situations in which the actor is engaged in solitary activity, for example, studying alone in a library. At the other end of the continuum are situations in which the actor is interacting with several persons simultaneously. The crucial question for the observer is which kind of situations are most useful for reducing his uncertainty about the actor. Certainly, observing persons engaged in solitary activities provides certain information to observers. For example, observers may be able to make confident and accurate attributions about motivational levels and interests of actors by observing their behaviour in solitary situations. However, it seems reasonable to suppose that contexts in which the actor is interacting with others may provide potentially more information than solitary situations. In more reactive contexts, the actor cannot only talk about his solitary activities but he also must respond to other persons. This line of argument suggests that observation in reactive situations is preferred to observation in solitary contexts for purposes of reducing uncertainty.

While the above discussion has emphasized the unobtrusiveness of the observer, it is worthwhile to note that there may be variations along this continuum as well. In small group situations, persons may be more or less obtrusive to the point where persons will comment upon their behaviour, for example, 'Wasn't he very dominant?' or 'He was so quiet I almost didn't know he was here'. It may be that new group members generally attempt to assume an unobtrusive observer role in order to observe the kinds of reactivity presented by other group members. This approach may be used when the new member is likely to be evaluated by the group at some future time; that is, the new member wishes to get the 'lay of the land' before he commits himself publically to positions on issues.

Passive Strategy II: Social Comparison

Social comparison theory (Festinger, 1954) postulates that persons have a 'drive' for self-evaluation. When persons are unsure or uncertain of their abilities or the appropriateness of their opinions or emotional responses, they will seek out others in order to determine their level of ability or the kinds of opinions or emotional responses they should display in unfamiliar social situations. Schachter's (1959) landmark research on the relationship between anxiety and affiliation, and subsequent research, provide considerable support for social comparison theory predictions. The theory further predicts that persons will not just seek out any other person or persons for social comparison purposes, but they will seek out others whom they perceive to be similar to themselves. Again, findings of Schachter's (1959) research tends to support this generalization.

When an individual experiences an epistemological deficit about another person's abilities, opinions, and emotional responses, that is, the individual is uncertain about the *other* rather than *himself*, it seems plausible that certain social comparison notions can be used to predict how the individual will cope with his uncertainty about the other. Specifically, we might expect the individual who wishes to learn about the other's abilities, opinions, and emotions to try to observe the other in situations where the other is interacting with persons *known* by the individual observer. If the observer knows little about those interacting with the actor, he stands to gain considerably less information about the actor. When known others are observed with the actor, the observer can make more confident inferences regarding the probable responses the actor would manifest if the observer and the actor actually came into face-to-face contact.

Probably, there is a *tendency* for those who are best known and understood by an individual to be *similar* to him. If this is the case, we would expect that when observers rely on known others as social comparison stimuli for the unknown target person, the observers by default are relying on *similar others* for comparison stimuli. However, it seems that information about an unknown other could be gained whether the unknown other was observed interacting with persons who are similar or dissimilar to the observer. More confident attributions might result from observations of the unknown person with similar others. In any case, the social comparison strategy suggests that observers prefer to observe the target person interacting with known others rather than with unknown others. It should be emphasized again that while social comparison is conceived of as a passive strategy, the cognitive effort required for the selection of optimal observational contexts may be considerable.

Passive Strategy III: Disinhibition Search

In the previous discussion of Jones and Davis's (1965) correspondent inference theory of attribution it was pointed out that in-role behaviour or behaviour which is highly constrained by social desirability norms is potentially less informative to the observer. According to Jones and Davis (1965), in such situations observers have a difficult time making confident inferences about actors' dispositions from observations of their behaviour.

Given the attribution problems associated with observations in formal interaction situations, it is reasonable to suggest that observers prefer to collect data about unknown others in social situations in which interaction is less constrained by social norms and rules. Observers will search for social contexts in which the actor is likely to enact a wider range of behaviours, that is, where inhibitions are likely to be fewer. Of course, there is one problem with this strategy. The kinds of social situations in which inhibitions are likely to be lower are more private in nature. Thus, if an observer wishes to be unobtrusive, there may be a severe limitation on his ability to make observations in situations where inhibitions are likely to be lowered.

Active Stragegy I: Asking Others About the Target

By contrast to the passive uncertainty reduction strategies outlined above, the active strategies require the observer to take overt steps in order to procure information about the actor or to arrange circumstances in such a way that he is able to glean information about the actor. However, the difference between active and interactive strategies is that in active strategies, the observer does not engage in direct communication with the actor. Interactive strategies are those which require direct symbolic exchanges between actor and observer.

One way to gain information about another is to ask persons who already know the other well. Of course, there are several potential limitations to this strategy for knowledge generation. First, the verbal reports of informants may be distorted either intentionally or unintentionally. Second, the informants may tell the actor that the observer has been seeking information about him thus influencing the behaviour of the actor in ways which lead both the observer and informants to erroneous inferences.

An interesting question in this regard is what kinds of informants are preferred by observer-inquirers. In all likelihood, observers tend to choose informants who are in frequent, direct contact with actors. Moreover, informants who have access to the private lives of actors are most probably preferred. Informants who have such access are likely to observe the behaviour of actors under conditions which promote disinhibition. Finally, observers might be prone to recruit informants who are similar to themselves for the reasons discussed under the passive strategy of Social Comparison. The preceding discussion implies that the same criteria for selecting observational contexts within the passive strategies category may be employed to select informants as well.

The strategy of using informants is not employed solely in situations where the observer does not have direct contact with the actor. After a particular observer and actor engage in face-to-face interaction, the observer may ask informants how the actor responded to him. This situation may be produced by the observer's concern for the actor's evaluation of him. Under these conditions, the same criteria for informant selection may be used by the observer and the risks associated with informant disclosure cited above are present.

Active Strategy II: Environmental Structuring

The strategy of environmental structuring is similar to one kind of research strategy used to study behaviour in the laboratory. In a typical interaction experiment, the experimenter will arrange a set of conditions by employing confederates, instructions, etc., and then unobtrusively observe the effect of these manipulations on behaviour, for example, record interaction from behind a one-way mirror. The question here is whether persons employ similar strategies in their everyday lives. Also, we can ask whether persons ever structure environments and then do not themselves interact with the actor but assume a relatively passive observer role. The answer to these questions is most probably affirmative. For example, a person who wishes to learn something about another may arrange seating patterns in a meeting in such a way that one of his informants is seated next to the target person. After the interaction is over, the informant can report his observations to the observer. Also, in inviting the persons to a social gathering, those hosting the party may engineer their guest list so that at least some 'reliable informants' will be present to share their views of 'newcomers'. Of course, since persons most probably tend to invite those who are similar to themselves to such social gatherings, the similarity between the observer and the informants probably is great. Such similarity may act to enhance the value of the information given to observers by their informants.

It is important to note that environmental structuring may involve both the physical and the social environment. Controlling seating arrangements with place cards, placing certain magazines on coffee tables, hanging particular paintings on walls in order to gather information about an actor are examples of structuring the physical environment. Making sure that certain persons are present in the same social environment as the target person at the same time in order to observe the responses of the target person to the others present is an example of structuring the social environment. In both cases, responses of the target person may be either directly observed by the observer or reported to the observer by informants. The important attribute of the environmental structuring strategy as well as the strategy of asking others about the target is the active role taken by the observer-inquirer. However, it should be kept in mind that when we refer to active strategies we do not mean to imply that the observer and actor are in direct communication with each other. Strategies in this category are considered next.

Interactive Strategy I: Verbal Interrogation.

When actors and observers engage in face-to-face communication, one of the most obvious ways the participant-observer can gain information about the actor is to ask him questions. Berger and Calabrese (1975) argue that high levels of uncertainty produce high rates of question asking in initial interactions. As the interaction progresses and uncertainty is reduced, the number of questions asked tends to decrease. Calabrese (1975) found support for this proposition.

While question asking is an obvious strategy, it is not.without several limitations (Berger, Gardner, Parks, Schulman, and Miller, 1976). First, there is little doubt that there are limits upon the *number* of questions that may be asked per unit of time in many social interactions. When these limits are exceeded, the interaction takes on the character of a formal interview and the person being asked the questions is likely to become reticent to answer them. In addition, the person being interrogated is likely to begin to dislike the question asker. Not only is there an apparent upper limit on the number of questions that may be asked per unit of time, but there is also a norm which requires that persons be willing to answer questions that they ask of others. This reciprocity norm (Gouldner, 1960) not only governs question asking behaviour but also exerts control on intimacy of disclosure (Ehrlich and Graeven, 1971; Sermat and Smyth, 1973). Finally, merely because one is able to ask direct questions to another does not guarantee that the person answering the question will reply truthfully.

In initial interaction situations there is an additional constraint which the observer-interrogator must face. Because it is generally inappropriate to begin initial interactions by asking highly intimate questions (Gardner, 1976), the observer-interrogator in such a situation cannot 'get to' highly intimate information very quickly. If he moves too fast, he is likely to be perceived negatively by the target of his question asking. The norm of *gradual incrementalism* prevents the observer from acquiring highly intimate information in initial interactions through verbal interrogation. Thus, although question asking seems to be an obvious strategy for reducing uncertainty, it may be that the limitations cited above considerably reduce its usefulness. However, more research effort should be directed toward patterns of question asking as relationships develop.

Interactive Strategy II: Self-Disclosure

In discussing the Verbal Interrogation strategy above, mention was made of the reciprocity norm which appears to govern both question asking behaviour and intimacy levels of self disclosure. A number of studies have shown that the more intimate information an individual discloses about himself to another, the greater the likelihood that the other will disclose more intimate information about himself (Ehrlich and Graeven, 1971; Jourard, 1971; Sermat and Smyth, 1973). It is important to remember that the information exchanged in such situations might be intimate but not truthful. Recognizing this limitation, there seems to be little doubt that disclosing information about one's self to another is a potentially powerful way to induce the other to disclose similar information about himself.

It should also be kept in mind that the strategy of self-disclosure does not just refer to the disclosure of intimate information. Disclosure can beget disclosure of any number of different intimacy levels. Thus, if one wishes to find out where a stranger is from, he might disclose his home town to the stranger. On the other hand, if a person wishes to learn something about another's political attitudes, he might proffer certain information about his own political attitudes. Of course, there is always the possibility that even when such information is given, the person receiving it will not respond in kind. When this occurs, the probability that the relationship will fail to grow increases.

Interactive Strategy III: Deception Detection

In outlining the previous two strategies, the possibility of falsification of information was raised. There is little doubt that when persons interact with each other they sometimes brag, ingratiate, and attempt to manipulate each other by falsifying information. Falsification may occur in at least two ways: (1) withholding of information, and (2) distortion of information. Thus, a given individual may fail to mention the fact that he has been fired from several jobs because of his heavy drinking. Or, a person may exaggerate his prowess in athletics. These tendencies towards distortion represent problems for the observer who wishes to know and understand another to a significant extent.

When persons misrepresent themselves for the purpose of enhancing their esteem in the eyes of others, there are a number of strategies they may employ (Jones, 1964; and Jones and Wortman, 1973). Ingratiators can use opinion agreement, flattery, self-presentation (presenting one's self in a favourable light), and the rendering of favours to accomplish their objective. In these cases, the problem for the observer is to determine the sincerity of the potential ingratiator's behaviours. Several communication strategies might be used to accomplish this objective. First, if opinion agreement is suspected by the participant-observer, he may proffer a number of opinions on various issues to see whether the other agrees with all or most of them. If the other shows a high level of agreement on several issues, the participant-observer might then 'change his mind' on some of them to see whether the suspected ingratiator follows suit.

In the case of flattery, the observer might reject the compliment several times to determine whether the suspected ingratiator will continue to give the compliment. If the person rendering the compliment is willing to repeat the compliment several times, the participant-observer might be more prone to accept it as genuine. Not responding verbally to positive self-presentations may be a way of unmasking this ingratiation strategy. If a person continues to brag about his accomplishments in spite of the disinterest shown by the target, the target might well conclude that the person is engaging in ingratiation. A similar strategy might be used to detect favour rendering.

The above examples of strategies for the detection of deception assume that the potential deceiver may be misrepresenting himself or herself by presenting false information. However, deception can also occur when the deceiver *withholds information* about himself. Perhaps it is at this point that observers monitor more carefully the nonverbal cues that the suspected deceiver is emitting (Knapp, Hart and Dennis, 1974). This is not to say that nonverbal cues are ignored when a person is suspected of engaging in the ingratiation strategies outlined above; however, it may be that when verbal means for detecting deception are available in an interaction, they are preferred. When a person withholds information, observers may have to rely totally on nonverbal cues as sources of information about deception.

Deception can also be detected using both the active and passive modes for knowing outlined earlier. Persons who know the target can be consulted to check the veracity of the information given by the suspected deceiver. Observers can attempt to observe unobtrusively suspected deceivers. Thus, the deception detection process is not confined to the interactive category. However, when the observer can use his own communicative capacity to determine whether or not a given target is engaging in deception, he most probably runs the best chance of uncovering the deceiver.

MUTUAL UNDERSTANDING

Throughout the present chapter, the focus of the discussion has been upon the *individual's* quest for understanding. Little has been said about the joint seeking of two or more persons for such knowledge and understanding. The preceding discussions suggest that persons will achieve *mutual understanding* when they have generated and confirmed a significant number of causal attributions for various facets of each other's behaviour. Of course, it is possible that in a two person communication system one individual will have a high level of understanding of the other but the other will have a low level of knowledge about his partner. Such asymmetric situations are likely to be troublesome and to produce feelings of inequity, especially in the person who feels he has the higher level of understanding.

Another possibility worth mentioning is that in a dyadic communication system, various combinations of knowledge and understanding levels on the part of the interactants may produce differences in the kinds of knowledge generation strategies discussed above. Two persons who have very low levels of knowledge about each other may use strategies which differ from those employed in a situation where one person in the dyad has considerable information and the other very little. Finally, even when two persons have relatively high levels of understandings of each other, it is still necessary to update information to take into account changes which have happened to both of them. Certain of the strategies outlined here might be used for that purpose more frequently than others. At present, we are not in a position to predict exactly what strategies would most likely be used under which set of circumstances, however, this would seem to be one of the next issues that should be considered in this line of inquiry.

CONCLUSION

In this chapter, we have examined some antecedents to the knowledge generation processes involved in getting to know others. We have also attempted to outline some of the strategies which persons use to gain knowledge about others. Most probably, important alternative antecedents as well as several strategies have been overlooked. Moreover, no attention was given in the present chapter to the possible differences between *strategies* and *tactics* for the knowledge generation. Within each one of the strategies we have considered, there are numerous tactical variations possible for implementating the strategy. However, since the number of tactical variations is so large within any one strategy, it was impossible to consider them.

In spite of the above limitations, it is hoped that the reader has found the general approach to the study of relationship development presented here to be of heuristic value. For too long, those interested in relationship development have viewed *attraction* and *liking* as the crucial criterion variables to study. In the present view, such variables as knowledge and understanding deserve at least as much if not more consideration in the study of relationship development and disintegration. After all, when people develop what they call 'meaningful relationships' with others, they usually say that these relationships involve a high level of *understanding*. And, when significant relationships disintegrate, the persons involved are frequently heard to say that they lacked *understanding*. While such constructs as knowledge and understanding are difficult to conceptualize and operationalize, this very difficulty suggests their potential importance in relational growth and disintegration. Hopefully, future research and theoretical developments will shed more light on their role in interpersonal communication.

7

Why do Low-prestige Language Varieties Persist?

ELLEN BOUCHARD RYAN

During the past fifteen years, a host of language attitude studies conducted in several societies have demonstrated that the varieties of a particular language tend to enjoy differential prestige. Even the speakers of the lower-prestige styles frequently view those styles unfavourably. The purpose of this chapter is to explore possible reasons for the maintenance of these varieties despite pressures for their speakers to substitute styles which are viewed more positively.

EXISTENCE AND PERSISTENCE OF LOW-PRESTIGE LANGUAGE VARIETIES

Many languages have undergone a process of standardization resulting in the widespread acknowledgement within a given society that one particular variety, the standard dialect, incorporates a formal set of norms defining 'correct' usage. This high prestige standard is usually employed predominantly by the social group(s) with the highest social status in that society. Once this historical process has resulted in universal recognition of the standard, one might expect the other varieties to disappear over a generation or two. However, many regional, ethnic, and social class varieties (e.g. Schwyzerdeutsch in Switzerland, Canadian French in Canada, Appalachian and Black English in the United States, and Catalan Spanish in Spain) have tended to persist for centuries, surviving strong pressures to succumb in favour of the standard dialects (cf. Giles and Powesland, 1975; Macaulay, 1973).

The most widely utilized techniques for investigating speakers' views of speech was developed in Montreal during the 1950s by Wallace Lambert and colleagues. In the 'matched-guise' experiment, judges listen to a number of different voices reading the same passage and evaluate each of them on rating scales or bipolar-adjective scales. Although the judges are unaware of the use of guises, the different speech styles are represented by the same reader(s). With the matched-guise procedure, the Montreal research group has shown that French Canadian listeners view speakers of European French more favourably than speakers of their own Canadian French (Lambert, Hodgson, Gardner, and Fillenbaum, 1960; d'Anglejan and Tucker, 1973) and upper-class French Canadians speakers more favourably than lower-class French Canadian speakers (B Brown, 1969). In an adaptation frequently employed when believable matched-guises are unavailable, the contrasted speech styles are represented by distinct speakers. Cooper (1975) has suggested that the original procedure as well as the adaptation be referred to as 'verbal-guise' techniques.

Such verbal-guise procedures have been utilized in many situations where differential status has been associated with speech varieties. In Britain, Howard Giles and associates have established the overriding prestige attributed to 'Received Pronunciation' (RP) over regional and foreign accents (Giles, 1970; 1971a) and over lower-class accents (Bourhis, Giles, and Lambert, 1975; Giles, 1970; Giles and Bourhis, 1976b). Likewise, numerous studies conducted in the United States indicate agreement among majority and minority group members that standard English is the high status variety in contrast to Black English (Tucker and Lambert, 1969; Williams, Hewett, Miller, Naremore, and Whitehead, 1976), to lower-class white English (Labov, 1966; Shuy, 1969), and to Mexican American Accented English (cf., Ryan and Carranza, 1977). Egyptian students in a study by El-Dash and Tucker (1975) judged speakers more favourably in their Classical Arabic guises than in their Colloquial Arabic guises. In Italy, Bates (1975) reports that a strong preference for standard Italian over a local dialect was evident among speakers of the dialect even at age six.

Despite great variability in the English speech of his New York City informants, Labov (1966) found uniformity in their reactions to speakers in terms of judgements of job suitability. In fact, the speakers with the highest frequency of stigmatized pronunciations in their own speech showed the greatest tendency to downgrade others for their use of such features. In his discussion of these data, Labov (1972b) posed the obvious question: why do people not conform to the normative values they express? After considering a number of alternative explanations, Labov proposed that non-standard speakers did not want to adopt the dominant group's norms. Although they endorsed those norms in the test situation o(i.e., judgement of social status), an opposing set of values must have supported their vernacular forms.

More generally, the stubborn persistence of diverse language varieties within many societies demands an explanation. For example, despite the lure of social mobility and years of educational (and frequently political) efforts, there is no apparent move towards universal adoption of RP English in Britain, of standard English in the United States, of Castillian in Spain, or of European French in French Canada. In fact, throughout history one can find many instances of a low prestige vernacular dialect becoming a regional standard over a higher status variety, the most notable example being the displacement of a few classical languages in Europe by 'lowly' vernaculars such as French and Italian (Fishman *et al.*, 1966).

MULTIDIMENSIONALITY OF ATTITUDES TOWARDS LANGUAGE VARIETIES

In considering aspects of language preference which may account for the remarkable stability of nonstandard language varieties, we will follow the recommendation made by Weinreich (1970) that the meaning of the term prestige be restricted to 'advantage for social advancement'.

Language as Group Identity Symbol

The value of language as a chief symbol of group identity is one of the major forces for the perservation of nonstandard speech styles or dialects (Gubuglo, 1973). Glaser and Moynihan (1975) state that a rise of ethnicity has occurred across the world, with language as an important marker of the newly important ethnic groups. In a series of studies concerning ethnic identity, Taylor and associates have found language to be a critical dimension of identity (Taylor, Bassili and Aboud, 1973; Taylor, Simard and Aboud, 1972).

Just as ethnicity should be viewed as a matter of choice, not accident (Patterson, 1975), accent or dialect adoption should be considered as a matter due largely to conscious choice. Thus, although regional, ethnic, and lower-class individuals have limited access to opportunities for acquiring the prestige variety compared to members of the high status groups, much of the failure of these individuals to profit from whatever opportunities are available is due to counter-acting pressures favouring their native speech styles. Most importantly, a certain amount of language loyalty is natural in every language user because of the inescapable emotional involvement with one's mother tongue *as one learned it in childhood* (Weinreich, 1970).

The conscious aspect of accent choice is highlighted by the frequently occurring phenomenon of increased nonstandardness in the speech of adolescents as they attempt to distinguish themselves from the established prestige groups (Barker, 1947; Fisher, 1971; Weinreich, 1970). Recently, Ramirez (1974) has noted the deliberate return to a Chicano dialect of Spanish by youths in order to establish identity within their own cultural group as well as its adoption by fluent Spanish speakers as a way of establishing a feeling of brotherhood with the Chicano movement.

The relationship between speech and ethnic identity has been mentioned by a variety of authors. For example, Lambert (1967) describes the second-language learner's need to preserve something which separates him from the new language group. Otherwise, with fluent speech in the new language, he might begin to lose his original identity. In situations of intergroup conflict, an individual may feel it is especially important that his true group identity be reflected in his speech at all times. In a Quebec study, Gatbonton-Segalowitz (1975) discovered that the degree of French accent in the speech of French Canadians was related to their feelings of identification with their own group. Thus, those Québécois with the strongest attachments to the French ethnic group spoke English with the heaviest accents.

In his study of the social motivation of a sound change in Martha's Vineyard, Labov (1972a) observed that a high degree of nonstandard centralization of two diphthongs was closely correlated with expressions of strong resistance to the influence of the 'summer people'. In the most traditional area of the island, residents appeared particularly intent upon maintaining their distinctiveness. Since many of the lexical differences had become obsolete with the fading of the whaling industry and since the group was fighting against considerable pressures to maintain its identity, it is not unnatural to find phonetic differences becoming stronger (i.e., more nonstandard forms among the younger generations). In an interesting anecdote reported by Labov, the speech of one youth became markedly more like island speech after he returned to the island after mainland college. In fact, his speech represented hypercorrection in that he used the non-standard variants even more frequently than the most traditional local speakers. Having deliberately turned his back on 'outside' success in favour of an island life, this young man was apparently trying via his speech to become 'one of the islanders'.

Perhaps Brehm's (1972) theory of psychological reactance provides a basis for understanding this exaggeration of the nonstandard variety. He has proposed that threatened loss of freedom leads to behaviours such as choosing a threatened choice alternative as well as more favourable attitudes towards the threatened alternative. Thus, if the people in a minority group feel as though their freedom to continue using their style of speech is threatened, they might exhibit reactance by using their distinctive speech. Furthermore, in reaction to the perceived threat, they would be likely to intensify their performance of the threatened behaviour by using the style more frequently and/or by increasing its distinctiveness from the 'preferred' style. Individuals who have deliberately chosen to belong to the minority group might be expected to react most strongly to threats from the dominant group.

Regarding intergroup relations, Tajfel (1974) has proposed that members of a group are led by interactions with other groups to seek qualities of their own group which can serve to differentiate themselves favourably from the outgroup. Such positive ingroup distinctiveness allows for a positive social identity as well as satisfaction with one's own group membership. Bourhis and Giles (1977) have applied this theory specifically to language. Although speech convergence (shift towards an interlocutor's style) is the norm, speech divergence (shift away from the standard) is seen to be particularly popular means of establishing such ingroup distinctiveness. In their study, nonstandard speakers did engage in accent divergence during conversations with an argumentative standard speaker. Thus, as Lieberson (1970) has also suggested, language differences can serve two functions, with respect to maintenance of group identity: the strengthening of ingroup unity as a symbolization of group differences; and an increase in outgroup distance as a type of restriction on intergroup communication.

Language Attitude Studies Attempting to Isolate Distinct Dimensions

A number of speaker evaluation studies have reported that nonstandard speech is evaluated along several distinct dimensions. For example, although downgrading their own speech style on scales mainly concerned with social status or competence, nonstandard speakers in Great Britain have shown accent loyalty on personality rating scales related to social attractiveness and integrity (Cheyne, 1970; Giles, 1971b; Strongman and Woosley, 1967). In another British study (Giles, 1973a), regional speakers rated the quality of an argument higher when presented in standard accent than in regional, but the regionally accented argument was apparently more persuasive in that it resulted in greater change in views. Toughness emerged as a positive characteristic of nonstandard varieties in Labov's (1966) study of New York Speech and in d'Anglejan and Tucker's (1973) investigation of French Canadian speech. In another French Canadian study (with teenagers and male and female adults), Bruce Brown (1969) factor analysed personality evaluations of lower-class French speakers. For the three groups of subjects, the first factor always related to competence while the second varied between benevolence, sternness, or toughness. Whereas competence ratings were clearly dependent upon social class, ratings on the second factor were not predicted by actual or perceived social class.

At Notre Dame we have been tackling the issue of multidimensional language attitudes during the past five years. Three of our evaluative reaction studies have attempted to distinguish between status and solidarity as two important dimensions of social interaction affecting language use (R. Brown, 1965). According to Brown, status differences are characterized by demonstrable influence, power, and control. As we have already seen, ratings along this dimension for members of all groups in a society tend to reflect the relative socio-economic status of the speech groups represented. On the other hand, solidarity is characterized by Brown as being attributed to a person who is similar to the perceiver and is marked by frequent interaction, self-disclosure, and intimacy. Thus, one might expect higher solidarity ratings for a nonstandard style from members of a group associated with that language variety.

In situations where two stable language varieties exist, Fishman (1970) has indicated that one speech variety (the standard) is usually associated with status, high culture, and aspiration towards social mobility while the second variety (the non-standard) is typically connected with solidarity, comradeship, and intimacy within a low status group. The nonstandard speaker often reflects this distinction by choosing the appropriate language variety for specific situations. Presumably, if he cannot speak the official standard, his speech in formal, inter-group situations converges towards the standard as much as possible while it diverges from the standard in intimate, within-group situations.

In our investigations (Brennan, 1977; Carranza and Ryan, 1975; Ryan and Carranza, 1975), two sets of rating scales were employed: status-stressing ('intelligent', 'educated', 'wealthy', 'successful') and solidarity-stressing ('kind', 'likeable', 'good', 'trustworthy'). It was predicted that, whereas standard English speakers would be universally viewed more positively on status-stressing scales, Mexican Americans would prefer speakers of ethnic speech (either Spanish or Mexican American accented English) on scales related to solidarity. First of all, factor analyses of the ratings have strongly supported the original assignment of the eight scales to two distinct status and solidarity dimensions. Secondly, the difference between language varieties was much less on solidarity scales than on those related to status. However, the expected group differences, indicating stronger solidarity preferences for the nonstandard speech by Mexican Americans than by Anglo Americans, were not observed. It may be that the formal setting (a group study conducted in a high school classroom) inhibited the Mexican American students from revealing their true feelings of solidarity and identification with their ethnic speech. Use of a casual interview in the home or community centre would certainly provide a more sensitive measure of such feelings.

Some evidence already exists to indicate that attitudes of nonstandard speakers towards their own variety and the standard depends on the context within which they are used. Ryan and Carranza (1975) found that Mexican American accented English was downgraded relative to the standard more in a school context than in a home context. It should be noted that context was only manipulated minimally, in terms of the topic on which the speaker talked. El-Dash and Tucker (1975) reported that Classical Arabic was felt by Egyptian students to be the most suitable style for all situations except the home, where Colloquial Arabic was preferred and Classical Arabic was considered unsuitable. The importance of the situation in evaluating the social significance of speech differences was also highlighted by Gatbonton-Segalowitz (1975). In this study of French Canadian reactions to speakers of French accented and standard Canadian English, French Canadian Nationalist subjects preferred standard English speakers as leaders in an intergroup situation with both French and English Canadians but preferred French-accented speakers as leaders in an intragroup situation. Thus, further attempts to manipulate social context in language attitude studies seem warranted.

We have also begun to explore the value of a structured interview situation for illuminating the multi-dimensional nature of views towards ethnic and standard speech styles. Carranza (1977) employed a four-dimensional language preference (English v. Spanish) questionnaire as part of a sociolinguistic study of Mexican American parents residing in a large Latino district of a mid-western city. Based on Gardner and Lambert's (1972) contrast between instrumental and integrative motivation for second language learning, respondents were asked to indicate the degree of their preference for English or Spanish on instrumental items (i.e., to get ahead in life or to get a job) and for integrative items (i.e., to better understand people and their way of life and to allow interaction with a greater variety of people). In addition, items thought to reflect two other functions of language were included: affective (i.e., language liked best and one which would be preferred for use all the time) and communicative (i.e., language in which one can best express oneself and language in which one best communicates). Three dimensions emerged as distinct from analyses of the data: instrumental, integrative, and affective-communicative. An analogous but less refined procedure was employed for attitudes towards Mexican accented English; and again the instrumental and integrative dimensions were separable.

In summary, both evaluative reaction and questionnaire studies have revealed that nonstandard speech varieties may have low prestige but are associated with other values of importance for an ethnic group. It should be noted that the contrast between instrumental and integrative motivation appears to be quite similar to that between status and solidarity. In order to stress the sense of belonging which underlies the solidarity notion, one perhaps should have incorporated into the Carranza (1977) interview study, items such as language variety most important for one's identity or most important for use with good friends.

Suggestions for Further Research

A systematic series of studies must be conducted so that a well articulated explanation can be formulated for the maintenance of low-prestige language varieties. Of critical importance are questions concerning the separability and universality of dimensions. Do judges distinguish between standard and nonstandard speakers along separable dimensions, or does one overriding factor (e.g., social status) dominate to the exclusion of others? Given that several distinct dimensions of attitudes towards the standard and relevant nonstandard varieties could be isolated for one minority group, would the same dimensions be applicable for majority group members or for minority and majority individuals in different language variation situations? The outcome of this model of language attitudes includes both basic universal aspects (e.g., social status and group identity) as well as more superficial situation-dependent aspects (e.g., stereotypes associated with a given ethnic group).

In the search for the dimensions underlying language attitudes several issues must be addressed. First, the type of empirical procedures employed in deriving dimensions from rating scales contribute significantly to the ultimate result. Second, the joint use of direct and indirect attitude measures is a highly recommended cross-validation technique. Third, since the attitudes towards standard and nonstandard language varieties may vary quite dramatically within a group (especially within a minority group), it is important to ascertain the critical within-group characteristics and to investigate their interaction with postulated attitudinal dimensions.

With indirect rating scale studies, the proposed dimensions should be empirically validated by at least two methods: correlational and factor analyses of the ratings and predicted interactions of the dimensions with subjects and speech variables. In the past, the rating scales used in speaker evaluation tasks have been derived in two major ways. Lambert et al. (1960) and Williams et al. (1976) have stressed the importance of using scales spontaneously produced in pilot studies with representatives of the same ethnic and social groups as the subjects in the study. The logic underlying this procedure is that one does not wish to force subjects to make judgements in an experimental task which they would not make in a more open-minded or natural situation. On the other hand, we at Notre Dame have selected *a priori* dimensions, defended on the basis of previous research and on sociolinguistic theory. It is our belief that the use of predetermined dimensions is necessary in order to explore systematically the multidimensionality of language attitudes. However, pilot work is recommended as a means of establishing which rating scales best represent the given dimensions. The emphasis here should be on the selection of scales with widespread applicability across potential subject groups.

Both direct and indirect measures of language attitude appear to be critical. With direct measures, such as interview questionnaires, the interpretation of responses is subject to less controversy. Furthermore, the idea of asking people directly how they feel about various speech styles and their speakers is certainly appealing. In particular, open-ended interviews would be most useful for suggesting new or altered dimensions to be explored. However, the current literature provides many warnings that direct questions may not reflect the whole picture. On the basis of a variety of interview tasks, Labov (1966) proposed that informants tend to perceive their own speech in terms of the norms at which they are aiming rather than the sound actually produced. On the other hand, Giles (1970) provides some evidence for repressed recognition of the nonstandardness of one's own speech in that his listeners gave higher ratings for 'speech identical to your' than for their own dialect. On the other hand, the fact that fewer nonstandard pronunciations were actually used by Trudgill's (1972) speakers of a distinctive regional dialect than they reported using suggests that the local dialect enjoyed 'covert prestige', despite the feelings of inferiority revealed in interviews.

Of particular importance for an understanding of attitudes towards a minority group's language varieties is the consideration of within-group differences. Many members of a dominated group may attempt to improve their chances for economic and social success by associating themselves with the dominant group. Often, as Weinreich (1970) mentioned, only those individuals already enjoying favoured social status feel able to indulge in ethnic preservation activities while those in more subordinate social positions are eager for assimilation. Two subgroups likely to be favourable towards ethnic speech are those who are no longer trying to move up in society and the younger generation, who have been most influenced by social movements declaring 'Ethnic is beautiful'. Also, it appears that male–female differences in attitudes exist with males tending to respond more to peer group pressures favouring nonstandard speech and females inclined to respond more to the advantages for social advancement of the standard. An individual's language attitudes should also be related in some fashion to his own language abilities. Thus, one would expect different attitudes towards a group's nonstandard speech from members who spoke only the standard, members who were comfortable with both varieties, and members who spoke only the nonstandard form. For example, one could investigate the generalizability of Labov's (1966) finding that New York City speakers with the most nonstandard pronunciations were the most likely to downgrade the nonstandard style. In addition, it is likely that several personality or social psychological variables such as authoritarianism, anomie, or internal-external motivation affect language attitudes in a describable manner.

CONCLUSIONS

In conclusion, low-prestige speech varieties persist basically because the speakers do not want to give them up. The fundamental distinction developed in this chapter contrasts status or prestige, the value of a speech variety for social advancement, and solidarity, the value of a variety for identification with a group. As we have seen, many studies have found majority and minority group preferences for speakers of the standard language with respect to status and competence traits. On the other hand, the nonstandard variety has been viewed more favourable on other traits, especially those related to group solidarity. Failure to demonstrate actual minority group preference on solidarity characteristics for their nonstandard variety may be due to the 'standard-majority' test settings employed. Future research in ingroup solidarity-stressing settings should provide for a better assessment of the value of a minority language variety for the group.

We need to continue our investigations until we can specify the reasons why and the conditions under which nonstandard speech varieties are preferred over standard styles. Furthermore, the conditions under which the standard variety is viewed more favourably must also be specified.

One important consideration here is whether standard speakers are preferred because of the speech characteristics themselves or because of the inferences about the speaker made on the basis of the speech characteristics. Noting that a Spanish accent seems to enhance the image of an eminent professor or a man of obvious wealth, Ryan and Sebastian (1976) proposed that assumptions regarding social class may have led to the downgrading of accented speakers in earlier studies. In this study, speakers of either standard or accented English were presented to Anglo college students as middle-class or lower-class individuals. For trait ratings as well as social distance, a significant interaction reflected the fact that lower-class accented speakers were perceived much less favourably than the corresponding lower-class standard speakers while the differences associated with speech style for middle-class speakers were smaller. Thus, support was obtained for the notion that accent does not matter as much for individuals known to be from the middle class. It would be useful in future studies to search for the specific background and situational information which would elicit a preference for the accented speaker, even from majority group members.

A broad range of applications of these social psychological investigations could be suggested. Many texts on minority education stress the importance of high self-esteem as a foundation for good learning experiences. Part of an individual's self-image depends upon reactions of family and school towards his speech variety. On the basis of the research considered here, one would propose an approach towards language use that is neither a majority-oriented as the traditional standard-only practice nor as ingroup-oriented as the minority-only methods being discussed frequently in this decade. The emphasis in schools should be on enhancing the value of both standard and minority varieties. This can be accomplished by distinguishing between the formal uses of the standard in formal, intergroup situations and the informal uses of the minority styles in less formal, more person-oriented ingroup situations. Furthermore, the results of the Ryan and Sebastian study suggest that the negative reactions of Anglos towards minority speakers may be reduced by exposing the majority group members to members of the minority group of the upper or middle class. In fact, minority individuals too could often profit from contact with high status members of their own group who speak their nonstandard variety. The critical practical issues concern how to assist the minority individual to feel comfortable with the use of both standard and minority varieties, the former to enhance his image within the society as a whole and the latter to enhance his sense of identification with his own group.

8
Psycholinguistic Distinctiveness: Language Divergence in Belgium[1]

RICHARD Y. BOURHIS, HOWARD GILES, JACQUES P. LEYENS, and HENRI TAJFEL

Many social groups can be readily categorized by their distinct language varieties, and for many ethnic and national groups, these can be among the most salient dimensions of their social identities (Taylor, Bassili, and Aboud, 1973; Giles, Taylor and Bourhis, 1977; Giles, Taylor, Lambert and Albert, 1976; Ryan and Carranza, 1977). Indeed, for many ethnic group members, language spoken is often the major embodiment of their ethnicity given its distinctly human character and the fact that it can be used to attain and maintain cultural distinctiveness (Fishman, 1972, 1977). For instance, a number of ethnic minorities (e.g., the Welsh, Catalans and Québécois) are redefining their statuses in a more favourable direction and expressing this via language. Although many authors have discussed the linkage between language and ethnicity, few as yet have linked these to the dynamics of inter-ethnic group relations in any coherent fashion (see however, Lukens, in press). Moreover, when one examines social psychological accounts of intergroup relations, little attention is afforded language behaviour. Given the current prominence of such issues all around the world, this is a somewhat surprising state of affairs.

In an attempt to take account of these theoretical deficiences, Giles, Bourhis and Taylor (1977) proposed a framework for understanding the role of language in ethnic group relations. Firstly, the model describes the socio-structural factors which can influence whether an ethnolinguistic minority will or will not seek to establish its own ingroup language as a viable mode of communication. Secondly, it attempts to outline some of the socio-psychological processes operating between ethnolinguistic groups in contact which allow us an explanation of the linguistic strategies they adopt. This latter psychological approach, which is of prime interest to us in the present context, can be regarded as a theoretical integration of two independent conceptual systems: Tajfel's (1974; 1978) theory of intergroup relations and social change, and Giles's theory of interpersonal accommodation through speech (Giles, 1973; Giles and Powesland, 1975).

Let us very briefly examine each theory in turn, and then discuss certain aspects of their integration. Tajfel has suggested that when members of a group interact with members of another, they compare themselves on a number of value dimensions with this other group. He claims that these intergroup social comparisons will lead group members to search for characteristics of their own group which will lead them to differentiate themselves favourably from the outgroup. Such positive ingroup distinctiveness will not only allow individuals satisfaction in their own group membership but will afford them a positive social identity.

Giles has been concerned with understanding why people shift their speech in different social contexts, and especially in interaction with others. He has suggested that in many social interactions, speakers desire their listeners' social approval. One tactic (consciously or unconsciously conceived) is for the former to modify his speech in the direction of the latter, a process termed speech *convergence*. On the other hand, there might arise situations where the speaker might wish to dissociate himself from the other – perhaps because of his undesirable habits, appearance, etc. – and hence accentuate their linguistic differences, a process termed speech *divergence*.

Giles, Bourhis and Taylor (1977) were concerned with showing how the speech strategies of convergence and divergence (among others) could be understood in an inter-ethnic group context by means of Tajfel's theory. For instance, it was suggested that when members of a subordinate group considered their inferior status to be just and fair, they would attempt to 'pass' into the dominant group socially and psychologically. They might also do this linguistically, and hence in interaction with a member of the dominant group would converge towards him. However, if group members considered their inferior status to be illegitimate and the intergroup situation to be unstable, they would redefine their group attributes, socially and psychologically, in a more positive direction. They might also do this linguistically, and hence in interaction with a member of the outgroup might accentuate their own ingroup characteristics by means of speech divergence. In such an interaction, one might expect the dominant group member to adopt reciprocal strategies of divergence in an attempt to retain his own positively-valued distinctiveness.

Therefore, it was proposed that in certain intergroup situations, members of an ethnic group might search for a positively-valued distinctiveness from the outgroup on *linguistic* dimensions they valued highly, a process Giles, Bourhis and Taylor termed 'psycholinguistic distinctiveness'. By diverging (or emphasizing) their own ethnic accent, dialect or language, ingroup members would accentuate the differences between themselves and the outgroup on a salient and valued dimension of their group identity.[2]

Bourhis and Giles (1977) designed an experiment to demonstrate the use of *accent* divergence among Welsh people in an inter-ethnic context, and to investigate the conditions which facilitate its occurrence. The study was conducted in a language laboratory where people who valued their national group membership and its language highly were learning the Welsh language; only 26 per cent of Welshmen can speak the national language. During one of their weekly sessions, Welshmen were asked to help in a survey concerned with second language learning techniques. The questions in the survey were verbally presented to them in English in their individual booths by a very English-sounding speaker, who at one point arrogantly challenged their reasons for learning what he called 'a dying language which had a dismal future'. Such a question was perceived by them to threaten their feelings of ethnic identity, and the informants broadened their Welsh accents in their replies as compared with their answers to an emotionally-neutral question asked earlier. In addition, some informants introduced Welsh words and phrases in their answers, while one woman did not reply for a while, and then was heard to conjugate Welsh verbs very gently into the microphone.

The study showed then that when ingroup members are ethnically threatened by an outgroup speaker they will make themselves psycho-linguistically distinct from him by accent divergence. Interestingly, even when he asked a neutral question of them, the informants emphasized their Welsh group membership in terms of the content of what they said in their replies (termed, 'content differentiation'), demonstrating that psycholinguistic distinctiveness can occur in different linguistic forms. The subjects in this experiment did not have a productive command of the Welsh language and the symbol of their Welsh identity would have been their Welsh accents in English (cf. Bourhis, Giles and Tajfel, 1973). The authors raised the question as to whether in truly bi- or multilingual contexts, where the language itself for speakers might be a symbol of group solidarity, psychological differentiation would be manifest in terms of an actual language shift to own-group usage (i.e., *language divergence*). Bourhis and Giles also speculated that perhaps there was a hierarchy of strategies of psycholinguistic distinctiveness, some of which are more symbolic of ethnic dissociation than others, with language divergence being among the most potent given its extremely overt character.

The first study to be reported here was designed to look into these notions in the multilingual setting of Belgium. Yet before outlining the nature of the investigation, an overview of the language situation in this cultural context needs to be provided.

THE BELGIAN SITUATION[3]

Prior to presenting a necessarily brief account of the language situation in Belgium, it must be stressed that it is extremely difficult to do justice to the complexity of the situation. From the outset, and still today, Belgium is made up of two main linguistic areas: the Francophone area is situated in the south, and known as Wallonia; the Dutch area is situated in the north, and known as Flanders. The capital of Belgium, Brussels, is situated in the southern part of Flanders and is predominantly French-speaking, although officially bilingual.

According to the last linguistic census figures (taken in 1947), 53 per cent of Belgians were Dutch-speaking, while 42 per cent were French-speaking, with 18 per cent of the overall population reporting to be bilingual. In addition, there is also a small German-speaking area which is situated in the eastern part of Belgium (for more recent estimates and trends see Coppieters, 1974).

Belgium was created and recognized as a nation state in 1830. Its creation through a bourgeois revolt had been spearheaded by Walloons, Gallicized Flemings and French-speaking inhabitants of Brussels (the Bruxellois). Belgium, then, was the creation of the *Francophone* bourgeoisie (Kelly, 1969). This had the consequent effect that French was instituted as the administrative language of the leading circles in Belgium. Without French, social promotion in the public or state sector was denied. Indeed, Francophones in Belgium, influenced as they were by nineteenth-century nationalism, had the goal of incorporating the Flemings (more than half the total population) as rapidly as possible into the French linguistic group in order to develop a state which was strongly unitary and linguistically homogeneous (Fleerackers, 1973). At this time, then, the prospects for the Dutch (Flemish) language were bleak since it was denied most of the institutional rights and supports afforded to French in the new nation state. According to Lorwin (1972), Flemish intellectuals complained: 'To be Belgians we have to cease being Flemish.' In other words, to succeed in Belgian society, the Flemings had to 'pass' into the dominant group by adopting Francophone ways (cf. strategies of social mobility, Tajfel, 1974; and with reference to language, Giles, Bourhis and Taylor, 1977). It could be said that the weakness of the Dutch language in Belgium in those days reflected the economic and social plight of the Flemish people themselves and of their region in Flanders.

In the mid nineteenth century, French-speaking Wallonia was second only after Britain to industrialize and prosper principally because of the localization of natural resources (coal) (Kelly, 1969). Its urban workers became radicalized while the élites in Brussels were a liberal bourgeoisie and in complete control of the new state. The dominance of the French language right up to the Second World War reflected the political and economic dominance of the Francophones at all levels of private and government activity throughout Belgium. Well into the early twentieth century, education in Flemish was limited to primary school, while the secondary school and university curricula was exclusively French even in Flanders itself.

It was only in 1930 that the University of Ghent was transformed into the nation's first all-Dutch language university. For the first time, Flemish élites could be trained entirely in Flemish instead of in French. In 1932, laws were passed to give Flemish equality with French as the official language in the administration, in primary and secondary education, and in the courts and the army. In the late 1930s, attempts at institutionalized bilingualism for all in Belgium were thwarted by Francophones in Wallonia and Brussels who considered Dutch a language of restricted practical use. The unilingual Walloons did not want to learn Dutch and they opted for unilingualism of the Belgian regions instead of bilingualism across the whole country. As a result, Flanders in the north became officially unilingual Dutch, while Wallonia in the south remained officially French. The nation's capital, however, was to remain officially bilingual, although in reality it was predominantly French.

One of the most drastic changes in the relationship between the two linguistic communities occurred after the Second World War. Belgium's second industrial revolution occurred in Flanders, not Wallonia. Wallonia's heavy industries and coal production were no longer profitable after the War, and the region's industrial structure and its social services began to decay. In Flanders, on the other hand, an increasingly self-confident and dynamic Flemish élite had been formed within the span of three decades to manage and operate the modern industries with its massive influx of new, mostly American, capital. The industrial centres of gravity shifted towards the Flemish ports. Indeed, industrial production in Flanders is still to this day increasing five times faster than its Walloon counterpart (Fleerackers, 1973). In the decades following the war, Flanders began to prosper economically, socially, and culturally, while Wallonia rightly complained of the State's failure to promote the modernization of their region. Meanwhile, Brussels remained resolutely Francophone, archliberal and fastidiously bourgeois. As long as the Bruxellois earned half again as much as the average citizen in Belgium, and since French remained an international language, the capital's Francophone had every reason to remain distinct from both the Flemish and the Walloons (Kelly, 1969). For the same reasons, the Bruxellois had every reason to prefer Belgium as a unified state with a strong centralized government based in Brussels rather than as a decentralized state with much regional autonomy. Through the postwar years, the conflict of interest between the two linguistic communities became more acute and the division of parliamentary seats between the traditional political parties came to reflect more and more the linguistic cleavage within the country (Lorwin, 1972).

In the 1960s a series of laws polarized the relations between the two ethnolinguistic communities which in turn stimulated each group to increase its demands on the political system (Dunn, 1972; Hill, 1974).

The first of these attempted to establish the language frontiers between Flanders and Wallonia. The shifting of some relatively small districts from one side of the linguistic frontier to the other in order to make each region as linguistically homogeneous as possible caused much opposition between the Walloons and the Flemish. The second law was designed to provide better educational and cultural facilities for the Flemish minority in Brussels and to halt the 'Frenchification' of Brussels' Flemings by preventing them from sending their children to French schools. This law was seen by most Flemings as a necessary step to protect the status of the Flemish language in the nation's capital, and by the Francophones as an infringement of individual liberties. A third law sought to improve the position of Flemish as a language in the administration of the municipalities of the Brussels region while, at the same time, creating certain French language facilities in some Flemish communes on the outskirts of Brussels. This latter law was seen as a natural extension of human liberties by the affluent Francophones who in increasing numbers moved from the capital to the small Flemish countryside towns, thus turning them into Francophone suburban enclaves. Much of this movement occurred before the Francophones were fully aware that they were infringing the territorial rights (*droit du sol*) of the Flemish area surrounding Brussels. To the Flemish, the extension of French language facilities in these areas was perceived as a threat to the cultural and linguistic integrity of their territory: the beginning of a Francophone 'oil spot' spilling beyond the Brussels agglomeration at the expense of Flanders. Indeed, for a long time, Flemish spokesmen had denounced Brussels as a national capital in which they, the Flemish, the majority of Belgian citizens, did not feel home. That the Francophone 'oil spot' might be allowed to spread onto Flemish territory as a result of these language laws was extremely infuriating and threatening to the Flemish in Flanders.

The effect of these laws on the relationship between the communities by the mid 1960s has been summarized by Lorwin (1972) in the following way:

> The nation has become an amalgam of one oppressed majority and two oppressed minorities. There are the old historical grievances of the Flemish, the newer grievances of the Walloons, and those of the Bruxellois under Flemish pressures. If the situation is new, it follows an old rule: many are oppressed, but no-one oppresses. (Lorwin, 1972)

So, in spite of, if not because of, the laws passed in the early 1960s, whose purpose had been to take the language issues out of politics, the language issues instead came to dominate Belgian politics in the

1960s and 70s. For a short while in the mid-60s, a number of governments defused the language problem by creating a permanent commission whose task was to improve relations between the linguistic communities so that the government could focus its attention on the other matters, such as the economy.

Yet in 1968, the linguistic truce was broken by the problems of the Catholic University of Louvain in southern Flanders. Since the 1960s, the 10,000 French-speaking students and professors living in Louvain with their own special Francophone grade schools and facilities had been considered by the Flemish as an additional Francophone enclave on Flemish soil. Finally, the situation became explosive when the Francophone section of the university announced its plans for the expansion of the language facilities to Louvain (Leuven, to the Flemish). Tempers rose, and after numerous demonstrations, clashes with the police, and street fights between Flemish and Francophone students, as well as a toppled government, the problem of the Catholic University of Louvain had to be dealt with. The new government voted a massive increase of subsidies to both the Flemish and Francophone sectors of the higher educational system which allowed the Catholic University of Louvain (Francophone section) to rebuild all its facilities at Ottignies (as Louvain la Neuve), 18 kilometers away in Wallonia.

Temporarily this measure restored the linguistic truce, but other problems were looming. Among the laws promulgated in 1963, one stipulated that the distribution of parliamentary seats between the Flemish and Walloons was to be established in proportion to the demographic ratio existing between them. But by the late 1960s, the increasing demographic preponderance of the Flemish led to a redistribution of parliamentary seats which gave the Dutch-speaking ministers a distinct majority over their French-speaking counterparts. Again tempers rose until a fragile compromise over the representation issue was negotiated between the two groups to keep the peace. After the trauma of the incidents at Louvain and the problem of representation at the national parliament, a definite start was made by the government to reform the constitutional structure of the Belgian state. Through the constitutional revision of 1971, Belgium was divided into three cultural communities (the Dutch, French and German) and four linguistic areas (the Dutch language area, Flanders; the French language, Wallonia; the bilingual area of Brussels, the capital; and the German language area in the east) each being responsible for their own social, economic, educational and linguistic matters. The central parliament remained responsible for the Brussels region with local matters in the capital being entrusted to Dutch and French cultural commission which had equivalent power and jurisdiction. For affairs dealt with by the central government, and equal number of French- and Dutch-speaking representatives were allocated to the national parliament. Through these, and other complicated compromises within the new constitution (see Dunn, 1974, Coppieters, 1974 for further details), the French and Dutch communities in Belgium hoped to steer a course mid-way between a unitary and federal state. From a centralistic and French-speaking state in 1830, Belgium had become a bicultural state in which the regions and cultures had a certain degree of internal autonomy.

The plans for this new constitution were not, however, well received by the French majority in Brussels. The Francophones strongly objected to the clause that gave the Flemish minority in Brussels an equal number of high functionaries in municipalities and local authorities. This situation repolarized the opinions of the two linguistic communities across the whole of Belgium and led to the downfall of the government. These issues are not yet resolved, and since 1971 more than five governments have toppled on issues directly, or indirectly, related to the problem of the two linguistic communities. Indeed, it is Brussels which remains the major point of contention between the two. The range of alternatives concerning the future of Brussels within Belgium is the topic of much heated debate for both linguistic communities (Inglehart & Woodward, 1972).

THE EMPIRICAL WORK

The first investigation we carried out in Belgium involved different groups of trilingual Flemish students being recorded in two types of encounters ('Neutral' and 'Aggro') with a Francophone outgroup speaker. The language in which the interaction was initiated was in English, given that many Flemish students and some Walloons and Bruxellois sometimes converse in English—it being an emotionally-neutral language (Scotton, 1976) (from now on the latter two groups will be referred to as Francophones in this chapter). The context of the interaction was, like the Bourhis and Giles study, that of a language laboratory where, as it happens, the participants were there to improve their English-speaking skills. Unlike the previous Welsh study, however, two variables were included in the design. First, the informants had some prior knowledge about the speaker; some were told he was sympathetic with their ethnolinguistic aims, others that he was not. It was thought that the more negative the ingroup's view of the speaker, the more likely it would be that the situation had potential for language divergence to occur. Second, the intergroup categorization was made explicit and salient between the Francophones and Flemings for some subjects, while only implicit for others. It was felt that the more the encounter was couched in ethnic group terms, the more likely it would be that psycholinguistic distinctiveness would operate. Indeed, Giles and Taylor (1978) have shown that when intergroup relations are made salient for Welshmen, they tend to identify more closely with other (Welsh) ingroup members and to dissociate themselves cognitively from relevant (English) outgroup members. On the basis of the above discussion, the aims of the investigation were as follow:

I. To provide evidence for the notions of psycholinguistic distinctiveness in Belgium via language divergence. It was hypothesized that Flemish subjects would switch from English into Flemish when confronted with a Francophone speaker who attacked a salient dimension on their ethnic identity.

II. To investigate the factors affecting the frequency of occurrence of language divergence in this context. It was hypothesized that more subjects would switch to Flemish when being threatened by an outgroup speaker (a) when intergroup categorization was made explicit rather than implicit, and (b) when the ingroup had the prior knowledge that he was unfavourably rather than favourably disposed towards their ethnolinguistic desires.

METHOD: STUDY I

Experimental Design

The subjects (Ss) for the experiment were randomly divided into four groups. Two of these were assigned to the 'Implicit Categorization' conditions, while the others were assigned to the 'Explicit Categorization' conditions. The former did not have their ethnic group membership made salient by the experimenter (E), nor were they informed explicitly that they would be talking to an ethnic outgroup speaker. The latter, on the other hand, were formally labelled, 'The Fleming Group', and were told repeatedly that they would be addressed by a Francophone Belgian. In addition, they were told that some of their replies would be played back afterwards, publicly, thereby heightening perceived accountability within their own ingroup for their reactions to the outgroup speaker. These two conditions were further divided into those Ss who received information that the tape-recorded speaker was either sympathetic or unsympathetic to their position on the language issue in Belgium (the Pro- and Anti-conditions respectively). Ss in all four conditions were required to undergo the same three situations: (1) to provide baseline data of their speech in the language laboratory situation (the Precondition); (2) to reply to the tape-recorded speaker's emotionally-neutral question (the Neutral condition); (3) to reply to the speaker's ethnically-threatening question (the Aggro condition). The study thus constituted a $2 \times 2 \times 3$ matrix design.

Subjects

Forty-eight Flemish students attending the University of Louvain volunteered as Ss for the experiment. They were predominantly middle class in social background and were taking English as their major course at the university. On the basis of post-experimental self-ratings (using a nine-point scale where $1 =$ low and $9 =$ high), they claimed to speak Flemish fluently ($\bar{X} = 8.31$) but French only moderately well ($\bar{X} = 4.83$). They claimed to speak and understand English very well ($\bar{X}_s = 6.21$ and 4.08 respectively). They also reported feeling very Flemish ($\bar{X} = 7.01$), identified very strongly with Flemish issues ($\bar{X} = 7.62$) and were quite dissatisfied with the government's handling of Flemish affairs ($\bar{X} = 3.32$).

The Ss were randomly assigned to four experimental groups of 12 informants each, half of whom were female and the other half male, and all subsequently reported understanding the English of the stimulus speaker with great ease ($\bar{X} = 7.58$). The Ss' self-ratings were subjected to statistical analyses, and no differences emerged between the four groups on the linguistic and social indices mentioned above.

Materials

The materials consisted in the main of three items:

(a) A language laboratory with playback and tape-recording facilities in each booth.

(b) A stimulus tape of a male (trilingual) Francophone interlocutor with a distinctive French accent in his English asking questions first of an emotively-neutral nature, and then of an ethnically-threatening one.

(c) A post-experimental questionnaire tapped Ss' social and linguistic attitudes (already reported), and their perceptions of the experimental situations. Ss were asked in both the Neutral and Aggro conditions to recall (by means of nine-point scales) their impressions of the stimulus speaker on the following scales: the extent to which he had a French accent in his English, seemed provocative, insulting, disturbing, and had an understanding of the issues involved. In addition, Ss were asked to rate the extent to which they agreed with his opinions, would like to have met and helped him in the future, had found the fact that he was a Francophone affected them, and had emphasized their Flemishness in their replies. The questionnaire, which was printed in Flemish, also allowed Ss plenty of opportunity to express openly any other comments on, or reactions to, the experimental situations.

Procedure

The Ss were assembled in four separate groups and were administered the task on separate occasions. These occasions were, in fact, times when they would have had instruction in English at the language laboratory anyway, but had agreed to participate in some research on foreign language learning. E arrived in the class and introduced himself (in English) as a Canadian student spending three months in Belgium as part of his graduate studies; it was felt that such a person would be viewed as ethnically-neutral. He explained that a colleague of his was conducting research into second language learning techniques. Unfortunately, that person could not turn up personally but had recorded some questions on audio-tape for them to answer. E stressed the fact that his survey was totally unrelated to the university and was not concerned with examining their English language skills. However, before E played the tape, he told them it might be worthwhile to determine whether each of the recording machines in the booths was operative. To facilitate this task, he asked Ss to talk for about 3 or 4 minutes into the microphone (in English) about their experiences that previous weekend. This procedure was actually conducted so as to provide baseline speech data for that context (the Pre-condition). Having elicited the baseline data, E informed Ss about the nature of the task to follow. They were told they would hear a question (in English) from the E's colleague over their headphones and would be given another four minutes to reply.

E then told Ss that his colleague thought it might be useful for them to have a little background information about himself, and so he had prepared a few autobiographic notes for this purpose. Two groups received information which included a sympathetic attitude towards the Flemish language (the Pro-conditions), while the others received information suggesting that the speaker was unsympathetic to the language (the Anti-conditions).

One group of Ss in both the Pro- and Anti-conditions had no further information about the speaker other than he was E's colleague.[4] When listening to the speaker, however, they would have known immediately by his accent that he was a Francophone Belgian from pilot work we had undertaken. Ss in these two groups represented the 'Implicit Categorization' conditions. The other two groups had the above instructions qualified in the sense that it was specified repeatedly that the speaker was indeed a Belgian Francophone, while having a card displayed in their individual booths indicating that they were members of 'The Flemish Group'. In addition, E told them that after they had responded to the speaker they, as a group, would hold a discussion about the issues involved. To facilitate this, a number of the group's replies would be played back in public for discussion. For these two groups, then, inter-ethnic group relations was made very salient, and they represented the 'Explicit Categorization' conditions.

Therefore, two of the groups had inter-ethnic group relations made salient to them, the others did not. These two groupings were further divided into those who perceived the speaker as being basically Pro- or Anti-Flemish.

E then played the stimulus tape. In the prologue on the tape, it was made clear that the speaker Ss were to hear was trilingual in English, French and Flemish, and that he preferred English from them in their replies, but would accept French. In other words, there were strong and implicit social constraints against the use of Flemish in this context. He asked them (in English because it was an English language group) an emotionally-neutral question about their reactions to the language learning laboratory method. While Ss were listening to the question, they were being tape-recorded unknowingly at the same time. Ss were then allowed four minutes to answer this question. All Ss in fact answered this question within the time designated, and they then heard the second question over the headphones. This constituted the Aggro condition since the speaker suddenly shifted topic to downgrading the use of the Flemish language in Brussels and spoke for the exclusive use of French in the capital. Ss then had four minutes to respond to this question. Once again, any movements or verbal reactions they might have given while the speaker was encoding his 'aggressive' question would have been tape-recorded, unknowingly to the Ss. In addition, the tape-recording equipment was left on after the procedure was presumed to be over (the Post-condition). They were told that unfortunately there would not be sufficient time left for a group discussion and so a short questionnaire was administered which would allow them an opportunity of expressing their feelings of the situation. This questionnaire was concerned with eliciting their self-rated language and social attitudes and their perceptions of the experimental situations.

E then did in actual fact open discussion with the groups and invited comments while debriefing them as to the true purpose of the experiment. The whole experimental procedure lasted about 50 minutes per group.

RESULTS

The Ss' perceptions of the experimental situations were subjected to analysis, as were their tape-recorded replies.[5]

Ss' perceptions of the situations

Ss' ratings of the questionnaire items were subjected to a $2 \times 2 \times 2$ analysis of variance consisting of the factors of *group* (Explicit/Implicit Categorization), *information about outgroup speaker* (Pro-/Anti-group), and *stimulus conditions* with repeated measures (Neutral/Aggro).

Significant main effects for stimulus conditions emerged on most scales. It was found that Ss considered the speaker to have less understanding of the issues involved (F = 25.68; d.f. = 1.47; p < 0.01), sounded more provocative (F = 57.57, p < 0.01), insulting (F = 63.09; p < 0.01), and French-accented (F = 5.10; p < 0.05) in the Aggro than the Neutral condition. Moreover, Ss disagreed with him more (F = 42.18; p < 0.01); were more disturbed by him (F = 36.95; p < 0.01), and affected by the fact that he was a Francophone in the former than the latter condition. Also, Ss felt that they would have helped the speaker more (F = 4.38; p < 0.05), but would have less likely wanted to meet him personally (F = 14.99; p < 0.01) after the Aggro than the Neutral condition. Finally, Ss recalled that they emphasized being Flemish more in the Aggro than the Neutral condition (F = 82.61; p < 0.01). These results suggest that Ss perceived the Aggro condition in the way it was intended, and found it threatened their sense of ethnic identity.

Significant main effects also emerged from the other factors. Ss considered the speaker to be more provocative (F = 6.85; p < 0.05) and felt that they themselves emphasized their Flemishness more (F = 4.97; p < 0.05) in the Anti- than Pro-conditions. Also, Ss claimed that they would have liked to meet the speaker more (F = 12.47; p < 0.01) and would have helped him more (F = 6.59; p < 0.05) when intergroup categorization was implicit rather than made explicit. No significant interaction effects emerged on any scale between any of the factors.

Language measures

The Ss' replies in Pre-, Neutral and Aggro conditions were analysed to determine language(s) spoken. It can be seen from Table 8.1, that threatening Flemings' identity when intergroup categorization is only implicit does not cause them to diverge into their own ethnic language in the present context. However, when intergroup categorization is made explicit, and when Ss have prior knowledge that the speaker considers their ethno-linguistic aims illegitimate (Anticondition), 50 per cent of the Flemings in that cell diverged away from the Francophone interlocutor into Flemish. Interestingly, this divergent shift occurred in a particular manner. These Ss would respond to the Aggro question immediately in English and then after about a minute would virtually restate their position but this time in

Table 8.1 *Study I: Number of* Ss *in each experimental condition replying in Flemish**

Groups		Stimulus conditions		
		pre-	neutral	aggro
Implicit categorization	Pro- (n=12)	0	0	0
	Anti- (n=12)	0	0	0
Explicit categorization	Pro- (n=12)	0	0	1
	Anti- (n=12)	0	1	6

*The remainder of the Ss in each cell would have replied in English.

Flemish (an English to Flemish shift). This suggests that speech divergence is not simply an immediate, emotional response mediated by lack of attention or speech monitoring (see Brook, 1963; Labov, 1970), but rather can, at least in some instances, be regarded as a deliberate tactic of ethnic dissociation and psychological distinctiveness.

Across conditions, however, it was generally found that Ss tended to reply to the stimulus speaker in English. A phonological analysis of speech proved to be unfruitful and did not appear to yield differences between groups or stimulus conditions. For instance, we found that Ss did not sound more Flemish in the English in the Aggro than the Neutral condition, probably due to their restricted speech repertoire (cf. Segalowitz, 1976). Furthermore, an analysis of the content of Ss' replies yielded little of interest between groups or conditions. Ss definitely and consistently disagreed with the speaker in the Aggro condition and there tended to be a great deal of homogeneity in the nature of their response. Nevertheless, Ss thereby did distance themselves from the outgroup speaker by means of 'content differentiation' (Bourhis and Giles, 1977). There was, unlike the Bourhis and Giles study, no evidence of content differentiation in the Neutral condition at least in terms of their stressing their Flemish group membership.

As mentioned in the Method section, the experimental setting also allowed us to record Ss' more covert reactions to the speaker when he was delivering his message. These reactions we will call 'covert', since they were not for public consumption and sometimes were manifest by whispers under the breath, other times by muttered comments. Usually, they were spoken in Flemish and, more often than not, constituted aggressive, derogatory and obscene remarks directed against the speaker. As can be seen from Table 8.2, there was no evidence of such covert responses occurring in the Neutral condition, yet 44 per cent of the subject sample produced such reactions in the Aggro condition. It is interesting to note that this, what we may call 'covert psycholinguistic distinctiveness', tended to occur slightly more often when intergroup categorization was made explicit than implicit, and more often when the speaker was perceived to be anti- rather than pro-ingroup. It was also possible to detect responses at the end of the experimental tape-recording session (the Post-condition) when Ss presumed the tape-recording equipment was not 'on'. It was found that the number of Ss who found it necessary to make comments to their compatriots (in Flemish) in adjoining cubicles varied between the groups. It would appear that there was a greater need for intra-group communication after a threatening encounter with an outgroup speaker when intergroup categorization was made explicit than when it was implicit. Naturally enough, statistical analyses of the covert and overt responses was deemed inappropriate given the small sample involved.

Table 8.2 *Study I: Number of Ss making covert responses in Flemish during the experimental procedures and after it*

Groups		Experimental conditions		
		Neutral	Aggro	Post-
Implicit categorization	pro-	0	2	2
	anti	0	4	0
Explicit categorization	pro-	0	3*	2
	anti-	0	5*	4

*One covert response was manifest in English.

DISCUSSION

The study has shown that explicitness of intergroup categorization, perception of ethnic threat, and knowledge of the outgroup speaker's belief structure are important determinants of how individuals view an ethnic group interaction. The influence of these factors was well reflected in the Ss covert and overt behaviour. (Indeed, the study has substantiated the notions of psycholinguistic distinctiveness via language divergence and thereby satisfies the first aim of the study.) It was found that when a Francophone interlocutor threatened the identity of Flemish listeners, they polarized the speaker as sounding more Francophone—a process we may term *perceptual* divergence (cf. perceptual convergence, Larsen, Martin and Giles, 1977)—and themselves as feeling more Flemish. This cognitive dissociation was manifest behaviourally at a covert level in terms of whispered or muttered disapproval while the Francophone interlocutor was speaking, and at an overt level, as hypothesized, through shifts to own group language (Flemish).

The second aim of the experiment was also satisfied in that factors affecting the frequency of occurrence of language divergence have been elucidated to a certain degree. Our second hypothesis was confirmed to the extent that the variables of explicit *v.* implicit categorization, and knowledge about the outgroup speaker being pro- *v.* anti-ingroup, had the predicted effects on the number of Ss diverging. Nevertheless, they were only operative at all in the present context in an additive fashion. It was found that only when intergroup categorization was made explicit, and when the speaker had been known from the outset to be antithetical to ingroup ethnolinguistic goals, did language divergence emerge—and then for only half the sample. This is not to say, however, that psycholinguistic distinctiveness was not occurring for the remaining Ss under the Aggro condition, since all Ss in their replies 'content differentiated' themselves from the Francophone speaker.

In the present study, there was no condition, such as represented in Bourhis and Giles (1977), where Ss had *no* information prior to the interaction about the outgroup speaker's attitudes towards them as a group. It would have been interesting to have included a condition such as this (cf. Simard, Taylor and Giles, 1976) so as to determine whether Ss would have perceived the outgroup speaker in an ambiguous, intermediary position between the Pro- and Anti-conditions, or whether, they would have stereotypically attributed him negatively as Anti- from the outset. If the former had been the case, we would have expected about 25 per cent divergence, while if the latter was found to be more valid, 50 per cent divergence may still have occurred with this group.

Nevertheless, we still have not arrived at what may be considered the minimally sufficient conditions for language divergence to occur for the vast majority of group members. It may well have been that the instructions in this study attenuated the Flemings' tendencies towards divergence to their own ingroup language. It may be recalled that the speaker preferred that replies be addressed to him in English, and if not that language, then French. It could be argued that more Ss would diverge when such constraints operating against the use of Flemish are not apparent. Furthermore, it is felt that language divergence would occur more easily if the Francophone speaker himself diverged into French while threatening the Ss, thereby making him an even less desirable target person with whom to identify. Study II was designed to investigate these expectations.

METHOD: STUDY II

Experimental Design

The Ss for this second experiment were also randomly divided into four groups. Two of these were assigned to 'Explicit Categorization I' conditions, while the others were assigned to 'Explicit Categorization II' conditions. The former simply represented a replication of the Explicit Categorization conditions found in Study I. The latter were the same but with the added differences that the outgroup speaker made it clear in the prologue on the stimulus tape that he had no preferences as to which language he required Ss to use in reply. These conditions were once again further divided into those who received information that the speaker was either sympathetic or unsympathetic with their ethnolinguistic sentiments (the Pro- and Anti-conditions respectively). Ss in all four groups were required to undergo the same conditions as in Study I (i.e., Pre-, Neutral and Aggro), but this time were required to answer a second threatening question from the outgroup speaker who also diverged away from

English into the French language (the Aggro 2 condition). The study thus constituted a 2 × 2 × 4 matrix design.

Subjects

Thirty-two Flemish students attending the University of Louvain volunteered as Ss for the experiment. They were of predominantly middle class social origins and were taking English as their major at the University. On the basis of post-experimental self-ratings, they claimed to speak Flemish fluently ($\bar{X} = 8.50$) and French only moderately well ($\bar{X} = 5.00$). They also claimed to speak and understand English very well ($\bar{X}_s = 6.47$ and 8.40 respectively), and to a certain extent can be considered even more trilingual than our Ss in Study I. Once again, the Ss claimed to have moderately strong Flemish accents in their English and French ($\bar{X} = 4.31$ and 4.03 respectively). They also reported feeling very Flemish ($\bar{X} = 7.41$), identifying very strongly with Flemish issues ($\bar{X} = 8.32$), and being quite dissatisfied with the government's handling of Flemish affairs ($\bar{X} = 3.63$).

The Ss were from the same subject population as those in Study I and were randomly assigned to four experimental groups of eight informants each, again half of whom were of each sex. They all subsequently reported understanding the stimulus speaker's English and French ($\bar{X}_s = 7.35$ and 7.28 respectively) with great ease. These Ss' self-ratings were subjected to statistical analyses and no differences emerged between the four groups on the linguistic and social indices mentioned above.

Materials

The materials were exactly the same as those for Study I with the addition of another 45-second question (Aggro 2 condition) from the Francophone interlocutor on the stimulus tape. Since this question also involved the speaker's switching into the French language, an additional item on the post-experimental questionnaire tapped the extent to which the Ss understood the speaker's statements.

Procedure

The procedure followed was exactly the same for the Ss in this experiment as it was for Ss in the Explicit Categorization conditions in Study I, except that this time they were required to answer three questions from the speaker who was known to all as a Francophone Belgian. Intergroup categorization was made very salient for Ss and they all believed that they would be held responsible to the group later for their individual replies. The Ss who formed the Explicit Categorization I conditions represented a replication of the Explicit Categorization conditions in Study I, while Explicit Categorization II was different only in that on the prologue of the stimulus tape, the speaker claimed that he would accept English, French or Flemish from the Ss. These two conditions were further divided into Pro- and Anti- conditions by the same method as in Study I. After reacting to the three phases of the stimulus tape, Ss were again told that there was insufficient time for group discussion and were administered the questionnaire. Ss were also secretly tape-recorded while the speaker addressed them and at the close of the experimental procedure. E finally invited comments from the group in discussion, and debriefed them as to the true purpose of the experiment.

RESULTS AND DISCUSSION

The data arising from this investigation were analysed on three levels as in Study I, namely, Ss' perceptions of the situations and their overt and covert responses to it.

Ss' perceptions of the situations

Ss' ratings of the questionnaire items were subjected to a $2 \times 2 \times 3$ ANOVA consisting of the factors of *group* (Explicit I/Explicit II intergroup categorization), *information about outgroup speaker* (Pro-/Anti-ingroup), and *stimulus conditions* with repeated measures (Neutral/Aggro 1/Aggro 2).

It was found (see Table 8.3) that Ss perceived the speaker to have less understanding of the issues involved, disagreed with him more, were less prepared to help him, considered him more provocative and insulting, and tended to emphasize their Flemishness more as they moved from Neutral through to Aggro 1 to Aggro 2 conditions. In addition, they thought that the fact that the speaker was a Francophone affected them more in the two Aggro conditions than the

Table 8.3 *Study II: F values and mean reactions to the speaker under three conditions*

Rating scales*	Experimental conditions			F values (d.f.=2,63)
	Neutral	Aggro 1	Aggro 2	
Understanding	6.16	3.91	3.78	24.16
Agree	5.91	3.31	2.63	31.94
Helpfulness	5.69	4.75	4.44	4.44
Disturbed	2.19	6.25	5.97	32.33
Francophone	2.50	4.94	4.68	12.12
Provocative	3.38	7.13	7.59	60.67
Insulting emphasize	2.47	6.25	6.97	52.10
Flemishness	1.97	6.28	6.41	39.97

All F values have $p < .01$
* The higher the mean rating, the more understanding, disturbed, insulting, etc., the Ss felt.

Neutral condition, and were more disturbed by him in the former than the latter situations. Ss also found him to be more provocative ($F = 4.35$; $p < 0.05$) when he allowed them a language choice in their replies (Explicit Categorization II) than when he stated his preferences (Explicit Categorization I). No perceptual effects emerged for the Pro-/Anti-conditions, nor for any of the interactions.

Overt language measures

As in Study I, Ss' replies to the stimulus speaker's question were analysed to determine the language(s) spoken. As can be seen from Table 8.4, the Ss in Explicit Categorization I conditions corroborated the language differences found in the Neutral and Aggro conditions in the previous investigation. The only appreciable amount of language divergence occurred when the listeners had prior knowledge that the speaker was anti-group. Once again, this situation elicited 50 per cent of Ss in this cell replying to the Aggro (1) question in English and after a minute switching into Flemish (the English to Flemish shift).

The addition of the conditions whereby the speaker allowed the Ss

Table 8.4 *Study II: Number of Ss in each experimental condition replying in Flemish**

Groups		Pre-	Stimulus conditions Neutral	Aggro 1	Aggro 2
Explicit categorization 1	pro- (n=8)	0	0	1	3
	anti- (n=8)	0	1	4	8
Explicit categorization II	pro- (n=8)	0	2	0	4
	anti- (n = 8)	0	1	0	7

*The remainder of Ss in each cell would have replied in English.

complete language freedom in their replies did not, however, have the expected results. No subject in the Explicit Categorization II conditions used Flemish in Aggro 1, whereas paradoxically enough, three informants adopted an English to Flemish shift in response to the Neutral question. These are admittedly curious findings, and it might be that allowing listeners to reply in one of the three languages explicitly is such an unusual concession for an *outgroup* speaker to make as to add cognitive confusion to the situation.

Nevertheless, the addition of Aggro 2, whereby the outgroup speaker diverged away from the Ss into French, did have the expected result in that this condition elicited far more divergence than Aggro 1. In fact, when Ss had prior knowledge that the speaker was unsympathetic to their ethnolinguistic desires, almost 100 per cent of Ss diverged into Flemish. Moreover, although the Pro-/Anti-conditions had little effect on Ss' recalled perceptions of the inter-group encounter, they did have a marked effect on Ss' language behaviour; those in the Pro-conditions were almost half as likely as those in the Anti-conditions to diverge. It may be that giving inconsistent information about the speaker's true position regarding salient language issues (that is, positive information on the card prior to interaction, and negative during it), makes Ss unsure about his real intentions, and thereby attenuates their tendencies to dissociate themselves completely from him by means of a divergent language shift. Indeed, these results suggest that the divergence occurring in the Anti-conditions cannot be attributed solely to a simple reciprocity mechanism (Gouldner, 1960).

However, not only did the introduction of the Aggro 2 condition affect the magnitude of divergent responses from Ss, it had an effect on their *nature* as well. It may be recalled that in Study I the form of the divergent response in the Aggro condition was in terms of an English to Flemish shift. In the main, that was the nature of the divergent shifts in Study II as well. Yet out of the fifteen informants who diverged in the Anti-conditions in Aggro 2, five of them commenced in Flemish and then restated their position in English after a minute (i.e., a Flemish to English shift), while two others commenced and remained totally in Flemish.

Covert language measures

As in study I, attention was also paid to Ss' responses to the speaker as he was questioning them, and as to whether interaction between participants ensued after the procedure was over. From Table 8.5, it can be seen that in three out of four conditions, there was a tendency for more Ss to make covert remarks at the speaker when he diverged away from them (Aggro 2) than when he threatened them in English

Table 8.5 *Study II: Number of Ss making covert responses in Flemish during the experimental procedures and after it.*

Groups		Neutral	Experimental conditions Aggro 1	Aggro 2	Post-
Explicit categorization 1	pro-	0	3*	4	2
	anti-	0	5*	1	6
Explicit categorization II	pro-	1*	3	6*	6
	anti-	3	3*	4*	5

*One covert response was manifest in English.

(Aggro 1). This finding, of course, corresponds well with the more overt language switches found in Ss' behaviour towards the speaker. Also, more Ss in Study II engaged in communication with their partners after the experiment than in Study I, which would support the contention that the amount of intra-group communication can be directly related to the extent of outgroup threat perceived by the ingroup. Again, however, we have an anomaly with regard to Ss' responses in Explicit Categorization II conditions in that four Ss made covert responses even to Neutral questions. In this case, the novelty of the language freedom situation may have aroused some general level of responsiveness in Ss as these comments, unlike those in the ensuing threatening conditions, were not derogatory.

It has been shown, then, that the Aggro 2 condition elicited less favourable impressions of the speaker, more covert derogatory remarks while he was speaking, and more divergent responses in reply than in Aggro 1 condition. Unfortunately, we cannot with any degree of certainty attribute these effects solely to the outgroup speaker's own divergence. It may be that the accumulation of two threatening questions, or the specific nature of the Aggro 2 question, actually elicited these reactions from Ss. Alternatively, the increased divergence may have been due to some combination of these factors. It is our guess, particularly in view of the post-experimental discussion held with informants by E, that the outgroup speaker's use of French was in fact primarily responsible for the increased linguistic and social dissociation from the Flemish Ss. Obviously, further research will help elucidate the causal agents more precisely.

GENERAL DISCUSSION

We have found that in the multilingual situation of Belgium, the perception of ethnic threat from an outgroup Francophone speaker voiced in an emotively-neutral language (English) was greeted by vocal strategies of psycholinguistic distinctiveness from ingroup (Flemish) recipients. All Flemish Ss disagreed vehemently with the outgroup speaker, and hence differentiated themselves from him in terms of the content of their replies. However, half of those who knew the speaker to be negatively disposed towards them from the outset, and who had viewed the interaction explicitly in ethnic group terms, actually voiced their disagreement in their own ingroup language (Flemish). Such language divergence was observed in nearly all of the sample but this time in *his* owngroup language (French). Moreover, it was found that the nature of these divergent responses changed as the threat experienced by the ingroup became more intense. Naturally enough, one has to be extremely cautious in generalizing these findings to other ethnic group situations and consider that the present research was conducted with a given group of informants, on a specific issue, at a particular point in time, and in a certain setting.

It was found in Wales (Bourhis and Giles, 1977) that when a member of an English outgroup threatened a salient dimension of a Welshman's ethnolinguistic identity when intergroup relations between the two groups was salient for *S*s, the ingroup replied by broadening their Welsh *accents* in English. In their work, Bourhis and Giles proposed that an actual language shift might be a more potent signal of ethnic dissociation. The present results tend to support this contention in that hardly any individuals shifted to Flemish when the Francophone interlocutor threatened them from a supposedly sympathetic position. Yet as the situations were perceived to be more threatening, divergence gradually emerged. For instance, only 50 per cent of Flemings diverged under the most threatening conditions in Study I whereas nearly 100 per cent diverged under the even more threatening situations in Study II. The present studies also underline the notion that language divergence can take on many forms as has been shown with language convergence (Giles, Taylor and Bourhis, 1973). We have found that divergence was manifest by English to Flemish shifts in Aggro 1, whereas there was a tendency for Flemish to English, and even complete Flemish shifts, to appear in Aggro 2. It can be suggested that situations more threatening than those adopted in this research (perhaps through use of derogatory language from an outgroup speaker physically present) would produce 100 per cent complete Flemish shifts. In other words, not only may there exist a hierarchy of speech divergence strategies as suggested by Bourhis and Giles, but there may be a subhierarchy of *language* divergences, some of which speakers (and listeners) may feel are ethnically more dissociative than others. However, our studies also point to the need for the development of an instrument which might inform us as to the type of situations ingroup listeners subjectively feel as more or less threatening to their sense of ethnic identity. Certainly, the variables of intergroup categorization explicitness, attributions of the out-group's beliefs, outgroup divergence/non-divergence would be important dimensions in this respect.

The usefulness of the language laboratory setting as an economic situation to gather interactive data again has been demonstrated (Giles and Bourhis, 1976a). We have also shown that it is possible to gather information by means of subtle, covert cues of how people are reacting via language to others' messages. Further work could look more closely at these reactions and determine the differential rates of occurrence of whispers and comments in one language rather than another, the exact nature of the comments as well as differential rates of breathing and bodily movements, etc. In the present investiga-tions, there was a fairly close correspondence between the overt and covert levels of language use. In other cultural and verbal contexts no such clear correspondence may exist, perhaps because of stringent social norms for speech behaviour. In such cases, an analysis at these covert levels might be valuable in determining people's true reactions to others' behaviour (cf. d'Anglejan and Tucker, 1973; Lieberman, 1975).

The present studies have, of course, raised a number of questions for further research besides those of cross-cultural validation, only a few of which will be explicitly considered here. For instance, would the same amount of language divergence have occurred if the out-group speaker had been of a higher or lower status, and would the fact that the interaction was not face-to-face have attentuated or accentuated the patterns observed? Would the Ss' own belief struc-tures about the inter-ethnic group situation (Turner & Brown, 1978), the specific social context and purpose of the interaction as well as the nature of the relations between the groups have affected their reactions? What are the phenomenological experiences of lan-guage divergence as encoded by an ingroup speaker and as decoded by the outgroup recipient, and how does the latter handle such signals of ethnic dissociation? Until such questions have been explored, we must be cautious in generalizing our findings to real life encounters, to other subject populations, and to other social con-texts. Nevertheless, it is our contention that such processes do oper-ate in social reality and that they are particularly pertinent in con-texts where members of ethnic and social groups have an inadequate social identity, or are redefining their previously inferior group identity in a more positive direction as an ethnic collectivity (that is, with groups who have high to medium *ethnolinguistic vitality*; see Giles, Bourhis and Taylor, 1977).

We have shown, then, how language in a multilingual context can be used by ingroup speakers to heighten psychological distinctiveness. In the present ethnic context, different strategies of language divergence from English to Flemish were adopted by Flemish students whose ethnolinguistic identity was being threatened to various extents by a tape-recorded Francophone interlocutor. This demonstration of psychological differentiation by means of language divergence underlies the value of examining the role of language in ethnic group relations through Tajfel's theory of intergroup behaviour and Giles's theory of speech accommodation. Moreover, it adds a new dimension to the already established literature on bilingual code-switching (e.g., Herman, 1961; Gumperz and Hernandez-Chavez, 1972).

9
Language as a Factor in Intergroup Relations[1]

WALLACE E. LAMBERT

One of the many puzzling features of the world in the mid 1970s is the surprisingly large number of break-away movements of ethnolinguistic groups, as witnessed in such places as Brittany, French Canada, Scotland and Wales. It is as though in certain parts of the modern world, a need for ethnic or ethnolinguistic identity has increased to a boiling point, and/or a new form of xenophabia has taken root, making it uncomfortable if not impossible for certain ethnolinguistic groups to live together harmoniously within a common social system. This is not to say that the break-away phonemenon is universal, for there are grounds for hope, as Jean-François Revel has argued so splendidly (Revel, 1970), that in the United States, perhaps as a consequence of extensive and sustained social unrest and conflict, a new form of mutual respect and appreciation for ethnic and ethnolinguistic diversity may be evolving in that multi-cultural and multi-linguistic setting. Whatever the real explanation may be for this phenomenon of separatism, it is nonetheless clear that today a strong case can be made for the social significance of language and the role it plays in person-to-person interaction, group-to-group contacts, and group-to-society relationships.

As I see it, ethnolinguistic identity is based on a belief that one's own group is distinctive in socially important ways (see Lambert and Klineberg, 1967); the underlying logic seems to be: we have our own unique culture and language and these give us distinctive styles of personality and distinctive modes of thought. Today there is a warning attached: Trespassers or potential eroders, beware!

In my own attempts to understand the social importance of language, I have come to question the very commonly held notion that culture and/or language really affect personality; I am inclined rather to the position that culture and language may affect styles of expression, but likely not basic personality dynamics (Lambert, 1974; Lambert, Frasure-Smith and Hamers, 1976). Similarly, I am not persuaded by the evidence available that culture or language have any real impact on thought. It also seems to me that many people living in bi- or multi- 'cultural' settings come to similar conclusions, in the sense that, through inter-cultural and inter-lingual contacts, they too come to question the supposedly distinctive characteristics of culture and language. Through cross-cultural and cross-lingual experiences, one begins to realize, whether consciously or not, that within-group variation is large and it usually outweighs across-group variation. The alternative view, then, is that the similarities of people through time, across settings, and across language boundaries are at least as socially significant as the differences between groups we are prone to assume.

Once a person begins to entertain this alternative and starts to question the notion of ethnolinguistic group distinctiveness, he is then likely to realign and amalgamate in his thinking the notions of 'culture' and 'language', making *language* differences—which are real enough—the important component of what is thought of as cultural-linguistic distinctiveness. It follows that the more important it is for a particular ethnolinguistic group to maintain its 'culture and traditions', the more salient and personally important *language* becomes for the group. Thus, language can come to mean 'language and culture', and 'culture maintenance' can come to mean language maintenance. In this way, language functions as a very senstitive filter through which one's perception of self, own group, and others must pass.

Using the province of Quebec and selected bicultural settings in the United States as frames of reference, much of our own research over the past twenty-five years has explored the social significance of language and dialect differences. Linguistic differences of this sort, in fact, have been used as means of eliciting the perceived characteristics of one's own ethnolinguistic group relative to various other contrasting groups. For example, in the late 1950s, our research group at McGill devised the 'matched-guise' procedure (Lambert, Hodgson, Gardner and Fillenbaum, 1960; Lambert, 1967), and by applying that procedure, we found in an early set of studies that English Canadians (ECs) tended to perceive French Canadians (FCs) in a pejorative manner, relatively. That is, ECs saw a bilingual person using his French language guise as being less intelligent, less trustworthy, shorter and less attractive (and so forth) than he was when using his English language guise. FCs, rather than reciprocating a comparable sentiment about Anglos, instead downgraded members of their own ethnolinguistic group relative to ECs. In fact, except for the trait of 'kindness', an instance where their own group was favoured, FC judges were more extreme than EC judges in the degree of negative sentiment directed towards FC relative to EC speakers. It should be mentioned that we certainly do not believe there is any truth to these stereotyped beliefs, neither the EC's stereotypes that their group is better in any sense than the FCs, nor the FC's stereotypes that their group is in any sense less good than ECs. But truth apparently plays little part in these explosive interpersonal and inter-group matters!

Negative views of one's own ethnic group of this sort and of this intensity are believed to colour interpersonal and inter-group relationships, often providing those in minority positions with a subjective justification for the existing differences in standards of living and status that separate subgroups in society. Negative views of this sort also often promote shifts in values, behavioural styles, and in the case where a different language is involved, socially important shifts away from the use of one's own language or dialect to that of the more prestigious group's language or speech style.

But the awareness that one is shifting can itself have profound psychological and social consequence. For example, one can become confused about one's personal identity, or begin to behave as though one actually were inadequate and inferior. As these sentiments spread through a social system, members of the system may be prone to give up and accept one's 'inferior' fate, at the same time as they ready themselves to counter-react in the sense of rejecting the accepted image of one's group, starting often with an exploration of the opposite view—that one's own group is as good if not better than the high prestige group. As the counter-reaction gains social force, the relative attractiveness and status of the two or more ethnolinguistic groups in the society can change.

Mechanisms of this sort are believed to underlie the 'French Canadian revolution' of the sixties which took shape at the same time as similar revolutions evolved in the United States, where demands for respect and identity for one's own racial, ethnic or linguistic group were often put forward in the context of threat and violence. The thinking seemed to be: If the system has not spontaneously generated tolerance and fairness, it is futile to hope for improvement by waiting. Better to band together and generate fear, hate, and social cleavages. It seems that our sociolinguistic research in the late fifties was reflecting a general feeling among FCs of personal inferiority and possibly even own group denigration, and as that research became public, it may have contributed indirectly to counter-reactions against such feelings.

Negative own-group feelings can have deep ramifying roots, and, regardless of surface signs, are not changed easily. For example, teachers can continue to differentially encourage students, though grading and moral support, to accommodate their speech styles to 'proper' standards or to essentially foreign standards, as in the case for FC students who are taught to model their speech on Continental French (see Frender, Brown and Lambert, 1970). Other research showed us that speech style can be more important than composition writing, artistic work, or personal appearance in teachers' judge-ments of pupils' capabilities (Seligman, Tucker and Lambert, 1972). Furthermore, in a recent study by Sylvie Lambert (1973), it was found that even in the 1970s FC ten year olds downgraded their own ethno-linguistic group relative to FF (French from France) compari-son persons (whose voices were incorporated into a matched-guise procedure) and on a certain set of characteristics relative to EC persons. What is most significant in this last study is that the teachers themselves were found to hold essentially the same views as the children did about the relative worth of representatives of the FF, EC and FC societies!

Parents, too, can perpetuate the feelings of inferiority by the ways they find to rationalize their choice of schooling for their chil-dren—home language instruction or other language instruction (Frasure-Smith, Lambert and Taylor, 1975). Thus, sizeable sub-groups of FC parents who hold particular views of themselves and their families in relation to FC and EC sub-societies in Canada chose to send their children to English language schools. We are beginning in this line of research to uncover the motivational bases of such choices. Much more encouraging is the finding that substantial subgroups of EC parents are choosing French language schooling for their children, and this seems to be a wide spread phenomenon, one that is spontaneously worked out by parents with little or no support or encouragement from the school systems involved (see Frasure-Smith, Lambert and Taylor, 1975).

We have been fascinated with our involvement in a community-based attempt to reduce intergroup tensions by offering French 'immersion' schooling for EC youngsters in Montreal and in various communities across Canada (Lambert and Tucker, 1972; Swain, 1976). In immersion programmes, EC children start schooling at kindergarten with a monolingual French speaking teacher, and the first three years of schooling are taught almost exclusively via French, until a balance 50/50 programme in French and English is reached from grade 4 to the end of the elementary years. This 'home-to-school language switch' programme provides the means for the prestigious language group to become fully functional in other languages—in this case French—with no signs of falling behind in their skills with the home language. Furthermore, these programmes tend to liberalize and improve the attitudes of EC youngsters toward the FC society.

In an important sense, the immersion experience equips the EC youngster with all the knowledge and skills needed to make social and personal contact with members of the FC society around him. Well equipped as their youngsters are, however, there are many signs suggesting that neither the EC parents nor the EC community really encourage interaction or close social contact with FCs. Nor does the FC society as yet seem too anxious to open its doors to the bilingual EC youngsters. As one watches the societal impact of this programme, one begins to re-evaluate the process of ethnic group self-segregation. One asks: Are ethnically concentrated neighbourhoods or communities symptoms of cultural solitude or are they comfortable and perhaps necessary corners of peace where people can be what they are? Have attempts to dissolve ethnic-group clustering in the name of democracy actually improved life in modern societies or might more respect for self and others be generated if societies were to encourage and support such clusterings and appreciate the sentiments underlying such clusterings? In other words, the potential values (in contrast to the drawbacks) of ethnolinguistic group concentration need to be explored.

A sharp contrast is drawn in our thinking between the enormous potential of immersion programmes for developing bilingual and bicultural skills for members of high prestige ethno-linguistic groups on the one hand; and on the other, the need to develop quite different educational programmes for members of less prestigious groups, such as the FCs in Canada or most hyphenated American subgroups in the United States. The former experience what we refer to as 'additive' bilingualism in the sense that a new language (or new languages) can be acquired or added with no concern at all that the base language and 'culture' are in any way jeopardized, whereas for the latter, a movement towards bilingualism usually represents a 'subtractive' experience wherein the other language is likely to swamp and submerge the home language (Lambert and Tucker, 1972; Lambert, 1974). We contend that in bilingual communities where differential prestige is accorded the languages and the ethnolinguistic groups involved, then attention should be placed by *both* linguistic groups on the development of skills with the language more likely to be overlooked. Thus, rather than exploring early immersion-in-English programmes, the FC community should consolidate and deepen its control of French and branch into English language training as early as possible but only when it is certain that full competence in the potentially neglected home language has been attained. In this way trends towards subtractive forms of bilingualism or biculturalism can be transformed into additive ones.

An American example of this sort of transformation is now becoming available. This is the case of French-Americans in northern New England who have only recently been given a chance to be schooled partly in their home language, French (Dubé and Herbert, 1975a and 1975b; Lambert, Giles and Picard, 1975; Lambert, Giles and Albert, 1976). In the northern regions of Maine, some 85 per cent of families have kept French alive as the home language or as one of two home languages even though traditionally all public schooling has been conducted in English. Our research group was asked to participate in an experiment wherein a quasi-random selection of schools in the area permitted to offer about a third of the elementary curriculum in French and where a second sample of schools, with children of comparable intelligence scores and socio-economic backgrounds, served as a control or comparison in the sense that all their instruction was in English. After a five year run, the children in the partial French schools clearly out-performed those in the control schools on various aspects of *English* language skills, on content, such as mathematics, learned partly via French, and, of course, in French language skills which for them were made much more literate (in contrast to mainly audio-lingual) because of the reading and writing requirements of the French schooling. In fact, the French trained children have stayed consistently ahead of the control children in English language achievement test scores as well as in grade placement levels. This means that they have a real chance to compete with other American children in enterprises that call for well developed educational abilities; they apparently have been lifted up from the low standing on scholastic achievement measures (always tested via English, mind you) that characterizes many ethnolinguistic groups in North America. An important element in this transformation appears to be a change in the self views of the French-trained youngsters who, our research has shown, begin to reflect a powerful pride in being French, and a realization that their language is as important a medium for education as is English (Lambert, Giles and Picard, 1975). Similar community-based studies are underway in the American South-west, and these, too, are based on the belief that ethnolinguistic minorities need strong educational experiences in their *own* languages and traditions before they can cope in an 'all-American' society or before they will *want* to cope in such a society.

In sum, the research described here has been based on a social psychological approach to intergroup behaviour and we feel that this perspective has made us more sensitive to a wider band of possible influence sources and has provided us with a more comprehensive means of explaining phenomena transpiring in these societies than a purely psychological, sociological or anthropological approach would have. By focusing on the language and its use, we are trying to gauge the views that members of each linguistic community hold of their own group in contrast to other groups, and this leads us to see the importance each group attaches to its linguistic identity, which becomes in large part its cultural identity. Then through educational experiments in which the language of instruction is varied, we are beginning to explore ways in which bi- or multi-cultural societies can be made more fair, more productive, and most important, more comfortable and more interesting.

10
Social Psychological Aspects of Second Language Acquisition

R. C. GARDNER

The learning of a second (or foreign) language in the school situation is often viewed as an educational phenomenon, and 'second languages' as a curriculum topic is considered in much the same light as any other school subject. The thesis proposed here is that such a perspective is categorically wrong, and that 'second languages,' unlike virtually any other curriculum topic, must be viewed as a central social psychological phenomenon. The rationale underlying this view is that most other school subjects involve learning elements of the student's own cultural heritage. Whether the topic is mathematics, history, chemistry, or anthropology, the student is placed in a situation of acquiring knowledge which is part of his own culture. Even anthropology or history, though they might focus on other cultural bases, are presented and viewed from the perspective of the student's own culture. Hence, one could reasonably conclude that most school learning involves the acquisition of knowledge or habits which are already part of the makeup of the culture with which the student identifies.[1] Such is not the case with second languages, however.

In the acquisition of a second language, the student is faced with the task of not simply learning new information (vocabulary, grammar, pronunciation, etc.) which is part of his *own* culture but rather of *acquiring* symbolic elements of a *different* ethnolinguistic community. The new words are not simply new words for old concepts, the new grammar is not simply a new way of ordering words, the new pronunciations are not merely 'different' ways of saying things. They are characteristics of another ethnolinguistic community. Furthermore, the student is not being asked to learn about them; he is being asked to acquire them, to make them part of his own language reservoir. This involves imposing elements of another culture into one's own lifespace. As a result, the student's harmony with his own cultural community and his willingness or ability to identify with other cultural communities become important considerations in the process of second language acquisition.

Such a perspective places second language acquisition at the centre of social psychology. Language is a symbolic representation of culture and it is a primary means of maintaining interaction between individuals. Thus, it is central to social psychology. But inter-ethnic interaction is also a major focus of social psychology (see Chapters 7, 8 and 9). Hence, if second language acquisition is viewed as a process whereby an individual from one ethno-linguistic community is concerned with adopting symbolic representations of another ethnolinguistic community, it becomes a central social psychological issue. It not only involves individuals and groups, but also language, culture, and intergroup interaction.

The orientation proposed here is not unique. The social psychological implications of second language acquisition have been considered at least since 1945. In a review of the literature on bilingualism to that time, Arsenian (1945:85) posed as one of many important researchable questions the query, 'In what way do affective factors, such as social prestige, assumed superiority, or contrariwise assumed inferiority, or enforcement of a hated language by a hated nation affect language learning in a child?'

Lambert (1963b) was, quite probably, the first to propose a social psychological theory of second language acquisition, though it was not really detailed. He stated (Lambert, 1963b: 114),

> This theory, in brief, holds that an individual successfully acquiring a second language gradually adopts various aspects of behaviour which characterize members of another linguistic-cultural group. The learner's ethnocentric tendencies and his attitudes toward the other group are believed to determine his success in learning the new language. His motivation to learn is thought to be determined by his attitudes and by his orientation toward learning a second language.

This formulation has served as the foundation for considerable research (see, for example, Gardner and Lambert, 1972; Lambert, 1972); however, it lacks precision. The purpose of the present chapter is to elaborate a theoretical model and to discuss some empirical findings relevant to it.

In its schematic form, the model is very simplistic, but such a representation highlights the major elements. Figure 10.1 presents the basic model in its most recent form, which differs in some important respects from an earlier version (Gardner and Smythe, 1975) which has been discussed by Schumann (1976).

The model consists of four segments: Social Milieu, Individual Differences, Second Language Acquisition Contexts, and Outcomes. It is hypothesized that the *Social Milieu* will determine the importance to second language acquisition of various *Individual Difference* variables. Furthermore, it is postulated that the individual difference variables will influence the extent to which learners achieve the possible outcomes in second language acquisition primarily through their interaction with the demands placed on them by the *Second Language Acquisition Context*. The model is consequently a social psychological one which focuses its major attention on individual difference variables as they relate to the achievement of *Outcomes* of second language acquisition. It treats the Social Milieu and the Second Language Acquisition Context both as causative and moderator variables in this relationship. It assumes, further, that the extent to which the various outcomes are achieved in the process of acquiring a second language will have a profound effect on at least some of the relevant individual difference variables. As such, it is also a developmental model.

The *Social Milieu* is explicitly included as a component in the model to emphasize the fact that the second language learning process must be considered in the larger context in which the individual and the second language learning programme exists. The major process variable here is labelled *Cultural Beliefs*. That is, it is proposed that the social milieu gives rise to many expectations in the minds of teachers, parents and students concerning the entire second language acquisition task. A student resident in a community where bilingualism is an expected part of his cultural heritage will have and will encounter cultural beliefs which are of a different order from those of a student resident in a community where unilingualism is the norm. Similarly, if a student resides in a community where speakers of the other language are not valued, or where debate exists concerning the value of that language or the reasons for teaching it, the beliefs he takes with him into the language learning situation will differ from those he would hold if he were resident of an area where opposing cultural beliefs exist.

This emphasis on the social context is general. For example, in

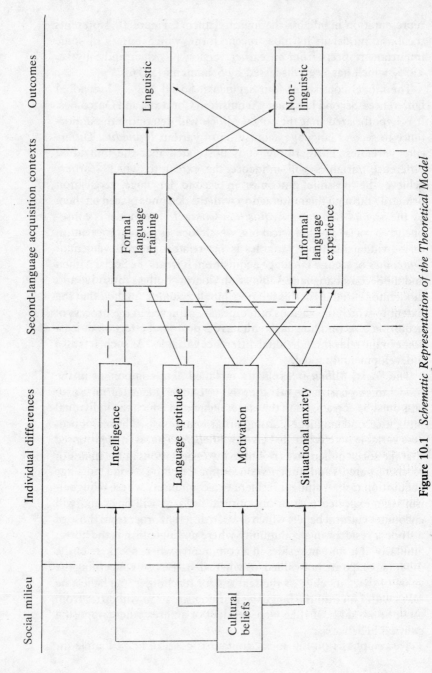

Figure 10.1 *Schematic Representation of the Theoretical Model*

Social milieu | Individual differences | Second-language acquisition contexts | Outcomes

Cultural beliefs

Intelligence

Language aptitude

Motivation

Situational anxiety

Formal language training

Informal language experience

Linguistic

Non-linguistic

addition to the situational beliefs referred to above, the present conceptualization would also encompass what Lambert (1974) has referred to as additive and subtractive bilingualism. This is a distinction in terms of the social implications of developing bilingual skills in which bilingualism is viewed as contributing to an individual's growth by offering him access to other cultural communities (additive) or as contributing to his feelings of loss of identity by orienting him away from his own cultural background towards another (imposed) one (subtractive). Obviously, this distinction depends not on the development of two language codes in the individual, but rather his belief and, quite likely, those of his immediate community concerning the implications of second language acquistion.

In the schematic model, direct lines are shown linking the cultural beliefs to four individual difference variables. This representation is used to indicate that these beliefs can influence the extent to which the various individual difference variables mediate achievement in a second language. It is not intended to suggest that cultural beliefs influence the development of such variables, though undoubtedly an individual's experiences with his social environment might have some effect. In fact, it will be argued later that an individual's motivation to learn a second language is highly influenced by such factors.

The second category of the model refers to individual differences—that is, characteristics of the student which will influence his approach to the second language acquisition process. In the figure, four major individual difference variables are listed: *intelligence, language aptitude, motivation,* and *situational anxiety*. Intelligence refers to a general class of abilities which account for individual differences in the extent to which students understand the nature of any task to be learned. Language aptitude refers specifically to the capacity to learn languages and is typically assessed in terms of students' verbal abilities. Although they appear to be quite similar, intelligence and language aptitude have been shown to be factorally independent (Gardner and Lambert, 1965). Motivation refers to those affective characteristics which orient the student to try to acquire elements of the second language, and includes the desire the student has for achieving a goal, and the amount of effort he expends in this direction. Finally, situational anxiety refers to those anxiety reactions aroused in specific situations involving the second language; examples would be French classroom anxiety or French use anxiety. Situational anxiety should not be confused with general anxiety. There is ample evidence to suggest that general anxiety does not play a role in second language acquisition (Gardner and Lambert, 1959; Gardner and Smythe, 1975; Tarampi, Lambert and Tucker, 1968) whereas situational anxiety does (Clément, Gardner and Smythe, 1977a; Gardner and Smythe, 1975).

The third aspect of the model refers to second language acquisition contexts. In this respect, we differentiate between *Formal Language Training* and *Informal Language Experience*. Formal language training refers to that instruction which takes place in the classroom or any other teacher/student context. Informal language experience, on the other hand, refers to those situations which permit the student to acquire competence in second language skills without direct instruction. Instances of such experiences would be speaking with members of the other cultural community, watching movies or television, listening to the radio, or reading material in the other language.

In Figure 10.1, solid lines are shown linking the four individual difference variables, intelligence, language aptitude, motivation, and situational anxiety to the formal language training context. This representation is used to indicate that all four variables would appear to influence the formal language situation. It seems obvious that differences in intelligence would reflect themselves in differences in schools taught second language skills simply because the more intelligent student would profit more from instruction since he could more easily understand the task. Language aptitude refers to those verbal abilities which are necessary to acquire specific second language skills (such as vocabulary, grammar, pronunciation, etc.); therefore, it seems reasonable that it too would play a direct role in a situation where such skills are specifically taught. Motivation would be expected to play a direct role in the formal language training situation because it would serve to keep the student in the programme, influence his perceptions of the training situation, and serve as the basis for many reinforcements which might be obtained in the classroom. Situational anxiety, specifically French classroom anxiety, would be expected to influence achievement in the formal situation because the arousal of such anxiety would result in negative reinforcements and a tendency to withdraw from the situation. In short, the four individual variables, intelligence, language aptitude, motivation, and situational anxiety would seem particularly important in the formal language training situation, but for different reasons.

In Figure 10.1, broken lines are shown relating intelligence and language aptitude to the informal language experience, while motivation and situational anxiety show direct links. The broken lines are meant to suggest that the influence of both intelligence and language aptitude would be less direct in informal situations than either motivation or anxiety, since the former variables would be influential only if the individual became exposed to these contexts. Motivation and situational anxiety would be more influential simply because they would determine whether or not students became involved in such situations.

As indicated in the model, both formal language training and informal language experience are shown as having direct effects on both linguistic and non-linguistic outcomes. The term linguistic outcomes refers to second language knowledge (of such structural aspects of the language as vocabulary, grammar, etc.) and specific second language skills (i.e., reading, writing, understanding and speaking). Non-linguistic outcomes, on the other hand, refer to those extra-language attributes which might develop as a function of second language training and experience. Examples of such non-linguistic outcomes are favourable attitudes towards the other cultural community, a general appreciation of other cultures, interest in further language study, etc. Although both linguistic and non-linguistic outcomes would develop from both formal language training and informal language experience, the specific outcomes developed would depend upon the nature of these contexts. For example, the so-called traditional approach to second language training may foster development of such linguistic outcomes as vocabulary, grammar and reading comprehension (but not oral fluency), and such non-linguistic outcomes as a greater understanding of the other cultural community. Oral/aural programmes could produce different outcomes (cf. Smythe, Stennet and Feenstra, 1972). Similarly, the nature of the informal language experience would influence outcomes. Listening to radio broadcasts, for example, might improve aural comprehension and promote an appreciation of the other community, while having a pen pal could improve writing skills and foster favourable attitudes towards some members of the community. In short, depending upon the nature of the particular formal language training or informal language experience, it is possible that different linguistic and non-linguistic out-comes would develop.

The preceding description provides an overview of the basic model, and from it a number of straightforward hypotheses can be developed. It does not, however, explain the concept of motivation as it applies to the acquisition of a second language. This requires further elaboration. Before presenting this extension, however, it is necessary to consider the role that the social context might play in second language acquisition because although the concept of moti-vation refers to the specific act of learning the language, it would seem to have a broad social foundation and thus any theoretical model must be considered in terms of the social context.

It is assumed in the model that the social milieu will influence the extent to which achievement in a second language is mediated by the individual difference variables. It was suggested earlier that cultural beliefs about such things as the value of second language acquisition, the level of achievement which might be expected, etc., will deter-mine the role that such cognitive factors as intelligence and language aptitude, or such affective factors as motivation and situational anxiety would play in second language acquisition.

This emphasis on the cultural setting has not apparently been made previously, hence it is perhaps not surprising that researchers have not concerned themselves with assessing the beliefs of a particu-lar community with respect to second language acquisition. The often heard argument, however, that Europeans seem more able to learn languages than North Americans might actually reflect differ-ent expectations about bilingualism in the two regions (assuming there is any validity in the argument). One study (Smythe, Gardner and Smythe, 1976) has demonstrated that the community beliefs operating on the child in a monolingual area, at least, are complex. In this study, twelve different groups of respondents varying from school board administration to students to parents of students not studying French were investigated. The responses supported the generalization that in that community there exists a generally favourable atmosphere for students of French, though this is not pronounced, and there is plenty of material for students actually to obtain a contrary impression. Most groups demonstrated positive attitudes towards bilingualism and slightly positive attitudes towards French Canadians, and expressed the view that French should be taught to all students regardless of their ability. However, they tended also to rate French as less important, less difficult and less interesting than five other academic subjects presented to them. Parent groups, furthermore, generally indicated that they were less informed about the French programme than other ones. Finally, a majority of most groups sampled indicated that they felt that a French television channel was not needed in the community and that they personally would not view it when it became available. It is interesting and informative that although the parents of students studying French held such feelings they nonetheless reported that they would encourage their children to watch it. Such material displays the conflicting beliefs which the student of a second language can encounter, and highlights the need for a careful consideration of the cultural context in which language programmes operate.

Such surveys are expensive to conduct, however, so before initiating such a programme it seems imperative to determine whether in fact the social context can influence the relationships between the individual difference variables and achievement in the second language. Communities obviously differ in a number of ways, and one which seems particularly relevant is the extent to which the other language group is an active part of the community. Giles, Bourhis and Taylor (1977) have proposed a schema for assessing ethnolinguistic vitality in terms of status, demography and institutional support, and consideration of this system would facilitate the classification of communities as either bilingual or monolingual, largely on the basis of public information.

Admittedly, such a dichotomous representation of the communities is gross. Nonetheless it provides an initial test of whether social contexts do influence the relationships between individual difference measures and achievement in the second language. Some evidence already supports the hypothesis that in communities differing in terms of a bilingual/monolingual distinction, individual difference variables are not similarly related to achievement. In summarizing the results of studies conducted in Maine, Louisiana, and Connecticut, Gardner and Lambert (1972:56) state:

The MLAT [Modern Language Aptitude Test] battery and the one intelligence measure used in each study turn out to be strong predictors of achievement in reading, vocabulary and grammar as measured by the Cooperative French Test (CFT) in two of the settings, although somewhat less powerful in the third (Maine).

Of the three sites, Maine was the only bilingual area, which suggests that cognitive factors, at least, are less related to achievement in the second language in a bilingual community than in a monolingual one. Support for the proposition that ability may be relatively unrelated to second language achievement is provided in a study conducted in the Philippines (Gardner and Santos, 1970; also see Gardner and Lambert, 1972), since the measures of language aptitude were virtually unrelated to the criteria. The language aptitude tests, however, were developed especially for that study, so it is possible that they lacked either validity or reliability, or both.

We do, however, now have considerable data with which to assess whether the correlations between achievement and three of the four individual difference measures (language aptitude, motivation, and situational anxiety) are differentially affected by whether or not the setting is monolingual or bilingual. These data were gathered from seven regions in Canada. Four of these regions, Vancouver, Edmonton, Winnipeg, and Kent County, Ontario, can be reasonably classified as monolingual regions in that English is the language most commonly employed, and although French speaking communities exist in and around some of these areas, they do not dominate the language scene. Three regions, Ottawa, Montreal and Moncton, can be classified as bilingual communities in that both English and French are languages used extensively both in the business community and in social situations.

In five of the regions, students in grades 7 to 11 were investigated. In one region, students were in grades 8 to 12, while in another only samples from grades 9 to 11 were investigated. The number of students in the samples varied from 62 to 239, with a mean of 161. The students were tested on three separate occasions over the academic year. During the first testing, they completed the short form of the Modern Language Aptitude Test of Carroll and Sapon (1959), and on the second occasion they completed a battery of tests assessing attitudinal/motivational characteristics. The third testing session, which took place towards the end of the academic year, was devoted to assessing achievement in French. For all samples, this involved a series of objective paper and pencil tests of French achievement. In addition, French speech samples were obtained for 21 samples varying in size from 37 to 143 with a mean of 83.

The effects of situation on the correlations between the major individual difference measures are available for the variables of study, language aptitude, motivation, and situational anxiety. The index of language aptitude was the total score of a short form of the MLAT (Carroll and Sapon, 1959); the measure of motivation was a composite of scores on three measures, motivational intensity, desire to learn French, and attitudes towards learning French (each scale being standardized before summation); the index of situational anxiety was a measure of French classroom anxiety. Three measures of linguistic outcomes are considered here, scores on objective measures of French achievement, French course grades, and indices of speech proficiency.

Table 10.1 presents the average correlations, for samples drawn from monolingual and bilingual communities, of the three individual difference measures with the three indices of French achievement. For both the objective tests of French achievement and the French grades there were 20 samples from the monolingual regions and 13 from the bilingual ones. For the measure of speech proficiency, there were 10 samples drawn from the monolingual communities and 11 from the bilingual ones.

Table 10.1 *Average correlations in monolingual and bilingual regions of three individual difference measures with three indices of French proficiency*

	Monolingual	Bilingual	Z
Objective tests:			
Language aptitude	0.37	0.27	3.93**
Motivation	0.31	0.29	0.72
French classroom anxiety	−0.24	−0.28	1.00
Classroom grades:			
Language aptitude	0.43	0.37	2.24*
Motivation	0.40	0.38	0.59
French classroom anxiety	−0.33	−0.25	−2.32*
Speech proficiency:			
Language aptitude	0.36	0.29	1.76
Motivation	0.38	0.27	2.59**
French classroom anxiety	−0.33	−0.34	0.22

*p <.05
**p <0.1

The correlations for each sample were transformed to 'Fisher Z scores prior to calculating the averages following the procedure described by McNemar (1969:158). The comparison of these average correlations makes use of a standard normal deviate (Z) and the results are also shown in Table 10.1. Inspection of this table will reveal that, except for two comparisons involving the index of situational anxiety, the average correlations are higher for the monolingual regions than for the bilingual ones. In four instances, these differences are significant, indicating that the social context does, in fact, influence the relationships between the individual difference measures and achievement in the second language.

Because the operational definition of 'social context' in the present case is so gross (i.e., monolingual v. bilingual regional), there could be a number of reasons for the differences, including, of course, differences in cultural beliefs. One, however, could be simply the relative lack of availability of informal language experiences in monolingual contexts, and consequently the reliance on the classroom context for the development of second language skill. In such a context, performance on objective tests of achievement could be expected to vary with differences in ability, classroom grades could be related to both ability and classroom anxiety, and speech proficiency could covary with motivation, more than in situations where informal experiences are not only available but unavoidable. In monolingual contexts where second language achievement must depend largely on the classroom situation, and where students would have to seek out informal experiences, it is reasonable to predict that such school-taught skills as vocabulary and grammar would depend primarily on the student's ability to profit from the teaching. For exactly these reasons too, grades reflect classroom behaviour. Anxiety too would be implicated. Finally, motivation would relate to speech proficiency because motivation would largely determine whether a student found any opportunities to speak the language, and thus acquire extra skill. The availability of informal language experiences in bilingual areas would mean that many other factors could influence achievement in the language, or even in individual cases that the three individual difference variables studied here could interact to determine a student's level of proficiency.

It should be emphasized that the correlations presented in Table 10.1 are average correlations based on relatively large sample sizes, and that in all cases, they reflect significant covariation between the individual difference measure and achievement. The differences just discussed reflect differences between the average correlations derived in monolingual and bilingual regions; the explanations are tentative, but reasonable. What is important in these data is that they clearly demonstrate that the social context does influence the relationship between individual differences and achievement. This influence, however, is one of attenuating or magnifying the relationship, not of eliminating it. The three individual difference variables discussed here are clearly implicated in the acquisition of a second language, but social context obviously affects their relative potency.

Until now, the concept of motivation has been considered in terms of affect and effort. That is, the motivation to learn a second language has been conceptualized as a combination of a positive attitude (desire) to learn the language and effort expended in that direction. Both facets seem necessary. Circumstances might induce effort (an impending examination, a severe teacher, etc.) but little desire. A student may want to learn the language, but not expend the effort. It would seem that to obtain a meaningful index of motivation, a researcher must consider both desire and effort. Motivation, however, can be affected by many factors.

There are considerable data to suggest that motivation so defined is associated with attitudes towards a number of social objects and to the individual's orientation in second language study, and that this attitudinal/motivational complex is related to achievement in the second language (Gardner and Lambert, 1959, 1972; Gardner and Santos, 1970; Gardner and Smythe, 1975; Smythe, Stennett and Feenstra, 1972). This attitudinal/motivational complex has been referred to as an integrative motive (cf. Gardner, 1966), and has been shown to include, in addition to the motivational components, favourable attitudes towards the other language group and an integrative orientation towards language study (a goal which stresses learning the language in order to meet with, communicate with, and learn more about the other language community). It has been argued that this integrative motive facilitates second language learning, but until now the role of the attitudinal component has not been elaborated. It is suggested here, however, that social attitudes are relevant to second language acquisition not because they directly influence achievement but because they serve as motivational supports. Since attitudes are formed through interaction with one's social environment, they make a direct link between the cultural milieu and the motivation to acquire a second language, and ultimately proficiency in that language. Figure 10.2 presents a schematic representation of a fuller model with respect to motivation and second language acquisition. In its complete form, the model states that individual differences in a number of social attitudes give rise to individual differences in motivation which in turn are responsible for variability in achievement. Achievement can be viewed in terms of both linguistic and non-linguistic outcomes, and both can in turn influence the individual's attitudes. Thus the model is dynamic, not static.

The attitudes can be of a highly general nature such as ethnocentrism and anomie, or they can be specific to learning languages, as in an interest in foreign languages. They can relate to the group who speak the language (e.g., attitudes towards French Canadians), or towards the situation in which learning takes place (e.g., attitudes towards the language teacher and the course). When considering attitudes which can support a student's motivation, many can be proposed, and these differ along a number of dimensions, not simply one of specificity-generality. The important consideration is that the attitude serves to maintain the desire and effort in the long and tedious process of acquiring the language. Short range motivational props such as fear of failure, desire to do well in school, vague future job requirements, etc., do not have the staying power or the generality to maintain consistent levels of motivation over prolonged periods of time or diverse opportunities to develop proficiency. Attitudes which relate to the social aspects of language acquisition would seem to meet these requirements.

The validity of this model, of course, hinges on the validity of the assumption that attitudes are important because they serve as motivational supports rather than as major correlates of achievement. This would be supported if the following conditions were met:

1. The various attitude measures correlate appreciably with the index of motivation.

2. The index of motivation correlates appreciably with indices of achievement in the second language.

3. Any correlation of attitudes with achievement is attenuated if the effects of motivation are partialled out of the attitude measure.

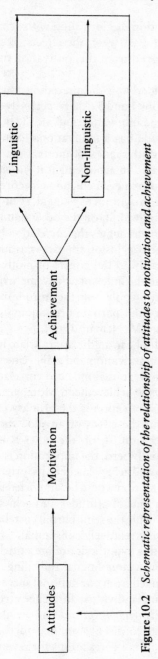

Figure 10.2 *Schematic representation of the relationship of attitudes to motivation and achievement*

4. The correlation of motivation with achievement is essentially maintained even when the effects of the corresponding attitude are removed from the motivation measure.

The rationale underlying the preceding four conditions merits discussion. Conditions 1 and 3 deal respectively with the association between attitudes and motivation and attitudes and achievement. If any particular attitude has a motivational component it should of course correlate with the index of motivation. Furthermore, if the attitude was implicated in achievement it should correlate appreciably with the index of achievement, and moreover should maintain a significant association with achievement even if the motivational component were removed. If, on the other hand, partialling out the effects of motivation attenuates the correlation between the attitude and achievement, the conclusion appears warranted that the association was due primarily to the effects of motivation. Because it is desirable to maintain the index of achievement intact and to remove the effects of motivation only from the attitude measure, semi-partial correlations (rather than partial correlations) are the appropriate statistics in this case (McNemar, 1969).

Conditions 2 and 4 bear on the appropriate interpretation of the association between motivation and achievement. First, it would be necessary for the motivational index to correlate significantly with the various measures of achievement. Moreover, following the logic described above, if motivation is the primary correlate of achievement, partialling out the effect of attitude should not materially influence this correlation. If, on the other hand, the semi-partial correlation is essentially zero, the implication is that the association between motivation and achievement is due primarily to the attitude. Thus, the basic assumption would be supported to the extent that the semi-partial correlations of attitudes and achievement were generally not significant, while the semi-partial correlations of motivation and achievement were relatively substantial.

Data relevant to this hypothesis are presented in Tables 10.2 and 10.3 for samples from a monolingual and bilingual area respectively. These data were derived from our national survey, and consequently the two non-attitudinal individual difference variables, *French Classroom Anxiety* and *Language Aptitude*, are available for purposes of comparison. The data consist of a summary of the first order correlations and the semi-partial correlations for seven attitude measures, the index of motivation, and the measures of *French Classroom Anxiety* and *Language Aptitude* with five criteria. These variables are:

1. *Interest in Foreign Languages.* This is an index of the student's degree of interest in learning foreign languages. The items comprising this scale refer to foreign languages in general and not any particular second language.

2. *Integrativeness.* This is a composite measure involving attitudes toward the specific second language community (in our case French Canadians, and the European French), and an integrative orientation in language study.

3. *Evaluation of the Learning Situation.* This is a composite of two measures assessing attitudes towards the French course and the French teacher.

4. *Instrumentality.* This is an index of the extent to which students feel that learning a second language is important for pragmatic or utilitarian reasons. No reference is made to a desire to communicate with members of the other language community.

5. *Parental Encouragement.* This is an assessment of the extent to which the student feels that he receives active encouragement from his parents to acquire the second language.

6. *Need Achievement.* This is a general measure of the desire to do well in any task the individual undertakes.

7. *Ethnocentrism.* This measure was adapted from Adorno, Frenkel-Brunswick, Levinson and Sanford (1950) and is an index of the extent to which an individual perceives his own group as superior and outgroups as inferior.

8. *French Class Anxiety.* This is a scale measuring the extent to which the student reports that he feels intimidated or anxious when speaking French in the classroom.

9. *Language Aptitude.* This measure consists of the short form of the Modern Language Aptitude Test (Carroll and Sapon, 1959).

10. *Motivation.* This is a composite measure involving three scales, Motivational Intensity (an index of the amount of effort expended to learn French), Desire to Learn French (an assessment of how much the student wants to learn French) and Attitudes towards Learning French.

The five criteria are:

1. *Behavioural Intention*: Ss were asked if they intended to re-enroll in French the next year. Their answers were coded 1 for 'no', 2 for undecided, and 3 for 'yes'.

2. *Opportunities to Use French*: Ss were asked if they had many opportunities to use French outside of the school setting during the preceding year. Their answers were coded 1 for 'no', and 2 for 'yes'.

3. *Canadian Achievement Test in French*: Three subtests from this battery were administered, for vocabulary, grammar and comprehension. The students' total scores provided an objective index of French achievement.

4. *Grades in French*: The classroom teachers supplied the final course grades for each student. Before computing the correlations, the grades were first transformed to standard scores within each class to remove variation in grades attributable to specific classes.

5. *Speech*: Samples of students were asked to describe in French a series of four cartoon panels after studying them for a two minute period. Responses were tape recorded and then rated by two judges for both fluency and pronunciation accuracy. Interjudge reliablilities varied over 21 samples from 0.62 to 0.96 and 0.65 to 0.95 with medians of 0.76 and 0.77 for fluency and pronunciation respectively. A second task required Ss to study a short passage of French prose and then read it aloud. These passages were also recorded and scored for fluency and accuracy. The reliabilities, in this case, ranged from 0.80 to 0.98 and 0.76 to 0.98, with medians of 0.86 and 0.83 respectively. The Speech score is the sum of the four ratings.

Table 10.2 presents a summary of the relevant correlations for a sample of 204 grade 11 students studying French as a second language in a monolingual anglophone milieu. (A sample of 82 students completed the speech task.) The first column of the table, r_1, presents the correlations of each of the 'predictor' variables with the index of motivation. It will be noted that all of these correlations, with the exception of that for *Language Aptitude* are significant, but that those involving *Interest in Foreign Languages*, *Integrativeness*, and *Attitudes towards the Learning Situation* are appreciably higher

Table 10.2 The relationship of ten predictor variables to motivation and five outcome variables in a monolingual setting

Predictor variables	Mot. r_1	Behav. inten. r_2	r_3	r_4	Opp. to use r_2	r_3	r_4	Catf. r_2	r_3	r_4	Grade r_2	r_3	r_4	Speech r_2	r_3	r_4
Interest in foreign languages	0.74**	0.33**	-0.07	0.40**	0.26**	0.00	0.24**	0.34**	0.09	0.19*	0.37**	0.00	0.34**	0.44**	0.07	0.31**
Integration	0.68**	0.36**	0.00	0.37**	0.24**	-0.01	0.27**	0.23*	-0.05	0.31**	0.31**	-0.04	0.39**	0.40**	0.05	0.35**
Attitudes toward learning situation	0.62**	0.33**	0.02	0.40**	0.18	-0.06	0.32**	0.12	-0.14*	0.39**	0.27**	-0.05	0.42**	0.39**	0.08	0.37**
Instrumentality	0.34**	0.24*	0.07	0.46**	0.06	-0.07	0.36**	0.00	-0.04	0.37**	0.15	-0.02	0.47**	0.19	0.01	0.49**
Parental encouragement	0.21*	0.20*	0.09	0.49**	0.03	-0.05	0.36**	0.04	-0.05	0.38**	0.04	-0.07	0.50**	0.15	0.03	0.51**
N-achievement	0.33**	0.07	-0.11	0.52**	0.08	-0.05	0.35**	0.23*	0.11	0.32**	0.34**	0.19*	0.41**	0.42**	0.26*	0.41**
Ethnocentrism	-0.31**	-0.07	0.09	0.52**	-0.05	0.06	0.36**	-0.35**	-0.24*	0.29**	-0.37**	-0.22*	0.41**	-0.41**	-0.26*	0.42**
French classroom anxiety	-0.33**	-0.29**	-0.13*	0.45**	-0.31**	-0.20*	0.27**	-0.33**	-0.22*	0.29**	-0.27**	-0.11	0.44**	-0.48**	-0.32**	0.39**
Aptitude	0.18	0.19*	0.11	0.49**	0.04	-0.02	0.36**	0.37**	0.31**	0.32**	0.48**	0.40**	0.42**	0.49**	0.40**	0.45**
Motivation		0.52**			0.36**			0.38**			0.50**			0.53**		

*p <.05
**p <.01

r_1 — Correlation of attitudes with motivation.
r_2 — Correlation of attitudes with outcome.
r_3 — Semi-partial correlation of attitudes (motivation removed) with outcome.
r_4 — Semi-partial correlation of motivation (attitude removed) with outcome.

than the others, Clearly, therefore, the various attitudes are related
to motivation to learn French but such motivation is most closely
linked with attitudes towards other languages, the ethnic community
concerned, and the learning situation. Language aptitude and motivation are virtually independent.

The columns labelled r_2 present the correlations of the attitude
measures with each of the five criteria. It will be noted that *Interest in
Foreign Languages, Integrativeness* and *Motivation* correlate significantly with all five of the criteria and moreover that *Motivation*
correlates higher with each criterion than any other predictor including the two other individual differences variables, *French Classroom
Anxiety* and *Language Aptitude. Instrumentality* and *Parental
Encouragement* are related only to the measure of *Behavioural
Intention to Continue French* study, which suggests that in a monolingual context these two attitudinal variables are not particularly
important for achievement. *Need Achievement* and *Language
Aptitude* are significantly related to all criteria except reported
Opportunities to Use French. Finally, *Attitudes towards the Learning Situation* and *Ethnocentrism* are significantly correlated with
only three of the five criteria. Both are correlated significantly with
French Grades and *Speech*; in addition, *Attitudes towards the Learning Situation* correlates significantly with *Behavioural Intention to
Continue French Study*, while *Ethnocentrism* relates to the *Canadian Achievement Test in French*. These various relationships (and
lack of relationships as well) are all quite meaningful and under-
standable given the nature of the variables.

The statistics presented in the columns labelled r_3 and r_4 give a
clearer indication of the dynamics operating. The r_3 columns are the
semi-partial correlation coefficients of each attitude measure with
that criterion once the contribution of motivation is removed from
the attitude measure. It will be noted that generally the correlations
are not appreciably or even significantly different from zero, suggesting that to a considerable extent the correlations between the various
attitude measures and the criteria can be accounted for by their
overlap with motivation. There are a few exceptions to this generalization, however: the significant semi-partial correlations between
the *Canadian Achievement Test in French* and *Attitudes towards the
Learning Situation*; those of *Ethnocentrism* with the *Canadian
Achievement Test in French, French Grades*, and *Speech*, and those
of *Need Achievement* with *French Grades* and *Speech*. Each of these

significant relationships indicate some extra-motivational associa-tion with these measures of achievement, but they are neither appreci-able or consistent. The overall conclusion seems appropriate that in most instances the correlations of the attitude variables with achievement can be attributed to their association with motivation. This, coupled with the relationships of the attitude variables with motivation, suggests that the attitude variables are instrumental in determining individual differences in motivation, but that their association with achievement is dependent upon their effect on motivation.

The pattern with respect to the individual difference measures of anxiety and aptitude is considerably different. The semi-partial cor-relations of *French Classroom Anxiety* with the various criteria are all significant with the exception of that with French grades. Lan-guage aptitude demonstrates significant semi-partial correlations only with the three criteria which one could expect to have appreci-able aptitude components, the *Canadian Achievement Test in French, French Grades* and *Speech*. It is obvious, therefore, that both French classroom anxiety and language aptitude contribute to the acquisition of a second language, and that their contributions are relatively independent of motivation.

The columns labelled r_4 summarize the semi-partial correlations of motivation with the corresponding attitude controlled. Here the results are extremely clear. In all cases, motivation relates to the criterion regardless of the particular attitude controlled!

Table 10.3 presents comparable data for a sample of 180 grade 11 Anglophone students learning French in a bilingual context (65 students completed the Speech task). The results agree with those obtained in a monolingual setting except for one correlate of motiva-tion and the relationship of attitudes and motivation to the criterion of speech. These differences are quite predictable given the differ-ences in social milieu between a monolingual and bilingual context.

Examination of Table 10.3 will reveal that motivation correlates significantly with all the predictor variables except *Ethnocentrism* and *Language Aptitude*, but that four variables, *Interest in Foreign Languages, Integrativeness, Attitudes towards the Learning Situa-tion*, and *Parental Encouragement*, are appreciably more highly correlated with *motivation* than the others. These results are com-parable to those obtained in the monolingual area except that paren-tal encouragement becomes a much more salient component of

Table 10.3 The relationship of ten predictor variables to motivation and five outcome variables in a bilingual setting

Predictor variables	Mot.	Behav.inten			Opp. to use			Catf.			Grade			Speech		
	r_1	r_2	r_3	r_4	r_2	r_3	r_4	r_2	r_3	r_4	r_2	r_3	r_4	r_2	r_3	r_4
Interest in foreign languages	0.76**	0.40**	−0.01	0.36**	0.27**	0.03	0.18*	0.20*	0.03	0.13	0.15*	−0.07	0.21*	0.14	−0.04	0.17
Integration	0.62**	0.23*	−0.13	0.51**	0.19*	−0.01	0.26**	0.31**	0.21**	0.05	0.12	−0.05	0.22**	0.02	−0.15	0.26*
Attitudes toward learning situation	0.48**	0.26**	−0.01	0.47**	0.05	−0.12	0.34**	0.03	−0.09	0.25**	0.07	−0.06	0.25**	−0.04	−0.16	0.27*
Instrumentality	0.29**	0.11	−0.04	0.53**	0.02	−0.08	0.33**	0.15*	0.08	0.20*	0.20*	0.14	0.20*	0.02	−0.05	0.22
Parental encouragement	0.51**	0.32**	−0.05	0.44**	0.33**	0.19*	0.18*	0.15*	0.03	0.19*	0.10	−0.03	0.23*	0.22	0.13	0.12
N-achievement	0.26**	−0.06	−0.20*	0.57**	0.01	−0.09	0.33**	−0.11	−0.18	0.27**	0.03	−0.03	0.25**	−0.07	−0.14	0.24*
Ethnocentrism	−0.02	−0.12	−0.11	0.54**	−0.06	−0.06	0.32**	0.03	0.04	0.24**	−0.12	−0.12	0.25**	−0.08	−0.08	0.22
French classroom anxiety	−0.18*	−0.19*	−0.10	0.51**	−0.35**	−0.30**	0.26**	−0.34**	−0.30**	0.18	−0.24**	−0.20*	0.21*	−0.64**	−0.61**	0.10
Aptitude	0.05	−0.11	0.08	0.53**	−0.06	−0.08	0.33**	0.06	0.05	0.23**	−0.27**	0.25**	0.23*	−0.04	−0.06	0.22
Motivation		−0.54**			0.32**			−0.24**			0.25**			0.25**		

*p <.05 r_1 — Correlation of attitudes with motivation.
**p <.01 r_2 — Correlation of attitudes with outcome.
   r_3 — Semi-partial correlation of attitudes (motivation removed) with outcome.
   r_4 — Semi-partial correlation of motivation (attitude removed) with outcome.

motivation. If direct comparisons are made between these correlations and those obtained in the monolingual area, in point of fact, these results suggest that *Parental Encouragement* is significantly more positively correlated with motivation, that *Ethnocentrism* is significantly less negatively correlated with motivation and that *Attitudes towards the Learning Situation* are significantly less positively correlated with motivation in the bilingual setting ($Z = -3.39$, -2.92, and 1.96 respectively). These results suggest that the social context can influence the attitudinal bases of motivation. In bilingual contexts where the other language group and their language are clearly salient factors, motivational levels are more related to students' perceptions of their parental encouragement, less related to their general ethnocentric tendencies, and less related to their evaluative reactions to the classroom setting.

When attention is directed to the attitudinal correlates of the various cirteria (the r_2 columns), it will again be noted that the similarities with the results obtained in the monolingual area outweigh the differences. In this context only French classroom anxiety and motivation correlate significantly with any of the other 'predictors'. *Interest in foreign Languages* correlates significantly with three criteria, *Behavioural Intention to Continue French Study*, *Opportunites to Use French*, and *Canadian Achievement Test in French*. The general superiority of these four predictors is comparable to that obtained in the monolingual area, except that their overall contribútions are somewhat reduced. (This, of course, is consistent with the results obtained above when the correlations of the three individual difference measures with achievement were compared in monolingual and bilingual regions.) *Parental Encouragement* assumes relatively greater prominence in this setting in that it correlates significantly with three criteria, quite possibly because of its greater association with motivation. The five variables, *Attitudes towards the Learning Situation*, *Need Achievement*, *Ethnocentrism*, *Language Aptitude*, and *Instrumentality*, are generally infrequent and poor correlates of the criteria, a result which is contrary to that obtained in the monolingual context for all 'predictors' except instrumentality, which it will be noted is a poor predictor in both contexts. Perhaps the major discrepancy involves the correlations for language aptitude. The only significant relation in this context is that with grades, though language aptitude is in fact the best correlate of grades. In other words, the relative importance of language aptitude in French achievement is considerably reduced in the bilingual context, even though it continues to be a strong predictor of classroom grades. *Motivation* and *French Classroom Anxiety* are generally the most consistent predictors of achievement in both contexts, but their importance relative to each other is reversed in this bilingual context. Whereas motivation was consistently a better predictor in the monolingual context, it is the best predictor only of *Behavioural Intention to Continue French Study* in the bilingual setting. *French Classroom Anxiety*, on the other hand, is the best predictor of *Opportunities to Use French* and the *Canadian Achievement Test of French* and *Speech*.

There is also considerable similarity between the monolingual and bilingual areas with respect to the two different types of semi-partial correlation coefficients in that the correlations with the criteria of the attitudes partialling out motivation (the r_3 columns) are generally low and not significant, while those involving motivation with the effects of attitudes removed are generally high and significant (the r_4 columns). As was the case with the monolingual areas, the semi-partial correlations of anxiety with the various criteria are significant, which suggests that motivation is not particularly involved in the association of anxiety with the various outcomes. Unlike the case with the monolingual areas, the semi-partial correlations for language aptitude are generally not significant; this finding is best attributed to the relatively unimportant role aptitude plays in the bilingual setting.

The semi-partial correlations for motivation are generally appreciable, indicating again that motivation is the major predictor, or determinant, of the various criteria and that the major role played by the various attitude measures is in sustaining the motivation. Such a generalization seems appropriate in the bilingual context for all criteria except *Speech* and the *Canadian Achievement Tests in French*. For these two criteria, the pure motivational component is much less influential, though still more so than the pure attitudinal ones, than was the case in the monolingual areas. It would seem that, given the greater opportunities to use the second language in informal contexts which characterize bilingual settings, and possibly different cultural beliefs, differences in motivation become less critical in determining differences in achievement. It is as though the non-motivated student simply cannot escape the opportunity of learning some aspects of the language. The anxious student either can avoid the situation, or simply perform less efficiently in situations assessing proficiency.

These results provide strong evidence in support of the assumption that attitudes are important in second language acquisition because they tend to support the student's level of motivation. The data also attest to the validity of the assumption that the social milieu influences the degree of contribution of the attitudinal variables, as well as the different major individual difference variables, aptitude, anxiety and motivation.

SUMMARY AND CONCLUSIONS

The purpose of this chapter was to present in some detail a social psychological theory of second language acquisition, to consider the role of the social milieu in this context, and to elaborate on the functions served by attitudes in providing the foundation for motivation. The theoretical analysis highlights features of the language learning process which heretofore have not been emphasized. Focusing on four individual difference variables, linking them conceptually to the social milieu, and indicating how they would interact with language acquisition contexts to produce different outcomes, explicitly brings together in one framework factors which have been discussed for many years. Theoretical presentations have tended to consider the cognitive (Carroll, 1963; Lambert 1963a) and affective (Lambert, 1963b) factors in relative isolation, though of course considerable research has investigated them in interaction (Gardner and Lambert, 1959, 1972; Gardner and Smythe, 1975; Smythe, Stennett and Feenstra, 1972). This, however, is the first presentation which attempts to provide a detailed examination of how these variables operate together in the acquisition process.

The empirical data presented here strongly suggest that the social milieu plays an important role in the acquisition of a second language. The milieux investigated involved a monolingual $v.$ bilingual distinction which would vary not only the opportunity for informal language experiences, but also quite probably beliefs about the value and consequences, etc., of second language acquisition. The relationships of the three individual difference measures to language achievement were appreciably influenced by this dichotomy, which suggests that further attention should be directed to a detailed analysis of the beliefs in a community *vis-à-vis* second language learning and their effects on the learning process.

The concept of the integrative motive was considered, and attention was directed to the function served by attitudes in this motivational complex. The hypothesis that attitudes were important for second language acquisition because they serve as motivational supports rather than as direct 'determinants' of achievement was supported in that correlations between attitudes and achievement were highly attenuated when the effects of motivation were partialled out, whereas the correlations between motivation and achievement were not similarly affected when the various attitudinal components were removed. The different social settings, monolingual *v.* bilingual, had predictable effects in the two complexes considered.

The theory presented here places considerable emphasis on the role the social context plays in the process of acquiring a second language. In the present analysis, social context was rather globally defined in terms of monolingual *v.* bilingual environments, but there are many other aspects of social context which could be considered. For example, all of the present data could be described as reflecting contexts where bilingualism could be viewed as additive in that the acquisition of French by Anglophone students could lead only to cultural enrichment, not a loss in cultural identity. In fact, it might very well be that the integrative motive is a potential determinant of second language achievement only in contexts where bilingualism could be viewed as additive. If potential bilingualism were seen as leading to cultural alienation (i.e., subtractive) it is difficult to see how a genuine interest in the other cultural community could serve as a potential motivational force facilitating achievement because *in this context* it also promotes personal dissatisfaction. Such speculation receives support from two recent studies investigating French Canadians learning English as a second language. Such a context could be viewed as reflecting supportive bilingualism if it assumed that French Canadians perceive bilingualism as a threat to their cultural identity—an assumption that is not without its support (cf. Taylor, Meynard and Rheault, 1977). In the first study (Clément, Gardner and Smythe, 1977a), it was found in two samples that an instrumental orientation to English study, which is viewed as particularly appropriate for French Canadians learning English, was associated with indices of personal dissatisfaction (feelings of anomie, ethnocentrism, negative evaluation of the self and French

Canadians). Such a pattern has not been reported in the studies of English Canadians learning French (Gardner and Smythe, 1975). In the second study, Clément, Gardner, and Smythe (1977b) found that fears of assimilation experienced while speaking English were appreciably and negatively associated with an integrative motive. That is, those who were integratively associated had no fear of assimilation into the English culture, or alternatively those who were fearful of assimilation were not integratively motivated. Such findings support the thesis underlying the theory presented here, *viz.*, that the social context must be considered in any formulation which seeks to explain the role of motivation in second language acquisition.

Future considerations should focus even greater attention on the social psychological aspects of second language learning. Within the framework proposed here, a number of issues can be raised which have both theoretical and practical implications. The ramifications of the additive/subtractive dichotomy on motivation could be considerable, primarily in those cultural settings where members of ethnic minority groups are concerned with acquiring the language of a majority group. Actually putting into operation the environmental parameters of additive and subtractive bilingualism would seem particularly important, especially given the findings presented here that the social context materially influences those factors operating in the language acquisition process. The actual interplay of the various individual difference variables with the two language acquisition contexts also requires further study. Although it is assumed that cognitive factors play a smaller role in developing skills in informal language acquisition contexts than do affective factors, this assumption has not been tested. Furthermore, the contribution of the two contexts to various outcomes requires investigation. Although many might see obvious associations between both contexts and linguistic outcomes, they might question whether the contexts have any considerable influence on non-linguistic outcomes. And, of course, it is not uncommon to hear the argument that the formal context does not, in fact, promote second language proficiency. Finally, focusing on the concept of motivation, further research could profitably be directed towards answering the question of how it facilitates language acquisition. Is it simply that motivated individuals work harder? Gliksman (1976) has in fact demonstrated that integratively motivated students volunteer answers in class more frequently than non-integratively motivated students. But it may not be that the positive affect associated with the motivation somehow makes it easier for the student to incorporate second language material. These, and many other questions of both theoretical and practical importance become salient when second language learning is viewed as a social psychological phenomenon rather than an educational one.

Contributors

Charles R. Berger

  Department of Communication Studies
  Northwestern University

Richard Y. Bourhis

  Department of Psychology
  McMaster University

John R. Edwards

  Department of Psychology
  St. Francis Xavier Univeristy

Robert C. Gardner

  Department of Psychology
  University of Western Ontario

Howard Giles

  Department of Psychology
  University of Bristol

Wallace E. Lambert

  Department of Psychology
  McGill University

Jacques P. Leyens

  Faculte de Psychologie
  Universite Catholique de Louvain

E. Allan Lind

Department of Psychology
University of New Hampshire

William O'Barr

Department of Anthropology
Duke University

Ellen B. Ryan

Department of Psychology
University of Notre Dame

Klaus R. Scherer

Psychologie
Der Justus Liebig-Universität Giessen

Robert N. St. Clair

Interdisciplinary Linguistics
University of Louisville

Philip M. Smith

Department of Psychology
University of Bristol

Henri Tajfel

Department of Psychology
University of Bristol

Notes

CHAPTER 1

1. I am grateful to Guy Fielding, Jennifer Williams, Philip Smith, Richard Bourhis, Robert St. Clair, Peter Trudgill, Donald Taylor and Klaus Scherer for their comments and time in discussion of the preparation of this chapter.

2. We shall deal with the decoding process in this book prior to the encoding one given the traditional emphasis in social psychology on viewing the individual more as an observer than an active interactant.

3. For some worthwhile integrative approaches, however, see Kelvin (1972), Harvey and Smith (1977) and Stotland and Cannon (1972).

4. Unfortunately, it is not within the scope of this chapter to review systematically the research that could fall under the rubric of 'the social psychology of language'. Nevertheless, the interested reader will be able to follow up on its disparate contents by means of references in this and subsequent chapters.

CHAPTER 2

1. I should like to thank Suzanne deLarichière for her assistance in this study, and Howard Giles for his comments upon an earlier draft.

2. Greaney, V. Personal communication, September 1976.

3. I have dealt elsewhere with characteristics of disadvantage (Edwards, 1976a, in press—a). The generally gross criteria employed here are adequate for present purposes.

4. Cell means, correlation matrices and other information referred to, but not shown (in the interest of brevity) in this chapter are available upon request from the author.

5. It should of course be remembered that self-reported data (what a respondent thinks or believes about something), such as those deriving from interviews, need not be directly related to what a respondent may actually *do*. Such data are still of interest, however, especially in combination with other approaches.

CHAPTER 3

1. We would like to express our gratitude to Donald Taylor and Richard Bourhis for their comments on earlier drafts of this manuscript.

2. For a review and rule-based analyses in communication theory, see Berger (1976).

3. For a short discussion of interpersonal accommodation on non-linguistic levels, see Fishman and Giles (1978).

4. On certain other evaluative dimensions such as social attractiveness, however, these British studies show that non-standard speakers are *more* favourably viewed than standard accented speakers (see also Bourhis and Giles, 1976). In this case, upward convergence would involve costs for the speaker in terms of a perceived loss of social attractiveness. Such costs are arguably minimal in many formal contexts (although obviously far from all of them) in relation to the potential rewards of increased competence involved.

5. For a more detailed review of Tajfel's theory and its relationship to language and ethnic group relations, see Giles, Bourhis and Taylor (1977).

6. See Giles and Powesland (1975: 166–70) for discussion of some of its limitations.

7. We wish to thank Valerie Walkerdine and her students at Northeast London Polytechnic for their co-operation in this investigation.

8. In this respect, see Eiser and Stroebe (1972: chapter 7) for their discussion of people attempting to achieve *evaluative*, as well as descriptive consistency in their social judgements.

CHAPTER 4

1. Social dynamism is a person perception dimension reflecting the power and the activity of the perceived individual.

2. The research project which included this observation and analysis of court speech and the experimental studies reported here was funded by a National Science Foundation Law and Social Science Program Grant (GS-42742), William O'Barr, Principal Investigator. In addition to the authors, others who contributed substantially to the project included Bonnie Erickson, John Conley, Bruce Johnson, and Laurens Walker. Inquiries concerning the analysis of the court speech should be addressed to W. M. O'Barr, Director, Law and Language Program, Department of Anthropology, Duke University, Durham, N.C. 27706.

3. For each sex of witness, the power tape differed considerably from the powerless tape with regard to the number of intensifiers, hedges, questioning forms, gesture-indicating phrases, polite forms, and hesitation forms used by the witness. The lawyer's speech and other aspects of the witness' speech was, to a very high degree, constant on all four tapes. Because there were some slight differences in the use of powerless features between the male witness-powerless speech tape and the female witness-powerless speech tape, we restricted our analysis of the results to comparisons within each sex of witness. A total of forty-six male and fifty female subjects participated in the experiment.

4. The social evaluation measures were constructed as follows: the competence dimension was the average of ratings of the witness on scales with

the labels 'competent', 'intelligent', and 'qualified'; the social attractiveness dimension was based on ratings of how 'likeable' the witness was; the trustworthiness dimension was based on a scale with the label 'trustworthy'; the social dynamism dimension was the average of ratings of the witness on scales with the labels 'powerful', 'strong', and 'active'; the convincingness dimension was the average of subjects' ratings of how much they believed the witness' testimony and of how convincing they felt the witness was.

5. This statement is based on ratings of the witness on a scale with the endpoint labels 'masculine' and 'feminine.'

6. Some indication of the differences between the narrative and fragmented tapes may be seen in the following indices. The average number of words in the witness' answers was 43.3 on the narrative tape and 8.6 on the fragmented tape. The lawyer asked 30 questions on the narrative tape and 131 questions on the fragmented tape. Eighty-two male and female undergraduates and 43 male and female law students participated in the experiment.

7. Among the major measures constructed from responses to this questionnaire were indices of competence (the average of ratings on scales labelled 'competent' and 'intelligent'). As noted, these measures were assessed both for subjects' own impressions of the witness and for their attributions concerning what the lawyer thought of the witness.

8. There is evidence from the analysis of partial correlations that it is likely that the subjects' own impressions of the witness were caused by their acceptance of the lawyer's perceived evaluations of the witness (see Asher, 1976, and Blalock, 1964, for a description of the analysis technique used).

9. As in the previous experiments, dimensions of speech variation other than that under study were controlled to provide an unambiguous test of the effects of the speech dimension of interest. In the present experiment, in addition to equating the substantive evidence presented on the four tapes, all of the tapes included approximately the same number of instances of simultaneous speech (except, of course, the control tape, which contained none), and these instances commenced with constant frequency at 'turn relevance places' and at other points in the original speaker's utterance. Further, the instances of simultaneous speech were distributed throughout the experimental testimony, and in half the instances of simultaneous speech the new speaker was the attorney while in the other half of the instances the new speaker was the witness.

10. Subjects in the experiment were thirty-eight male and forty-eight female undergraduates. Twenty to twenty-four subjects heard each testimony tape.

11. The authors wish to thank Dina Anselmi for her suggestions concering the interpretations of this effect.

CHAPTER 5

1. This chapter is based in part on research conducted by the author while at Harvard University and the University of Pennsylvania. Some studies and

parts of the analyses were supported by NIMH grant (MH-19-569-01) and DFG grant (Sche 156/1). The author gratefully acknowledges contributions by Barton Jones, Ursula Scherer, Sylvia von Borstel, Gudrun Herpel, Stephanie Kühnen, Reiner Standke, Hede Helfrich, and Janis Flint.

2. Since there is no consistent differential usage of the terms 'attitude change', 'persuasion', or 'social influence' in the literature, there will be no attempt in this chapter to define and distinguish these terms. Persuasion will be used loosely as that type of social behaviour in which predominantly verbal messages are used as influence mechanisms. Attitude change or behaviour change is seen as a possible result of such persuasive attempts.

3. The terminology in this area is a major obstacle to conceptual clarity and communicative accuracy. In this chapter we shall loosely follow the conventions proposed by Laver and Hutcheson (1972).

4. The author is much indebted to Barton Jones for contributing the description of the voice quality parameters, organization and realization of the rating sessions, as well as helpful criticism on the final version of the chapter.

5. The Giessen Speech Analysis System consists of a PDP 11/35 with the following periphery: 12-bit analog-to-digital converter and digital-to-analog converter, disk and magtape facilities, hardware Fourier processor and various input/output devices. Procedure for fundamental frequency extraction: excerpts of several minutes' duration for the individual juror's contribution to the discussion were digitalized with a 14-bit analog-to-digital converter. Individual speech frames of 62.5 msec duration each were then processed in such a way as to discard pauses and voiceless segments. An autocorrelation procedure was used to extract F_0.

6. This transcription system, the 'Giessen-Freiburger Transkriptionsschema', is the result of the joint effort of our Giessen psychology research group and a group of linguists under the direction of Prof. Dr. H. Steger at Freiburg University.

7. Most of these analyses were carried out by Janis Flint. A report of the results is in preparation. A preliminary write-up on the procedures used can be obtained from the author.

8. The jury sessions were videotaped in full. Unfortunately, due to a lack of resources at the time, most tapes had to be erased and reused before proper analyses could be made. A partial analysis of some video material of the American sessions is presented later in the chapter.

9. One, possibly important, factor which was not controlled in this study is the nature of the arguments used by the jurors. The cogency of the arguments could affect perceived influence independent of or in combination with vocal/verbal delivery style.

10. Given that there does not seem to be an interculturally effective 'voice of influence', one might also expect that males and females use different delivery styles in influencing others.

CHAPTER 6

1. These findings are based on a project conducted by members of a graduate seminar in interpersonal communication, Northwestern University in the spring of 1975.

CHAPTER 8

1. The research reported herein was supported by a grant from the S.S.R.C. We would like to express our gratitude to students and staff of the University of Louvain, and in particular L. K. Engels and A. Keuleers, for their co-operation in this project. We are also grateful to D. M. Taylor for his valuable comments prior to instigating experimental work, and to Ria de Bleser and Lois Huffines, for their comments on earlier drafts of this chapter.

2. Research by Parkin (1977) in Nairobi suggests that processes of psycholinguistic distinctiveness can operate even when groups are not marked by objective differences in linguisitic features. He found that Kenyan adolescents at school formed themselves into peer groups named 'societies' while those who had left school formed themselves into 'gangs'. Although their respective language behaviours were very similar, the societies *claimed* to speak far more in English, while the gangs claimed to speak more in Swahili. This situation was called one of 'putative psycholinguistic distinctiveness' (Giles, Bourhis and Taylor, 1977).

3. Since an historical interpretation may depend on the side one adopts and since the subjects chosen for our investigation were Dutch speaking and Flemish feeling' (as they say)—we have established the historical background from their point of view. A Walloon or Bruxellois reader would certainly object to some phrasing of this inevitably biased exposé. We are perfectly aware of this fact and ask them to understand our point of view; a study of highly subjective reactions must allow for some amount of subjective truth.

4. It is true that in the Implicit Categorization/Anti-condition, Ss will receive autobiographical information about the speaker which suggests that he is *likely* to be Francophone Belgian. Nevertheless, intergroup categorization is never made explicit by E.

5. No difference emerged between the sexes on any of the measures investigated within any of the subject groups, and hence they were combined for the analyses reported below.

CHAPTER 9

1. This paper was presented as part of a Symposium on Intergroup Behavior at the meetings of the International Congress of Scientific Psychology, held in Paris, July, 1976. It has been revised and expanded for this publication.

References

Aboud, F. E. and Taylor, D. M. *Ethnic interpersonal attraction: Do we ever prefer dissimilarity?* Unpublished manuscript, McGill University, 1973.

Abu-Sayf, F. K. and Diamond, J. J. Effect on confidence level in multiple-choice test answers on reliability and validity scores. *Journal of Educational Research*, 1976, 70, 62–3.

Adams, J. S. Inequity in social exchange. In L. Berkowitz (Ed.), *Advances in experimental social psychology*. New York: Academic Press, 1965.

Addington, D. W. The effect of vocal variations on ratings of source credibility. *Speech Monographs*, 1971, 38, 242–7.

Adorno, T. W., Frenkel-Brunswick, E., Levinson, D. J., and Sanford, R. N. *The authoritarian personality*. New York: Harper, 1950.

Agyris, C. Dangers in applying results from experimental social psychology. *American Psychologist*, 1975, 30, 460–85.

Allport, G. W. Historical background of modern social psychology. In G. Lindzey and E. Aronson (Eds.), *Handbook of social psychology* (Vol. 1). Reading, Mass.: Addison-Wesley, 1968.

Allport, G. W. & Cantril, H. Judging personality from voice. *Journal of Social Psychology*, 1934, 5, 37–54.

Altman, I. and Taylor, D. A. *Social penetration: The development of interpersonal relationships*. New York: Holt Rinehart & Winston, 1973.

Andersen, K. and Clevenger, J., Jr. A summary of experimental research in ethos. *Speech Mongraphs*, 1963, 30, 59–78.

Argyle, M. *Bodily communication*. London: Metheun, 1975.

Argyle, M., Alkema, F., and Gilmour, R. The communication of friendly and hostile attitudes by verbal and non-verbal signals. *European Journal of Social Psychology*, 1971, 2, 385–402.

Aronson, E. *The social animal*. San Francisco, Cal.: Freeman, 1972.

Arthur, B., Farrar, D., and Bradford, G. Evaluation reaction of college students to dialect differences in the English of Mexican-Americans. *Language and Speech*, 1974, 17, 255–70.

Arsenian, S. Bilingualism in the post-war period. *Psychological Bulletin*, 1945, 42, 65–86.

Asher, H. B. *Causal modeling*. Beverly Hills, Cal.: Sage Publications, 1976.

Bales, R. F. and Slater, P. E. Role differentiation in small decision-making groups. In T. Parsons and R. F. Bales (Eds.), *Family, socialization and interaction process*. New York: Free Press, 1955.

Baratz, J. C. Educational considerations for teaching standard English to Negro children. In B. Spolsky (Ed.), *The language education of minority children*. Rowley, Mass.: Newbury House, 1972.

Barker, G. C. Social functions of language in a Mexican American community. *Acta Americana*, 1947, 5, 185–202.

Barker, R. G. *The stream of behavior*. New York: Appleton-Century-Crofts, 1963.

Bates, E. *Pragmatics and sociolinguistics in child language*. Paper presented at the meeting of the Society for Research on Child Development, Denver, 1975.

Berdan, R. *The use of linguistically determined groups in sociolinguistic research* (Professional paper 26). Los Angeles, Cal.: Southwest Regional Laboratory, Educational Research and Development, 1973.

Bereiter, C. and Engelmann, S. *Teaching disadvantaged children in the preeschool*. Englewood Cliffs, New Jersey: Prentice-Hall, 1966.

Berger, C. R. *The acquaintance process revisited*. Paper presented at the annual convention of the Speech Communication Association, New York, November, 1973.

Berger, C. R. Proactive and retroactive attribution processes in interpersonal communication. *Human Communication Research*, 1975, 2, 33–50.

Berger, C. R. *Theory and research in interpersonal communication: An overview & second explication of issues*. Unpublished manuscript, 1976, Department of Communication Studies, Northwestern University.

Berger, C. R. and Calabrese, R. J. Some explorations in initial interaction and beyond: Toward a developmental theory of interpersonal communication. *Human Communication Research*, 1975, *1*, 99–112.

Berger, C. R., Gardner, R. R., Parks, M. R., Schulman, L. W., and Miller, G. R. Interpersonal epistemology and interpersonal communication. In G. R. Miller (Ed.), *Explorations in interpersonal communication*. Beverly Hills, Cal.: Sage Publications, 1976.

Berger, C. R. and Larimer, M. W. *When beauty is only skin deep: The effects of physical attractiveness, sex and time on initial interaction*. Paper presented at the annual convention of the International Communication Association, New Orleans, April 1974.

Berger, C. R., Weber, M. D., Munley, M. E., and Dixon, J. T. *Interpersonal relationship levels and interpersonal attraction*. Paper presented at the annual convention of the International Communication Association, Berlin, May 1977.

Berko-Gleason, J. Code switching in children's language. In T. E. Moore (Ed.), *Cognitive development and the acquisition of language*. London and New York: Academic Press, 1973.

Berkowitz, L. and Walster, E. Equity theory: Toward a general theory of social interaction. *Advances in experimental social psychology*, 1976, *9*.

Bersheid, E. and Walster, E. Attitude change. In J. Mills (Ed.), *Experimental social psychology*. London: Macmillan, 1969.

Blalock, H. M. *Causal inferences in non-experimental research*. Chapel Hill, North Carolina: University of North Carolina Press, 1964.

Boomer, D. S. Hesitation and grammatical encoding. *Language and Speech*, 1965, *8*, 148–58.

Borstel, S. von. Sprachstil und Persönlichkeit—Analyse des Zusammenhangs von Variablen Diplomarbeit. Unpublished manuscript, University of Giessen, 1976.

Bourhis, R. Y., and Giles, H. The language of cooperation in Wales: A field study. *Language Sciences*, 1976, *42*, 13–16.

Bourhis, R. Y., and Giles, H. The language of intergroup distinctiveness. In H. Giles (Ed.), *Language, ethnicity and intergroup relations*. London: Academic Press, 1977.

Bourhis, R. Y., Giles, H., and Lambert, W. E. Some consequences of accommodating one's style of speech: A cross-national investigation. *International Journal of the Sociology of Language*, 1975, *6*, 55–72.

Bourhis, R. Y., Giles, H., and Tajfel, H. Language as a determinant of Welsh identity. *European Journal of Social Psychology*, 1973, 3, 447–60.

Brehm, J. W. *Responses to loss of freedom: A theory of psychological reactance*. Morristown, New Jersey: General Learning Press, 1972.

Brennan, E. M. Accented speech: Linguistic analysis, scaling and evaluative reactions (Doctoral dissertation, University of Notre Dame). *Dissertation Abstracts International*, 1977, *38* (University Microfilms No. 77–19, 140 78 pp).

Brook, G. L. *English dialects*. London: Deutsch, 1963.

Brophy, J. E., and Good, T. L. *Teacher-student relationships: Causes and consequences*. New York: Holt, Rinehart and Winston, 1974.

Brown, B. The social psychology of variations in French Canadian speech. (Doctoral dissertation, McGill University.) *Dissertation Abstracts International*, 1969, *30*, 3093-B. (University Microfilm available through National Library of Canada.)

Brown, B. L., Strong, W. J., and Rencher, A. C. Perceptions of personality from speech: Effects of manipulations of acoustical parameters. *Journal of the Acoustical Society of America*, 1973, *54*, 29–35.

Brown, B. L., Strong, W. J. and Rencher, A. C. Fifty-four voices from two: The effects of simultaneous manipulations of rate, mean fundamental frequency, and variance of fundamental frequency on ratings of personality from speech. *Journal of the Acoustic Society of America*, 1974, *55*, 313–18.

Brown, R. *Social psychology*. London: Collier-Macmillan, 1965.

Brown, R. and Gilman, A. The pronouns of power and solidarity. In T. A. Sebeok (Ed.), *Style in language*. Cambridge, England: Technology Press, 1960.

Busemann, A. *Die Sprache der Jugend als Ausdruck der Entwicklungsrhythmik*. Jena: Fischer, 1925.

Busemann, A. *Stil und Charakter*. Meisenheim, Glan: Anton Hain Verlag, 1948.

Brunswik, E. *Perception and the representative design of psychological experiments*. Berkeley and Los Angeles, California: University of California Press, 1956.

Byrne, D. Attitudes and attraction. *Advances in Experimental Social Psychology*, 1969, 4, 35–89.

Byrne, D. *The attraction paradigm*. New York: Academic Press, 1971.

Calabrese, R. J. The effects of privacy and probability of future interaction on initial interaction patterns. (Doctoral dissertation, Northwestern University.) *Dissertation Abstracts International*, 1975, *30*, 4102–A. (University Microfilms No. 75–29, 595. 154 pp.)

Carranza, M. A. Language attitudes and other cultural attitudes of Mexican American parents: Some sociolinguistic implications. (Doctoral dissertation, University of Notre Dame.) *Dissertation Abstracts International*, 1977, *38*, 1693–A. (University Microfilms NO. 77–19, 519, 100 pp.)

Carranza, M. A., and Ryan, E. B. Evaluative reactions of bilingual Anglo and Mexican American adolescents toward speakers of English and Spanish. *International Journal of the Sociology of Language*, 1975, 6, 83–104.

Carroll, J. B. Research on teaching foreign languages. In N. L. Gage (Ed.), *Handbook of research in teaching*. Chicago: Rand McNally, 1963.

Carroll, J. B., and Sapon, S. M. *Modern language aptitude tests, form A.* New York: The Psychological Corporation, 1959.

Carswell, E. A. and Rommetveit, R. (Eds.). *Social contexts of messages*. London and New York: Academic Press, 1972.

Carter, R. S. How invalid are marks assigned by teachers? *Journal of Educational Psychology*, 1952, *43*, 218–28.

Cartwright, D., and Zander, A. *Group dynamics: Research and theory*. New York: Harper and Row, 1968.

Cheyne, W. Stereotypical reactions to speakers with Scottish and English regional accents. *British Journal of Social and Clinical Psychology*, 1970, *9*, 77–9.

Clément, R., Gardner, R. C., and Smythe, P. C. Motivational variables in second language acquisition: A study of francophones learning English. *Canadian Journal of Behavioral Sciences*, 1977, *9*, 123–33(a).

Clément, R., Gardner, R. C., and Smythe, P. C. Motivational characteristics of francophones learning English. 1977. (Research Bulletin, No. 408). University of Western Ontario. (b).

Clore, G. L., and Byrne, D. A reinforcement-affect model of attraction. In T. L. Huston (Ed.), *Foundations of interpersonal attraction*. New York: Academic Press, 1974.

Cooper, H. M., Baron, R. M., and Lowe, C. A. The importance of race and social class information in the formation of expectations about academic performance. *Journal of Educational Psychology*, 1975, *67*, 312–19.

Cooper, R. Introduction to language attitudes, II. *International Journal of the Sociology of Language*, 1975, *6*, 5–9.

Coppieters, F. Les problèmes communautaires en Belgique. Bruxelles: Institut Belge d'Information et de Documentation, 1974.

Dale, P. S. *Language development: Structure and function*. Hinsdale, Illinois: Dryden Press, 1972.

d'Angeljan, A. & Tucker, G. R. Sociolinguistic correlates of speech style in Quebec. In R. Shuy and R. Fasold (Eds.), *Language attitudes: Trends and prospects*. Washington, D.C.: Georgetown University Press, 1973.

Dittmar, N. *Sociolinguistics: A critical survey of theory and application*. London: Edward Arnold, 1976.

Doise, W., Sinclair, A. and Bourhis, R. Y. Evaluation of accent convergence and divergence in cooperative and competitive intergroup situations. *British Journal of Social and Clinical Psychology*, 1976, *15*, 247–52.

Dubé, N. C. and Herbert, G. *St. John valley bilingual education project*. (Report No. OEC–0–74–9331). Washington, D.C.: U.S. Department of Health, Education, and Welfare, August, 1975 (a).

Dubé, N. C. and Herbert, G. *Evaluation of the St. John valley, title VII bilingual education program, 1970–1975*. Unpublished manuscript, Madawaska, Maine, 1975 (b).

Duncan, S., Jr. Some signals and rules for taking speaking turns in conversations. *Journal of Personality and Social Psychology*, 1972, *23*, 283–92.

Dunn, J. A. Consociational democracy and language conflict. *Comparative Political Studies*, 1972, *5*, 3–39.

Dunn, J. A. The Revision of the Constitution in Belgium: A study in the institutionalization of ethnic conflict. *Western Political Quarterly*, 1974, *27*, 143–63.

Edwards, A. D. Social class and linguistic choice. *Sociology*, 1976, *10*, 101–10.

Edwards, J. R. Characteristics of disadvantaged children. *Irish Journal of Education*, 1974, *8*, 49–61.

Edwards, J. R. *Compensatory education and the characteristics of disadvantaged Children*. Dublin: Educational Research Centre, 1976 (a).

Edwards, J. R. Disadvantage. *Oideas*, 1976, *16*, 53–8. (b).

Edwards, J. R. Reading, language, and disadvantage. In V. Greaney (Ed.), Studies in Reading, Dublin: Educational Co., 1977, pp. 67–78.

Edwards, J. R. Speech of disadvantaged Dublin children. *Language Problems and Language Planning*, in press (c).

Edwards, J. R. Education, psychology and eclecticism. *Proceedings of the Second Educational Studies Conference*, in press (d).

Ehrlich, J. J. and Graeven, D. B. Reciprocal self-disclosure in a dyad. *Journal of Experimental Social Psychology*, 1971, *7*, 389–400.

Eiser, J. R. and Stroebe, W. *Categorization and social judgement.* New York and London: Academic Press, 1972.

El-Dash, L and Tucker, G. R. Subjective reactions to various speech styles in Egypt. *International Journal of the Sociology of Language*, 1975, *6*, 33–54.

Elyan, O., Smith, P., Giles, H. and Bourhis, R. Y. RP-accented female speech: The voice of androgyny? In P. Trudgill (ed.), *Sociolinguistic patterns in British English.* London: Arnold, 1978.

Ertel, S. Erkenntnis und Dogmatismus. *Psychologische Rundschau*, 1973, *23*, 241–69.

Ervin-Tripp, S. M. Sociolinguistics. *Advances in Experimental Social Psychology*, 1969, *4*, 91–165.

Eysenck, H. J. Manual of the Maudsley personality inventory. London: University of London, 1959.

Fanon, F. *Black skin, white masks.* New York: Grove Press, 1961.

Fasold, R. W., Bias, C., Shopek, L., Tully, B., and Louis, C. *Inferences on social lect level: Where you are and where your head is.* Unpublished manuscript, Indiana University Linguistics Club, Bloomington, Indiana, 1975.

Feldman, R. E. Response to compatriots and foreigners who seek assistance. *Journal of Personality and Social Psychology*, 1968, *10*, 202–14.

Ferguson, C. A. Foreword. In J. A. Fishman, *Sociolinguistics: A brief introduction.* Rowley, Mass.: Newbury House, 1970.

Festinger, L. A theory of social comparison processes. *Human Relations*, 1954, *7*, 117–40.

Fielding, G., and Evered, C. *The influences of patient's speech style and doctors' decisions in the diagnostic interview.* Unpublished manuscript, Social Psychology Department, University of Bradford, England, 1977.

Fielding, G. and Fraser, C. Language and interpersonal relations. In I. Markova (Ed.), *Language in its social context*. London: Wiley.

Fisher, I. When children's speech deteriorates. *The Speech Teacher*, 1971, *20* (3), 199–202.

Fishman, J. A. *Language loyalty in the United States*. The Hague: Mouton, 1966.

Fishman, J. A. (ed.). *Readings in the sociology of language*. The Hague: Mouton, 1968.

Fishman, J. A. *Sociolinguistics: A brief introduction*. Rowley, Mass: Newbury House, 1970.

Fishman, J. A. *Language and nationalism*. Rowley, Mass.: Newbury, 1972.

Fishman, J. A. Ethnicity and language. In H. Giles (Ed.), *Language, ethnicity and intergroup relations*. London: Academic Press, 1977.

Fishman, J. A. *et al. Language loyalty in the United States*. The Hague: Mouton, 1966.

Fishman, J. A. and Giles, H. Language and society. In H. Tajfel and C. Fraser (Eds.), *Introducing social psychology*. Harmondsworth, Middlesex: Penguin, 1978.

Flavell, J. H., Botkin, P. T., Fry, C. L. Jr., Wright, J. W., and Jarvis, P. E. *The development of role-taking and communication skills in children.* New York: Wiley, 1968.

Fleerackers, J. Flanders in Belgium. In M. Boey, J. Fleerackers and W. Sanders (Eds.), *Guide to Flanders: The Dutch-speaking part of Belgium*. Lannoo, Tielt and Utrecht, 1973.

Fleming, E. S. and Anttonen, R. G. Teacher expectancy, or My Fair Lady. *American Educational Research Journal*, 1971, *8*, 241–52.

Francis, H. Social background, speech, and learning to read. *British Journal of Educational Psychology*, 1974, *44*, 290–9.

Frasure-Smith, N., Lambert, W. E., and Taylor, D. M. Choosing the language instruction for one's children: A Quebec study. *Journal of Cross-Cultural Psychology*, 1975, *6*, 131–55.

Freijo, T. D. and Jaeger, R. M. Social class and race as concomitants of composite halo in teacher's evaluative ratings of pupils. *American Educational Research Journal*, 1976, *13*, 1–14.

Frender, R., Brown, B., and Lambert, W. E. The role of speech characteristics in scholastic success. *Canadian Journal of Behavioral Science*, 1970, *2*, 299–306.

Frender, R. and Lambert, W. E. Speech style and scholastic success:

The tentative relationships and possible implications for lower class children. *Georgetown Monographs on Language and Linguistics*, 1972, *25*, 237–71.

Gardner, R. C. Motivational variables in second-language learning. *International Journal of American Linguistics*, 1966, *32*, 24–44.

Gardner, R. C. *Social factors in second language acquisition and bilinguality*. (Research Bulletin, No 342.) University of Western Ontario, 1975.

Gardner, R. C., and Lambert, W. E. Motivational variables in second language acquisition. *Canadian Journal of Psychology*. 1959, *13*, 266–72.

Gardner, R. C. and Lambert, W. E. Language aptitude, intelligence and second language achievement. *Journal of Educational Psychology*, 1965, *56*, 191–9.

Gardner, R. C., and Lambert, W. E. *Attitudes and motivation in second language learning*. Rowley, Mass.: Newbury House, 1972.

Gardner, R. C., and Santos, E. H. *Motivational variables in second language acquisition: A Philippine investigation*. (Research Bulletin, No. 149.) University of Western Ontario, 1970.

Gardner, R. C. and Smythe, P. C. *Second language acquisition: A social psychological approach*. (Research Bulletin, No. 332.) University of Western Ontario, 1975.

Gardner, R. R. Information sequencing, background information and reciprocity in initial interaction. Unpublished doctoral dissertation, Northwestern University, 1976.

Gatbonton-Segalowitz, E. Systematic variables in second-language speech: A sociolinguistic study. Unpublished doctoral dissertation, McGill University, 1975.

Giffin, K. The contribution of studies of source credibility to a theory of interpersonal trust in the communication process. *Psychological Bulletin*, 1967, *68*, 104–20.

Giles, H. Evaluative reactions to accents. *Educational Review*, 1970, *22*, 211–27.

Giles, H. Ethnocentrism and the evaluation of accented speech. *British Journal of Social and Clinical Psychology*, 1971, *10*, 187–8 (a).

Giles, H. Patterns of evaluation in reactions to RP, South Welsh and Somerset accented speech. *British Journal of Social and Clinical Psychology*, 1971, *10*, 280–1 (b).

Giles, H. Communicative effectiveness as a function of accented speech. *Speech Monographs*, 1973, *40*, 330–1 (a).

Giles, H. Accent mobility: A model and some data. *Anthropological Linguistics*, 1973, *15*, 87–105 (b).

Giles, H. (Ed.). *Language, ethnicity and intergroup relations*. London and New York: Academic Press, 1977 (a).

Giles, H. The social context of speech: A social psychological perspective. *ITL: A Review of Applied Linguistics*, 1977, *35*, 27–42 (b).

Giles, H., Baker, S., and Fielding, G. Communication length as a behavioral index of accent prejudice. *International Journal of the Sociology of Language*, 1975, *6*, 73–81.

Giles, H. and Bourhis, R. Y. Methodological issues in dialect perception: A social psychological perspective. *Anthropological Linguistics*, 1976, *19*, 294–304 (a).

Giles, H. and Bourhis, R. Y. Black speakers and white speech: A real problem. In G. Nickel (Ed.), *Proceedings of the 4th AILA Congress*. Stuttgart: Hockschul Verlag, 1976 (b).

Giles, H., Bourhis, R. Y. and Taylor, D. M. Toward a theory of language in ethnic group relations. In H. Giles (Ed.), *Language, ethnicity and intergroups relations*. London: Academic Press, 1977.

Giles, H. and Powesland, P. F. *Speech style and social evaluation*. London: Academic Press, 1975.

Giles, H. and Taylor, D. M. National identity in South Wales: Some preliminary data. In G. Williams (Ed.), *Social and cultural change in contemporary Wales*. London: Routledge & Kegan Paul, 1978.

Giles, H., Taylor, D. M., and Bourhis, R. Y. Towards a theory of interpersonal accommodation through speech: Some Canadian data. *Language in Society*, 1973, *2*, 177–92.

Giles, H., Taylor, D. M., and Bourhis, R. Y. Dimensions of Welsh identity. *European Journal of Social Psychology*, 1977, *7*, 29–39.

Giles, H., Taylor, D. M., Lambert, W. E., and Albert, G. Dimensions of ethnic identity: An example from Northern Maine. *Journal of Social Psychology*, 1976, *100*, 11–19.

Glaser, N. and Moynihan, D. P. Introduction. In N. Glaser and D. P. Moynihan (Eds.), *Ethnicity: Theory and experience*. Cambridge, Mass.: Harvard University Press, 1975.

Gilksman, L. Second language acquisition: The effects of student attitudes on classroom behaviour. Unpublished Master's Thesis, University of Western Ontario, 1976.

Goldman-Eisler, F. *Psycholinguistics: Experiments in spontaneous speech*. New York: Academic Press, 1968.

Gough, H. G. and Heilbrun, A. B. *The adjective check list manual*. Palo Alto, California: Consulting Psychologists Press, 1965.

Gouldner, A. W. The norm of reciprocity: A preliminary statement. *American Sociological Review*, 1960, 25, 161–78.

Grimshaw, A. D. Sociolinguistics. In I. S. Pool and W. Schramm (Eds.), *Handbook of communication*. Chicago, Illinois: Rand-McNally, 1973.

Guboglo, M. N. *Linguistic contacts and elements of ethnic identification*. Paper presented at the meeting of the International Congress of Anthropological and Ethnographical Sciences, Chicago, 1973.

Gumperz, J. J. Linguistics and social interaction in two communities. *American Anthropologists*, 1964, 66, 137–53.

Gumperz, J. J., and Hernandez-Chavez, E. Bilingualism, bidialectalism and classroom interaction. In C. Cazden V. John, and D. Hymes (Eds.), *Functions of language in the classroom*. New York: Teachers College Press, 1972.

Gumperz, J. J. and Hymes, D. *Directions in sociolinguistics: The ethnography of communication*. New York: Rinehart and Winston, 1972.

Hamlyn, D. W. Person perception and our understanding of others. In T. Mischel (Ed.), *Understanding other persons*. Oxford: Blackwell, 1974.

Halliday, M. A. K. Language structure and language function. In J. Lyonds (Ed.), *New Horizons in linguistics*. Harmondsworth, Middlesex: Penguin, 1970.

Harré, R., and Secord, P. *The explanation of social behavior*. Oxford, Blackwell, 1972.

Harries, B. Children's language: The need for training students' attention and aural perception. *London Educational Review*, 1972, 1, 65–70.

Harris, M. B. and Baudin, H. The language of altruism: The effects of language, dress and ethnic group. *Journal of Social Psychology*, 1973, 97, 37–41.

Harrison, R. *Beyond words: An introduction to nonverbal communication*. Englewood Cliffs, New Jersey: Prentice-Hall, 1974.

Harvey, J. H., and Smith, W. P. *Social psychology: An attributional approach*. St. Louis, Missouri: Mosby, 1977.

Heider, F. *The psychology of interpersonal relations*. New York: Wiley, 1958.

Helfrich, H. and Dahme, G. Sind Verzögerungsphänomene beim spontanen Sprechen. *Zeitschrift für Sozialpsychologie*, 1974, *5*, 55–6.

Herman, S. Explorations in the social psychology of language choice. *Human Relations*, 1961, *14*, 149–64.

Herpel, G. *Sprechweise und Persönlichkeit – Analyse des Zusammenhangs zwischen Sprechweise-Variablen und- Persönlichkeitsvariablen*. Diplomarbeit: University of Giesen, 1976.

Hill, K. Belgium: Political change in a segmental society. In R. Rose (Ed.), *Electoral behavior*. New York: Free Press, 1974.

Hollander, E. P. *Principles and methods of social psychology*. New York: Oxford University Press, 1972.

Holsti, O. R. Content analysis. In G. Lindzey and E. Aronson (Eds.), *Handbook of social psychology*. Reading, Mass.: Addison-Wesley, 1968.

Homans, G. C. *Social behavior: Its elementary forms*. New York: Harcourt, Brace and World, 1961.

Hopper, R. and Williams, F. Speech characteristics and employability. *Speech Monographs*, 1973, *40*, 296–302.

Houston, S. H. A reexamination of some assumptions about the language of the disadvantaged child. *Child Development*, 1970. *41*, 947–63.

Hovland, C. I., Janis, I. L., and Kelley, H. H. *Communication and persuasion*. New Haven, Conn.: Yale University Press, 1953.

Hymes, D. H. *On communicative competence*. Paper presented at the conference on Mechanisms of Language Development, London, May, 1968.

Hymes, D. The scope of linguistics. *Items*, 1972, *26*, 14–18 (a).

Hymes, D. Models of the interaction of language and social setting. In J. J. Gumperz and D. Hymes (Eds.), *Directions in sociolinguistics: The ethnography of communication*. New York: Holt, Rinehart and Winston, 1972 (b).

Inglehart, R. F., and Woodward, M. Language conflicts and political community. In P. P. Giglioli (Ed.), *Language and social context*. London: Penguin, 1972.

Insko, C. A. and Schopler, J. *Experimental social psychology*. New York: Academic Press, 1972.

Jackson, D. N. *Manual for the personality research form*. Goshen, N. Y.: Research Psychologists Press.

Jaeger, R. M., and Freijo, T. D. Race and sex as concomitants of composite halo in teachers' evaluative ratings of pupils. *Journal of Educational Psychology*, 1975, 67, 226–37.

Jaffe, J., and Feldstein, S. *Rhythms of dialogue*. New York and London: Academic Press, 1970.

Jones, E. E. *Ingratiation: A social psychological analysis*. New York: Appleton-Century-Crofts, 1964.

Jones, E. E., and Davis, K. E. From acts to dispositions: The attribution process in perception. In L. Berkowitz (Ed.), *Advances in social psychology, II*. New York and London: Academic Press, 1965.

Jones, E. E., Davis, K. E., and Gergen, K. J. Role playing variations and their information value for person perception. *Journal of Abnormal and Social Psychology*, 1961, 63, 302–10.

Jones, E. E. and Gerard, H. B. *Foundations of social psychology*. New York: Wiley, 1967.

Jones, E. E., and Wortman, C. B. *Ingratiation: An attributional approach*. Morristown, New Jersey: General Learning Press, 1973.

Jones, R. G., and Jones, E. E. Optimum conformity as an ingratiation tactic. *Journal of Personality*, 1964, 32, 4–36.

Jourard, S. *Self-disclosure: An experimental analysis of the transparent self*. New York: Wiley, 1971.

Kalin, R., & Rayko, D. *The social significance of speech in the job interview*. Unpublished manuscript, Department of Psychology, Queen's University, Kingston, Canada, 1977.

Keaton, R. E. *Trial tactics and methods*. Boston, Mass.: Little, Brown and Company, 1973.

Keddie, N. *Tinker, tailor . . . the myth of cultural deprivation*. Harmondsworth, Middlesex: Penguin, 1973.

Kellaghan, T. Preschool intervention for the educationally disadvantaged. *Irish Journal of Psychology*, 1972, 1, 160–76.

Kellaghan, T. and Brugha, D. The scholastic performance of children in a disadvantaged area. *Irish Journal of Education*, 1972, 6, 133–43.

Kellaghan, T., and Greaney, B. A factorial study of the characteristics of preschool disadvantaged children. *Irish Journal of Education*, 1973, 7, 53–65.

Kellaghan, T., Macnamara, J., and Neuman, E. Teachers' assessments of the scholastic progress of pupils. *Irish Journal of Education*, 1969, 3, 95–104.

Kelly, G. A. Belgium: New nationalism in an old world. *Comparative Politics*, 1969, 1 (3), 343–65.

Kelly, H. H. Attribution theory in social psychology. *Nebraska Symposium on Motivation*, 1967, 14, 192–241.

Kelly, H. H. The process of causal attribution. *American Psychologist*, 1973, 28, 107–28.

Kelly, J. *Social forces and linguistic variability in teenage subcultures*. Paper presented at the 4th International Congress of Applied Linguistics. Stuttgart, September, 1975.

Kelman, H. C. Compliance, identification, and internalization: Three processes of attitude change. *Journal of Conflict Resolution*, 1958, 2, 51–60.

Kelvin, P. (1972). *The bases of social behavior*. London: Holt, Rinehart & Winston 1972

Key, M. R. *Male/female language*. Metuchen, N. J.: Scarecrow Press.

Kiesler, C. A. Group pressure and conformity. In J. Mills (Ed.), *Experimental social psychology*. New York: Macmillan, 1969.

Kiesler, C. A., Kiesler, S. B., and Pallack, M. S. The effect of commitment to future interaction on reactions to norm violations. *Journal of Personality*, 1967, 35, 585–99.

Kiesler, S. B. The effect of perceived role requirements on reactions to favour-doing. *Journal of Experimental Social Psychology*, 1966, 11, 198–210.

Knapp, M. L., Hart, R. P., and Dennis, H. S. An exploration of deception as a communication construct. *Human Communication Research*, 1974, 1, 15–29.

Kramer, C. Judgment of personal characteristics and emotions from nonverbal properties. *Psychological Bulletin*, 1963, 60, 408–20.

Kramer, C. Female and male perception of female and male speech. *Language and Speech*, in press.

Kraus, S. (Ed.). *The great debate*. Bloomington, Indiana: University of Indiana Press.

Krauss, R. M., and Glucksberg, S. The development of communicative competence as a function of age. *Child Development*, 1969, 40, 255–66.

Kühnen, S. *Stimme und Persönlichkeit – Analyse des Zusammenhangs von Stimmqualitat-variablen und Persönlichkeitsvariablen.* Diplomarbeit, University of Giessen, 1976.

Labov, W. The social motivation of a sound change. *Word*, 1963, *19*, 273–309.

Labov, W. *The social stratification of English in New York City.* Washington, D.C.: Center for Applied Linguistics, 1966.

Labov, W. The logic of non-standard English. *Georgetown University Monographs on Language and Linguistics*, 1969, *22*, 1–31.

Labov, W. The study of languages in its social context. *Studium Generale*, 1970, *23*, 66–84.

Labov, W. (Ed.). *Sociolinguistic patterns.* Philadelphia, Pa.: University of Pennsylvania Press, 1972 (a).

Labov, W. The social setting of linguistic change. In W. Labov (Ed.), *Sociolinguistic Patterns.* Philadelphia, Pa.: University of Pennsylvania Press, 1972 (b).

Lakoff, R. Language and woman's place. *Language and Society*, 1973, *2*, 45–79.

Lakoff, R. *Language and woman's place.* New York: Harper & Row, 1975.

Lambert, S. M. The role of speech in forming evaluations: A study of children and teachers. Unpublished Master's thesis, Tufts University, 1973.

Lambert, W. E. Psychological approaches to the study of language, part one—On learning, thinking and human abilities. *Modern Language Journal*, 1963, *14*, 51–62 (a).

Lambert, W. E. Psychological approaches to the study of language, part two—On second language learning and bilingualism. *Modern Language Journal*, 1963, *14*, 114–21 (b).

Lambert, W. E. The social psychology of bilingualism. *Journal of Social Issues*, 1967, *23*, 91–109.

Lambert, W. E. *Language, psychology and culture.* Stanford, California: Stanford University Press, 1972.

Lambert, W. E. Culture and language as factors in learning and education. In F. Aboud and R. D. Meade (Eds.), *Cultural factors in learning.* Bellinham, Washington: Western Washington State College, 1974.

Lambert, W. E., Frasure-Smith, N., and Hamers, J. *A cross-cultural study of child rearing values.* Unpublished manuscript, McGill University, 1976.

Lambert, W. E., Giles, H., and Albert, A. Language attitudes in a rural city in northern Maine. *La Monda Lingvo-Problemo*, 1976, 5, 129–44.

Lambert, W. E., Giles, H., and Picard, O. Language attitudes in a French-American community. *International Journal of the Sociology of Language*, 1975, 4, 127–52.

Lambert, W. E., Hodgson, R. C., Gardner, R. C., and Fillenbaum, S. Evaluational reactions to spoken language. *Journal of Abnormal and Social Psychology*, 1960, 60, 44–51.

Lambert, W. E., and Klineberg, O. *Children's views of foreign peoples: A cross-national study*. New York: Appleton-Century-Crofts, 1967.

Lambert, W. E., and Tucker, G. R. *Bilingual education of children*. Rowley, Mass.: Newbury House, 1972.

Larsen, K., Martin, H., and Giles, H. Anticipated social cost and interpersonal accommodation. *Human Communications Research*, 1977, 3, 303–8.

Laver, J., and Hutcheson, S. (Eds.) *Communication in face to face interaction*. Harmondsworth, Middlesex: Penguin, 1972.

Lennard, H. L., and Berstein, A. Interdependence of therapist and patient verbal behaviour. In J. A. Fishman (Ed.), *Readings in the sociology of language*. The Hague: Mouton, 1960.

Lieberman, D. Language attitudes in St. Lucia. *Journal of Cross-Cultural Psychology*, 1975, 6, 47–481.

Lieberman, P. *Intonation, perception and language*. Cambridge, Mass.: M.I.T. Press, 1967.

Lieberson, S. *Language and ethnic relations in Canada*. New York: Wiley, 1970.

London, H. *Psychology of the persuader*. Morristown, New Jersey: General Learning Press, 1973.

Lorwin, V. R. Linguistic pluralism and political tension in modern Belgium. In J. A. Fishman (Ed.) *Advances in the sociology of language, II*. The Hague: Mouton, 1972.

Lukens, J. Ethnocentric speech: Its nature and implications. *Maledicta: International Journal for Verbal Aggression*, in press.

Macaulay, R. K. S. Double standards. *American Anthropologist*, 1973, 75 (5), 1324–37.

Mahl, G. F., and Schulze, G. Psychological research in the extra-linguistic area. In T. Sebeok, A. S. Hayes and M. C. Bateson (Eds.), *Approaches to semiotics*. The Hague: Mouton, 1964.

Marwell, G., and Schmidt, D. R. Dimensions of compliance-gaining behavior: An empirical analysis. *Sociometry*, 1967, *30*, 350–64.

Matarazzo, J. D. A speech interaction system. In D. J. Kiesler (Ed.), *The process of psychotherapy*, Chicago: Aldine, 1973.

Mazanec, N., and McCall, G. J. Sex forms and allocation of attention in observing persons. *Journal of Psychology*, 1976, *93*, 175–80.

McAllister, A., and Kiesler, D. Interviewee disclosure as a function of interpersonal trust, task modeling, and interview self-disclosure. *Journal of Consulting and Clinical Psychology*, 1975, *43*, 428 ff.

McCroskey, J. C., and Mehrley, R. S. The effects of disorganization and non-fluency on attitude change and source credibility. *Speech Monographs*, 1969, *36*, 13–21.

McGuire, W. J. The nature of attitudes and attitude change. In G. Lindzey and E. Aronson (Eds.), *The handbook of social psychology, III.* Reading Mass.: Addison-Wesley, 1969.

McLuhan, M. *Understanding media.* New York: McGraw-Hill, 1964.

McNemar, Q. *Psychological statistics.* New York: John Wiley, 1969.

Mehrabian, A., and Williams, M. Nonverbal concomitants of perceived and intended persuasiveness. *Journal of Personality and Social Psychology*, 1969, *13*, 37–58.

Miller, G. R., Boster, F., Roloff, M., and Seibold, D. R. *Compliance gaining strategies: A typology of some findings concerning the effects of situational differences.* Paper presented at the annual convention of the International Communication Association, Portland, Oregon, April, 1976.

Miller, G. R. and Hewgill, M. A. The effects of variations in nor-fluency on audience ratings of source credibility. *Quarterly Journal of Speech*, 1964, *50*, 36–44.

Miller, G. R., Maruyama, Beaber, and Valone,

Miller, G. R. and Steinberg, M. *Between people: A new analysis of interpersonal communication.* Chicago: Science Research Associate, 1975.

Mills, J. Opinion change as a function of the communicator's desire to influence and liking for the audience. *Journal of Experimental Social Psychology*, 1966, *2*, 152–9.

Mills, J., and Jellison, J. M. Effect on opinion change of how desirable the communication is to the audience the communicator addressed. *Journal of Personality and Social Psychology*, 1967, *5*, 459–63.

Morrill, A. E. *Trial diplomacy*. Chicago, Illinois: Court Practice Institute, 1971.

Morris, C. G. and Hackman, J. R. Behavioral correlates of perceived leadership. *Journal of Personality and Social Psychology*, 1969, *13*, 350–61.

Moscovici, S. Communication processes and the properties of language. *Advances in Experimental Social Psychology*. 1967, *3*, 226–70.

Moscovici, S. (Ed.) The psycho-sociology of language. Chicago, Illinois: Markhan, 1972.

Moscovici, S. *Social influence and social change*. London: Academic Press, 1976.

Natalé, M. Convergence of mean vocal intensity in dyadic communication as a function of social desirability. *Journal of Personality and Social Psychology*, 1975, *40*, 827–30.

Newtson, D. Attribution and the unit of perception of ongoing behaviour. *Journal of Personality and Social Psychology*, 1973, *38*, 28–38.

Parkin, D. Emergent and stabilized multilingualism: Poly-ethnic peer groups in Urban Kenya. In H. Giles (Ed.), *Language, ethnicity and intergroup relations*. London: Academic Press, 1977.

Passow, A. H. *Deprivation and disadvantage: Nature and manifestation*. Hamburg: UNESCO Institute for Education, 1970.

Patterson, D. Context and choice in ethnic allegiance: A theoretical framework and Caribbean case study. In N. Glaser and D. P. Moynihan (Eds.), *Ethnicity: Theory and experience*. Cambridge, Mass.: Harvard University Press, 1975.

Pearce, W. B. The effect of vocal cues on credibility and attitude change. *Western Speech*, 1971, *35*, 176–84.

Pearce, W. B., and Brommel, B. J. Vocalic communication in persuasion. *Quarterly Journal of Speech*, 1972, *58*, 298–306.

Pearce, W. B., and Conklin, F. Nonverbal vocalic communication and perceptions of a speaker. *Speech Monographs*, 1971, *38*, 235–41.

Pellowe, J., Nixon, G. S., and McNeany, V. A dynamic modelling of linguistic variation: The urban (Tyneside) linguistic survey. *Lingua*, 1972, *30*, 1–30.

Peng, F. Communicative distance. *Language Sciences*, 1974, *31*, 32–5.

Powesland, P. F., and Giles, H. Persuasiveness and accent-message incompatibility. *Human Relations*, 1975, *28*, 85–93.

Raffler-Engel, W. von. *The unconscious element in inter-cultural communication*. Unpublished manuscript, Linguistics Department, University of Vanderbilt, 1977.

Ramirez, K. G. Socio-cultural aspects of the Chicano dialect. In G. D. Bills (Ed.), *Southwest Areal Linguistics*.San Diego, California: Institute for Cultural Pluralism. 1974.

Revel, J. F. *Ni Marx, ni Jésu*. Paris: Laffont, 1970.

Rist, R. C. Students social class and teacher expectations: The self-fulfilling prophecy in ghetto education. *Harvard Educational Review*, 1970, *40*, 411–51.

Robinson, W. P. *Language and social behaviour*. Harmondsworth, Middlesex: Penguin, 1972.

Rodnick, R. and Wood, B. The communication strategies of children. *Speech Teacher*, 1973, *22*, 114–124.

Rosenfeld, H. M. Effect of approval seeking induction on interpersonal proximity. *Psychological Reports*, 1965, *17*, 120–2.

Rosenfeld, H. M. Approval-seeking and approval-inducing functions of verbal and non-verbal responses in the dyad. *Journal of Personality and Social Psychology*, 1966, *4*, 597–605.

Rosenthal, R., and Rosnow, R. L. *Artifact in behavioral research*. New York: Academic Press, 1969.

Rubin, J. Z., and Brown, B. R. *The social psychology of bargaining and negotiation*. New York: Academic Press, 1975.

Ryan, E. B., and Carranza, M. A. Evaluative reactions towards speakers of standard English and Mexican American accented English. *Journal of Personality and Social Psychology*, 1975, *31* (5), 855–863.

Ryan, E. B., and Carranza, M. A. Ingroup and outgroup reactions toward Mexican American language varieties. In H. Giles (ed.), *Language, ethnicity and intergroup relations*. London: Academic Press, 1977.

Ryan, E. B., and Sebastian, R. J. *Social class effects on evaluation reactions towards accented speakers*. Unpublished manuscript, University of Notre Dame, 1976.

Sachs, J. Cues to the identification of sex in children's speech. In B. Thorne and N. Henley (Eds.), *Language and sex: Difference and dominance*. Rowley, Mass.: Newbury House, 1975.

Sacks, H., Schegloff, E. A. and Jefferson, G. A simplest semantics for the organization of turn-taking for conversation. *Language*, 1974, *50*, 696–735.

Schacter, S. *The psychology of affiliation: Experimental studies of the sources of gregariousness*. Stanford, California: Stanford University Press, 1959.

Scherer, K. R. *Nonverbale Kommunikation*. (IPK-Forschungsbericht). Hambury: Buske, 1970 (a).

Scherer, K. R. Attribution of personality from voice: A cross-cultural study of the dynamics of interpersonal perception. Unpublished doctoral dissertation, Harvard University, 1970.

Scherer, K. R. Randomized splicing: A note on a simple technique for masking speech. *Journal of Experimental Research in Personality*, 1971, *5*, 155–9.

Scherer, K. R. Judging personality from voice: A cross-cultural approach to an old issue in interpersonal perception. *Journal of Personality*, 1972, *40*, 191–210.

Scherer, K. R. Persönlichkeit, Stimmqualität und Persönlichkeitsattribution: Pfadenalytische Untersuchungen zu nonverbalen Kommunikationsprozessen. *Bericht über den 28. Kongress der Deutschen Gesellschaft für Psychologie*, Vol. 3. Gottingen: Hogrefe, 1974 (a).

Scherer, K. R. Acoustic concomitants of emotional dimensions: Judging affect from synthesized tone sequences. In S. Weitz (Ed.), *Nonverbal Communication*. New York: Oxford University Press, 1974 (b).

Scherer, K. R. Voice quality analysis of American and German speakers. *Journal of psycholinguistic Research*, 1974, *3*, 281–91 (c).

Scherer, K. R. Inference rules in personality attribution from voice quality: The loud voice of extraversion. Unpublished manuscript, University of Giessen, 1976.

Scherer, K. R., and Giles, H. *Social markers in speech*. Cambridge: Cambridge University Press, in press.

Scherer, K. R., London, H., and Wolff, J. J. The voice of confidence: Paralinguistic cues and audience evaluation. *Journal of Research in Personality*, 1973, *7*, 31–44.

Scherer, K. R., Rosenthal, R., and Koivumaki, J. Mediating interpersonal expectancies via vocal cues: Differential speech intensity as a means of social influence. *European Journal of Social Psychology*, 1972, 2, 163–176.

Scherer, K. R., Scherer, U., Rosenthal, R., and Hall, J. A. Differential attribution of personality based on multi-channel presentation of verbal cues. *Psychological Research*, 1977, 39, 221–47.

Scherer, U., and Scherer, K. R. Bürgernähe im Publikumsverkehr: Die Rolle des menschlichen Faktors in der Sozialplanung. In F.X. Kaufmann (Ed.), *Bürgernähe Gestaltung der sozialen Umwelt: Probleme und theoretische Perspiktiven*. Mesenheim, Glan: Anton Hain Verlag, 1977.

Schulman, L. S. Compliments, reciprocity and background information in initial interaction. Unpublished doctoral dissertation, Northwestern University, 1976.

Schumann, J. H. Affective factors and the problem of age in second language acquisition. *Language Learning*, 1976, 25, 209–35.

Schweitzer, D. A. The effect of presentation on source evaluation. *Quarterly Journal of Speech*, 1970, 56, 33–9.

Scotton, C. M. Strategies of neutrality: Language choice in uncertain situations. *Language*, 1976, 52, 919–41.

Segalowitz, N. Communicative incompetence and nonfluent bilingualism. *Canadian Journal of Behavioral Science*, 1976, 8, 122–31.

Segalowitz, N. and Gatbonton, E. Studies of the non-fluent bilingual. In P. Hornby (Ed.), *Bilingualism: Psychological and social implications*. New York: Academic Press, 1977.

Seligman, C. F., Tucker, G. R., and Lambert, W. E. The effects of speech style and other attributes on teachers' attitudes toward pupils. *Language and Society*, 1972, 1, 131–42.

Sereno, K. K., and Hawkins, G. J. The effects of variations in speakers nonfluency upon audience ratings of attitudes toward the speech topic and speakers credibility. *Speech Monographs*, 1967, 34, 58–64.

Sermat, V., and Smyth, M. Content analysis of verbal communication in the development of a relationship: Conditons influencing self-disclosure. *Journal of Personality and Social Psychology*, 1973, 26, 332–46.

Shannon, C., and Weaver, W. *The mathematical theory of communication*. Urbana, Illinois: University of Illinois Press. 1949.

Sherif, C. W., Sherif, M., and Nebergall, R. E. *Attitude and attitude change*. Philadelphia, Pennsylvania: Saunder, 1965.

Shuy, R. W. Subjective judgments in sociolinguistic analysis. In J. E. Alatis (Ed.), *Linguistics and the teaching of standard English to speakers of other languages on dialects*. Arlingon, Virginia: The Center for Applied Linguistics, 1969.

Shuy, R. W. Language and success: Who are the judges? In R. W. Bailey and J. L. Robinson (Eds.), *Varieties of Present-day English*. New York: Macmillan, 1973.

Shuy, R. W. Problems of communication in the cross-cultural medical interview. *ITL: A Review of Applied Linguistics*, 1977, 35.

Siebold, D. P. *A formalization of attribution theory: Critique and implications for communication*. Paper presented at the annual conference of the Central States Speech Association, Kansas City, April, 1975.

Siegman, A. *The voice of attraction: Interpersonal attraction and verbal behavior in the initial interview*. Unpublished manuscript, Department of Psychology, University of Maryland, Baltimore County, 1977.

Siegman, A., and Feldstein, S. *Nonverbal behavior* and communication. Hillsdale, New Jersey: Lawrence Erlbaum Associates, Inc., in press.

Simard L., Taylor, D. M., and Giles, H. Attribution processes and interpersonal accommodation in a bilingual setting. *Language and Speech*, 1976, 19, 374–87.

Slobin, D. *Psycholinguistics*. Glenview, Illinois: Scott, Foresman & Co., 1971.

Smythe, P. C., Gardner, R. C., and Smythe, C. L. *A survey of attitudes and opinions concerning the French programmes in the London public system*. (Research Bulletin, No. 11). Language Research Group: University of Western Ontario, 1976.

Smythe, P. C., Stennett, R. G., and Feenstra, H. T. Attitude, aptitude and type of instructional programs in second language acquisition. *Canadian Journal of Behavioral Science*, 1972, 4, 307–21.

Stein, R. T. Idenitfy emergent leaders from verbal and nonverbal communications. *Journal of Personality of Social Psychology*, 1975, 32, 125–35.

Stein, R. T., Geis, F. L., and Damarin, F. Perception of emergent leadership hierarchies in task groups. *Journal of Personality and Social Psychology*, 1973, 28, 77–87.

Stevenson, H. W., Parker, T., Wilkinson, A., Hegion, A., and Fish, E. Predictive value of teachers' ratings of young children. *Journal of Educational Psychology*, 1976, *68*, 507–17.

Storms, M. D. Videotape and the attribution process: Reversing actors' and observers' points of view. *Journal of Personal and Social Psychology*, 1973, *27*, 165–75.

Stotland, E., and Canon, L. K. *Social psychology: A cognitive approach*. Philadelphia, Pa.: Saunders, 1972.

Strickland, L. H., Aboud, F. E., and Gergen, K. J. *Social psychology in transition*. New York: Plenum, 1976.

Strongman, K. T., and Woosley, J. Stereotypical reactions to regional accents *British Journal of Social and Clinical Psychology*, 1967, *6*, 164–7.

Sudnow, D. (Ed.). *Studies in social interaction*. New York: Free Press, 1972.

Swain, M. Bibliography: Research on immersion education for the majority child. *The Canadian Modern Language Review*, 1976, *32*, 592–6.

Tajfel, H. La catégorization sociale. In S. Moscovici (Ed.), *Introduction à la psychologie sociale*. Paris: Larousse (Translation), 1972.

Tajfel, H. Social identity and intergroup behavior. *Social Science Information*, 1974, *13*, 65–93.

Tajfel, H. (Ed.). *Differentiation Between Social Groups: Studies in intergroup behavior*. London: Academic Press, 1978.

Tajfel, H., and Fraser, C. *Introducing social psychology*. Harmondsworth, Middlesex: Penguin, 1978.

Tajfel, H., and Israel, J. (Eds.). *The context of social psychology*. London: Academic Press, 1972.

Tajfel, H., and Wilkes, A. L. Classification and quantitative judgment. *British Journal of Psychology*, 1963, *54*, 101–14.

Tarampi, A. S., Lambert, W. E., and Tucker, G. R. Audience sensitivity and oral skill in second language. *Philippine Journal for Language Teaching*, 1968, *6*, 27–33.

Taylor, D. A., and Altman, I. Self-disclosure as a function of reward-cost-outcomes. *Sociometry*, 1975, *38*, 18–31.

Taylor, D. M., Bassili, J. N., and Aboud, F. E. Dimensions of ethnic identity: An example from Quebec. *Journal of Social Psychology*, 1973, *89*, 185–92.

Taylor, D. M., and Clément, R. Normative reactions to style of Quebec French. *Anthropological Linguistics*, 1974, *16*, 202–17.

Taylor, D. M., Meynard, R., and Rheault, E. Threat to ethnic identity and second-language learning. In H. Giles (Ed.), *Language, ethnicity and intergroup relations*. London: Academic Press, 1977.

Taylor, D. M., and Simard, L. Social interaction in a bilingual setting. *Canadian Psychological Review*, 1975, 16, 240–54.

Taylor, D. M., Simard, L. M., and Aboud, F. E. Ethnic identification in Canada: A cross-cultural investigation. *Canadian Journal of Behavioral Science*, 1972, 4, 13–20.

Thibaut, J. W., and Kelley, H. H. *The social psychology of groups*. New York: Wiley, 1959.

Thibaut, J. W., and Walker, L. *Procedural justice: A psychological analysis*. Hillside, New Jersey: Lawrence Erlbaum Associates, 1975.

Thorne, B., and Henley, N. (Eds.). *Language and sex: Difference and dominance*. Rowley, Mass.: Newbury House, 1975.

Timney, B., and London, H. Body language concomitants of persuasiveness and persuasibility in dyadic interaction. *International Journal of Group Tensions*, 1973, 3, 48–67.

Tinsely, H. A. and Weiss, D. J. Interrated reliability and agreement of subjective judgments. *Journal of Counseling Psychology*, 1975, 22, 358–76.

Triandis, H. C. Cognitive similarity and communication in a dyad. *Human Relations*, 1960, 13, 175–83.

Trudgill, P. Sex, covert prestige and linguistic change in the urban British English of Norwich. *Language and Society*, 1972, 1, 179–96.

Trudgill, P. *Sociolinguistics*. Harmondsworth, Middlesex: Penguin, 1974.

Tucker, G. R., and Lambert, W. E. White and negro listeners' reactions to various American English dialects. *Social Forces*, 1969, 47, 463–68.

Turner, J. C., and Brown, R. J. Social status, cognitive alternatives and intergroup relations. In H. Tajfel (Ed.), *Differentiation Between Social Groups: Studies in intergroup behavior*. London: Academic Press, 1978.

Walster, E., Berscheid, E., and Walster, G. W. New directions in equity research. *Journal of Personality and Social Psychology*, 1973, 25, 151–76.

Warr, P., and Knapper, C. *The perception of people and events*. London: John Wiley, 1968.

Webb, J. T. Interview synchrony: An investigation of two speech rate measures in an automated standardized interview. In A. W. Siegman and B. Pope (Eds.), *Studies in dyadic communication*. Oxford: Pergamon, 1970.

Weinreich, U. *Languages in contact*. The Hague: Mouton, 1970.

Welkowitz, J., and Feldstein, S. Relation of experimentally manipulated interpersonal perception and psychological differentiation to the temporal patterning of conversation. *Proceedings of the 78th Annual Convention of the American Psychological Association*, 1970, 5, 387–8.

Williams, F. Psychological correlates of speech characteristics: On sounding disadvantaged. *Journal of Speech and Hearing Research*, 1970, 13, 472–88.

Williams, F. The identification of linguistic attitudes. *International Journal of the Sociology of Language*, 1974, 4, 21–32.

Williams, F., Whitehead, J. L., and Miller, L. Relations between language attitudes and teacher expectancy. *American Educational Research Journal*, 1972, 9, 263–77.

Williams, F., Hewett, N., Miller, L. M., Naremore, R. C., and Whitehead, J. L. *Explorations of the linguistic attitudes of teachers*. Rowley, Mass.: Newbury House, 1976.

Wolff, H. Intelligibility and inter-ethnic attitudes. *Anthropological Linguistics*, 1959, *I*, 34–41.

Wrightsman, L. S. *Social psychology in the seventies*. Monterey: Brooks/Cole, 1972.

Index

187–92; awareness in, 127–34; development of, 9, 122–44; future interaction in, 131–4; initial interaction in, 123–4, 130, 131, 140
Interruption, 4, 107
Intonation contours, 88, 93, 104
Ireland, 22–44
Italian, 146

Judgemental process, 5, 7

Kinetic behaviour, 6–7
Knowledge, 125, 193; cognitive uncertainty and, 125–6; generation of, 123, 126, 127–31, 134–44; in interpersonal relations, 122–44 *passim*; levels of, 126, 143

Language: convergence in, *see* Convergence; divergence in, *see* Divergence; function of, vii, 186; general features of, 17; as group identity symbol, *see* Group identity; interpersonal relations and, 186–92; as reflection of disadvantage, 23, 38, 43; shift in, *see under* Accent, Speech shift; social psychology of, 18; study of, vii, 1
Language aptitude, 196–220; definition of, 198; measures of, 209
Language attitudes: language ability and, 155; measures of, 154; study of, 145, 150, 152, 153
Language behaviour, vii, 3, 7, 16, 53, 111, 122–3; as cues, *see* Cues; decoding processes of, *see* Decoding; encoding

processes of, *see* Encoding; in role, 125, 130; interpersonal relations and, 122–44; as rule governed, 45, 47, 122, 123, 125, 130, 131; social context of, *see* Social context; theory of, 1
Language divergence, *see* Divergence
Language instruction, vii, 189–90, 191, 192, 198, 199, 200–20 *passim*
Language learning, 10, 12, 45, 52, 148, 152, 160, 189–90, 191, 192; anxiety and, 197–8; 199–220; aptitude for, 196, 197, 198–220; formal, 198, 199; *'immersion schooling'*, 190; informal, 198, 199, 204; Language learning, motivation and, 152, 194, 196, 197, 198–220; social psychological aspects of, 193–220
Language loyalty, 148, 150–2
Language variables, *see* Speech variables
Language varieties, 1, 10, 45, 150–1, 158, 187; low prestige, 144–57; nonstandard, 23, 27, 90, 145–57; persistence of diverse, 145–57; Received-pronunciation, 8, 49, 52, 53, 57, 146, 147; standard, 8, 90, 91, 146, 147, 150, 151–3, 155; *see also* American English, Anglo-Canadian, Appalachian-English, Black American English, Castilian Spanish, Catalan Spanish, Chicano, English, Flemish, French, French American, French Canadian, German, Italian,